Humanitarian Intelligence

Security and Professional Intelligence Education Series (SPIES)

Series Editor: Jan Goldman

In this post–September 11, 2001, era there has been rapid growth in the number of professional intelligence training and educational programs across the United States and abroad. Colleges and universities, as well as high schools, are developing programs and courses in homeland security, intelligence analysis, and law enforcement, in support of national security.

The Security and Professional Intelligence Education Series (SPIES) was first designed for individuals studying for careers in intelligence and to help improve the skills of those already in the profession; however, it was also developed to educate the public in how intelligence work is conducted and should be conducted in this important and vital profession.

To view the books on our website, please visit https://rowman.com/Action/SERIES/RL/SPIES or scan the QR code below.

Humanitarian Intelligence

A Practitioner's Guide to Crisis Analysis and Project Design

Andrej Zwitter

ROWMAN & LITTLEFIELD
Lanham • Boulder • New York • London

Published by Rowman & Littlefield
A wholly owned subsidary of The Rowman & Littlefield Publishing Group, Inc.
4501 Forbes Boulevard, Suite 200, Lanham, Maryland 20706
www.rowman.com

Unit A, Whitacre Mews, 26-34 Stannary Street, London SE11 4AB

British Library Cataloguing in Publication Information Available

Library of Congress Cataloging-in-Publication Data

Name: Zwitter, Andrej, author.
Title: Humanitarian intelligence : a practitioner's guide to crisis analysis and project
   design / Andrej Zwitter.
Description: Lanham, Maryland : Rowman & Littlefield, 2016. | Series: Security
   and professional intelligence education series | Includes bibliographical references
   and index.
Identifiers: LCCN 2016033682 (print) | LCCN 2016038733 (ebook) |
   ISBN 9781442249486 (cloth : alk. paper) | ISBN 9781442249493 (electronic) |
   ISBN 9781786609465 (paper : alk. paper)
Subjects: LCSH: Humanitarian assistance—Management. | Humanitarian assistance—
   Safety measures. | Project management.
Classification: LCC HV553 .Z85 2016 (print) | LCC HV553 (ebook) |
   DDC 363.34/80684—dc23
LC record available at https://lccn.loc.gov/2016033682

Contents

List of Figures and Tables

FIGURES

TABLES

Tools and Step-by-Step Guides

Acknowledgment

This book is the result of research, teaching, and consultation work over the past decade. It would not have been possible without the support of my colleagues in the NOHA programme of the University of Groningen. I particularly wish to thank Maike Bennema for her insights and comments and my MA student Tamara van der Heijden for allowing me to use her research as an example of social network analysis. Furthermore, I am particularly indebted to my colleagues with whom I developed the Humanitarian Intelligence specialization within the master's programme in Humanitarian Action (NOHA), specifically Christopher Lamont, Joost Herman, Liesbet Heyse, and Rafael Wittek, but also everyone who contributed to the specialization over the past years. They have been a generous source of inspiration and provided reflection and critique. For a final set of comments regarding the framing of Humanitarian Intelligence I owe thanks to Nathaniel Raymond. Finally, I would like to thank my colleagues at the European Interagency Security Forum (http://www.eisf.eu) for contributing with their invaluable practitioner's points of view to previous drafts of parts of this manuscript.

It goes without saying that all errors and omissions are solely mine. I am grateful for the experience of writing this book and have to thank, last but not least, my partner and my mother for their patience in dealing with my mental and physical absence. Without their support and understanding this project would not have been possible.

Introduction

Humanitarian action is necessary to alleviate suffering, but it is also risky. It has the best chance of success when humanitarians are well prepared before entering the field. Given the mounting threats to humanitarian actors posed by criminals, militants, extremists, diseases, and other natural causes, while the demands for professionalization of aid are further increasing, there is likely to be an increasing need for well-planned humanitarian missions. In order to achieve that, well-planned humanitarian missions require good intelligence and solid risk assessment. "Humanitarian intelligence" is the term that describes this need for the process of data collection, analysis, and decision-making. When humanitarian analysis fails, it can lead to disasters for beneficiaries, for humanitarian actors themselves, and for the wider population.

The term "intelligence analysis" is usually occupied by intelligence agencies. While there is a justified resistance on the part of humanitarian actors to associate with intelligence organizations, there are important skills humanitarian analysts can and should learn from the rich and long experience of traditional intelligence analysis. In essence, as this book will point out, many of the analysis problems that humanitarian organizations face, such as threat assessments as well as complex stakeholder fields in adaptive and changing contexts, are similar to what traditional intelligence analysis encounters in day-to-day practice. To overcome the resistance to terminology resulting from cultural and political reasons, which also hampers learning from what intelligence analysis has to offer for the benefit of humanitarian analysis, is a first step toward improvement of the field of humanitarian analysis and intervention design. It is time to put this resistance to jargon aside and to allow the benefits that the accumulated knowledge and skills of traditional intelligence analysis can provide to the humanitarian field to be reaped.

The failures of intelligence services are sufficiently known and widely analyzed: from Stalin's failure at being his own intelligence analyst by not predicting Operation Barbarossa (1941), to the Mossad's failure to respond to evidence of an impending attack on Yom Kippur (1973), to the attacks of September 11, 2001, and the manufactured evidence to support weapons of mass destruction (WMDs) in Iraq. However, it is not only the governmental intelligence services that have experienced intelligence blunders. The same holds true for aid organizations as well:

- In 2003 terrorists attacked the UN headquarters in Baghdad killing 22 people, but the international nongovernmental organization (NGO) community did not respond immediately, assuming that their neutral and independent status would protect them. When it was followed by a series of kidnappings and attacks on the NGO community, the NGOs were not prepared and as a result their only feasible reaction was to evacuate their expatriate staff.
- When in 2005 the Ghana School Feeding Programme (GSFP) was set up by the Ghanaian government with the support of the Dutch embassy, the goal was straightforward and much applauded: by 2010, one million children were expected to benefit from the project and US$147 million would have been injected into the local economy. Due to faulty project assumptions relating to inaccurate judgments regarding the local and national capacity to run the program effectively, issues of corruption and mismanagement, and a misjudgment concerning the various stakeholders' willingness to collaborate, the Dutch government withdrew its support in 2007, and the early phase of the program until 2010 was ultimately considered a failure.
- In 2008 Cyclone Nargis hit Myanmar and resulted in more than 140,000 deceased and missing persons and left 2.4 million people in immediate need of humanitarian aid. In the initial assessment by the military junta, the generals thought it was just another typical cyclone and assumed that the regime could handle the situation. Furthermore, fear of invasion (in part prompted by the US offer to have aid distributed by US soldiers and by politicians like French foreign minister Bernard Kouchner demanding military humanitarian intervention) resulted in further resistance to foreign aid. Only intensive negotiations led by UN secretary Ban Ki-Moon and the ASEAN eventually calmed tensions and allowed for the entry of much-needed humanitarian assistance.
- The response to the 2010 Haiti earthquake has become infamous as an example of "well intended, but not well done." The UN Office for the Coordination of Humanitarian Affairs (OCHA) estimated that 12,000 NGOs would be present shortly after the earthquake, and it generated more than US$9 billion in public and private donations. Despite being one of the biggest relief aid responses in history, it was also considered one of the

biggest blunders. ALNAP (the Active Learning Network for Accountability and Performance in Humanitarian Action) analyzed the post-earthquake response situation and identified the following factors that hindered a more effective relief effort:[1]

○ a ceaseless flow of often-inexperienced small NGOs and in-kind donations;
○ a limited understanding of the context, particularly the urban setting;
○ by-passing of local authorities and civil society groups;
○ insufficient communication with affected populations;
○ lack of attention to how assistance could better support coping strategies;
○ weak humanitarian leadership structures, including a weak relationship with military leadership;
○ inadequate systems for data collection and analysis.

These are just a few of countless examples of humanitarian intelligence blunders. They illustrate that failures in intelligence analysis and project design can happen to any kind of actor (NGOs, states, international organizations) on various levels of analysis, operation, and planning. Furthermore, they elucidate that failures in humanitarian policy, programs, and projects can often be related back to:

a. lack of understanding of the operational *context*,
b. misjudgment of the *stakeholder* field (including cognitive biases),
c. faulty project key *assumptions* (relates to a and b), and
d. *coordination* failures (relates to b).

Humanitarian organizations are consumers and producers of intelligence at the same time. Moreover, there are different audiences for which the intelligence that has been used at different stages (planning, implementation and monitoring, evaluation) needs to be prepared in different formats and for different purposes. For example, in the planning and proposal writing phase the intelligence needs to serve at least three different purposes: (1) to plan the actual humanitarian operation, (2) to convince donors (e.g., the European Commission—ECHO, or USAID), and (3) to set the benchmarks for the monitoring of field activities.

Humanitarian analysts, to use a catch all term that encompasses rapid needs assessment teams, safety and security officers, project or programme planning teams, do hardly have any literature detailing useful current standards and important tools for their analysis needs. They have to rely on traditional intelligence and business intelligence methods to do their job, and this despite the fact that their needs are quite different. Also their strategic anchor points are different; for example, if a "hearts and minds" approach may be a common military strategy in enemy civilian areas in order to generate some working relationship with the local population, this shallow approach toward community acceptance would not suffice for a humanitarian organization. First, humanitarian organizations depend for their security, to a large degree, on genuine acceptance by the local population. Second, for the implementation of their projects with support in planning and execution by the local community, the relationship with this beneficiary community should exceed acceptance and progress ideally toward trust. Thus, it becomes clear to the reader that using pro forma "hearts and minds" techniques that would suffice for the military would certainly fall short of the desired effect humanitarian organizations need to achieve in order to establish what is called "humanitarian space," that is, operational space conducive to an effective and efficient humanitarian operation.

There are of course other constraints and strategic anchor points that determine the operational planning of humanitarian organizations. The "humanitarian principles," specifically the principles of humanity, impartiality, neutrality, and independence, define the relationship between the humanitarian organizations and other stakeholders. Many donor organizations and governments have obliged themselves to adhere to the principles of good humanitarian donorship, which in turn means that they also expect certain standards from humanitarian organizations. Depending on the background against which the humanitarian organization has been founded, there might be more elements defining their strategies, such as mission statement, core beliefs, internal policies, and other written and unwritten norms.

While in the past the operational security and many intelligence needs of humanitarian organizations were often taken care of by former military experts, today one increasingly finds civilians in the same positions. Both of these analysts require the right tools, and while military experts are well equipped to provide operational security, they sometimes lack an understanding of the specificities of humanitarian principles and the need for low profile security rather than hardening the targets; for example, many humanitarian organizations refuse military or security details to accompany them in the field in order not to become identified as mere proxies to foreign governments.

The problem that civilian analysts mostly face is that adequate training for humanitarian analysis is quite hard to come by. There are, of course, several university programs that focus on humanitarian action, such as the master's program of the Network of Humanitarian Action (NOHA) delivered by several European universities or the MA in Humanitarian Action by Fordham University. These university programs are, however, often either relatively general in their outlook or focus on specific areas such as international humanitarian law or supply chain management. BA and MA programs in intelligence studies focus predominantly on the traditional intelligence tradecraft and naturally lack an understanding of and a focus on the needs and constraints humanitarian actors face.

I.1 UTILITY OF HUMANITARIAN INTELLIGENCE

Humanitarian intelligence is an emerging field of study that is commonly covered by reports and guidelines prepared by the humanitarian community itself, drawing from a rich practical field experience. Within the larger academic domain of humanitarian studies there are fewer resources available to complement the practical work of the humanitarian community with the theoretical foundations it definitely needs to improve the conduct of humanitarian intelligence. This is exactly what the present book tries to accomplish—to bridge the gap between theory and practice, to provide practical tools for humanitarian analysis, and to cover the scientific background necessary to understand how these tools work and how they are best implemented.

Thereby, this book becomes useful both to practitioners and researchers in the domains of humanitarian action and to a large degree in the developmental sector. While both these fields are widely taught, their content is also quite diverse and needs to cover law, international relations, public health, psychology, management, anthropology, and not the least the analysis of contexts and actors. In the field of humanitarian studies and humanitarian action, this book will be of particular interest to humanitarian analysts, humanitarian managers, researchers, and students in humanitarian studies, international relations and foreign policy, as well as policymakers and consultants. To a large degree, particularly when it comes to practical tools for forecasting, scenario planning, stakeholder analysis, and context analysis, it will also benefit students, researchers, and practitioners in the fields of development, security as well as peace and conflict. Furthermore, experts in the area of civil protection and peacekeeping as well as intelligence analysis might find both practical tools and theoretical backgrounds benefiting their own analysis and project development. The study of humanitarian intelligence is also increasingly important for policymakers on a policy design level within the humanitarian and developmental sector as well as for practice-oriented researchers (think tanks) in the field of humanitarian and development aid and policy.

I.2 STRUCTURE AND LOGIC OF THE BOOK

In order to close the practice–theory gap for the emerging field of humanitarian intelligence, this book will provide an overview of the theoretical backgrounds against which many analytical tools have been developed, while at the same time providing step-by-step guidance on how to implement these tools in practice. To that end, it will cover:

- tools and methods of data gathering and analysis,
- standards of measurement and indicators in humanitarian action,
- interpretation strategies, and
- operational planning tools.

In order to achieve a better learning experience, the tools detailed in each chapter will be complemented with case studies and practical examples. Most of the cases will be of a hypothetical nature. The reason for using hypothetical cases is to provide for a clear illustration of the tools that are introduced without the distractions and differences in opinion and evaluation of data introduced by the complexities of a real case. This allows for keeping the explanations and applications for the purpose of accessibility on a level of complexity that does not exceed the scope of this book.

At the end of each chapter, review questions will allow the reader to reflect on the theoretical content of the chapter. In order to support the practical implementation of each tool, this book also provides step-by-step instructions for their use. An index of step-by-step guides, for quick access, can be found at the beginning of the book.

The overall book consists of four parts that introduce the humanitarian analyst to key elements of humanitarian intelligence (see Table I.1). These parts follow a general logic also applicable to the humanitarian intelligence cycle, which starts with a trigger inducing the need for principled and well-designed projects (part I), moves on to data collection and analysis of the context (part II), integrates stakeholders into the equation (part III), and concludes with evidence-based decision-making (part IV).

Part I contrasts humanitarian with traditional intelligence analysis and outlines the specific needs of the field of humanitarian action regarding intelligence techniques and tools as well as for particular skills of intelligence analysts. Furthermore, it juxtaposes the project and program cycle management with the intelligence cycle to illustrate the processes involved in humanitarian analysis, planning, and evaluation. One element of this part is also an introduction to the Logical Framework (LogFrame), a planning tool that has become a standard in humanitarian program and project development. Part II introduces the reader to data gathering and the assessment of reliability and validity of data, before providing the tools necessary to analyze data in the context within which the humanitarian operation shall be placed. The third part delves deeper into conducting strategic analysis and stakeholder networks. These insights will serve to develop tools for implementing all these elements into operational planning, that is, bridging the gap between knowledge, decision-making, and project design. This third part, "Actors and Interactions," takes a closer look at one of the most important aspects of humanitarian intelligence, the theories behind and the tools for the analysis of actors and their behavior. It covers perspectives, traditional stakeholder analytical tools, introduced by business intelligence and administrative sciences, and the relatively young but very powerful approach of social network analysis. The last part concludes the analytical process by discussing an approach to identifying present trends in the setup of complex contexts. It provides the transition to the designing of humanitarian projects by elaborating on different tools of planning entry and exit strategies as well as developing scenarios and tracking their progress with the help of indicators.

This book introduces in more depth the humanitarian analysis and intervention design (H-AID) framework, developed by the Groningen University team of the NOHA master's program on Humanitarian Action over the course of 15 years specifically for humanitarian analysts and researchers and made accessible to a wider audience in the book *Humanitarian Crises, Intervention and Security: A Framework for Evidence-Based Programming.*[2] Chapter 5 provides the foundations and the tools for the comprehensive context analysis (CCA). This tool can be used independently of the other tools of the H-AID framework as a stand-alone approach to in-depth context analysis. In addition, this chapter introduces two new tools not previously published: the capabilities/constraints analysis (section 5.3) and the relational analysis (section 5.4). Furthermore, chapter 7 provides an additional new tool that is also related to the H-AID framework; this helps the analyst to identify best and worst case trends in present situations. Chapters 5 and 7 are written with a view that they will function, on the one hand, as an introduction to the

Table I.1   Overview of the Structural Logic of Humanitarian Intelligence

I. Contextualizing Humanitarian Intelligence	Chapter 1: What is Humanitarian Intelligence
	Chapter 2: Humanitarian Intelligence in the Project Cycle Management
II. From Data to Context	Chapter 3: Information Collection, Reliability and Probability
	Chapter 4: Understanding Complex Contexts
	Chapter 5: Humanitarian Analysis and Intervention Design Framework (H-AID) – Comprehensive Context Analysis
III. Actors and Interactions	Chapter 6: Understanding Actors and their Impact
	Chapter 7: Social Network Analysis and Interpretation
IV. From Trends to Operational Planning	Chapter 8: Humanitarian Analysis and Intervention Design Framework (H-AID) – Actor-Based Trend Analysis
	Chapter 9: Operational Planning and Forecasting

much more elaborate book *Humanitarian Crisis, Intervention and Security.* This allows these chapters to be used in parallel with it. On the other hand, these chapters also introduce new tools previously not covered and thereby provide new approaches to those already familiar with *Humanitarian Crisis, Intervention and Security.* This book and the present title complement each other, while remaining complete books in their own right.

NOTES

1. Josh Harris, "Haiti Earthquake Response: Key Findings from ALNAP's Mapping and Analysis of Evaluations," *Trust.org—Thomson Reuters Foundation*, April 13, 2011, http://ww.trust.org/item/?map=haiti-earthquake-response-key-findings-from-alnaps-mapping-and-analysis-of-evaluations/.

2. Liesbet Heyse et al., *Humanitarian Crises, Intervention and Security: A Framework for Evidence-Based Programming* (London: Routledge, 2014).

Part I

CONTEXTUALIZING HUMANITARIAN INTELLIGENCE

Chapter 1

What Is Humanitarian Intelligence?

Humanitarian action has a great need for good analysis in order to improve humanitarian projects and interventions. However, resistance to learn from the rich experience and skills that traditional intelligence analysis has to offer stems in most part from a belief embedded in the culture of humanitarian action that all that is associated with intelligence agencies is negative. The fact that intelligence analysis provides exactly the skills and tools needed in the humanitarian field to improve humanitarian project development and programming makes a strong case to learn from this experience for the professionalization of humanitarian action. The concept of humanitarian intelligence intends to overcome this resistance, because the tradecraft needed for intelligence analysis can save lives and improve safety and security of aid workers.

The foremost aim of this chapter is to show that humanitarian analysis needs are in many respects similar to traditional intelligence needs. Besides answering the question posited in the title, this chapter covers the most important elements that constitute the operational parameters of humanitarian organizations. To define humanitarian intelligence means to first explain how the analysis needs of humanitarian aid workers changed over the past decades (1.1). Furthermore, it requires operationalizing the humanitarian principles and the concept of "humanitarian space" (1.2). The onset of the global war on terrorism, that is, the effect of terrorism and counterterrorism on humanitarian action more specifically (1.3), and the elements of professionalization that have been evolving in response to failures and lessons learned (1.4) also need to be explained. Finally, once we understand the processes set in motion by experiences regarding success and failures, we also understand how the global coordination mechanisms for humanitarian action evolved. Only then we can answer the question of what is humanitarian intelligence (1.5).

Going through these subquestions, this chapter establishes the terms and parameters that we will tacitly assume in subsequent chapters. In other words, this first chapter provides an intelligence perspective on the key parameters that any humanitarian analyst, whether working for a small nongovernmental organization (NGO) or for a large international organization, needs to understand and to a large degree also implement when planning operations. In other words, this chapter 1 forms the basis for all subsequent analysis and planning tools.

1.1   CHANGING NATURE OF HUMANITARIAN ANALYSIS NEEDS

Humanitarian action is not a new phenomenon. In fact, humanitarian aid in a structural and normatively embedded fashion has been provided to combatants since the onset of international law on the customs of war and the treatment of prisoners of war and those who can no longer fight (*hors de combat*). A historical turning point certainly was Henri Dunant's founding of the International Committee of the Red Cross (ICRC), an organization dedicated to alleviating the suffering of the hors de combat, the prisoners of war, and the suffering civilian population, in 1864. Subsequently, many international treaties were established to humanize warfare and to protect the suffering and the vulnerable.

A major turning point for the field of humanitarian action was the end of the Cold War, which led to a proliferation of humanitarian aid with the inclusion of many new NGOs and private groups dedicated to the delivering of aid to suffering populations whether affected by conflict or natural disasters, today simply referred to as "humanitarian organizations." The 1990s were marked by major humanitarian crises in Somalia, Rwanda, and Yugoslavia to name but a few. For example, while the humanitarian intervention in Somalia helped in saving an estimated 100,000 lives, it also cost many soldiers' and UN peacekeepers' lives. Militia leaders used stolen food aid to generate cash for purchasing weapons and keeping followers loyal, which perpetuated the conflict and created a political imbalance, the effects of which are shaping the political landscape even today.[1]

While certainly the goal of humanitarian aid workers and UN missions in general was to alleviate suffering in all these cases, the planning of many programs and projects had serious omissions, which led to disastrous consequences for beneficiaries, for the wider population, and for whole nations. Justifiably so, researchers and analysts heavily criticized the conduct of the international community and humanitarian organizations for unintentionally prolonging conflicts and causing negative consequences for beneficiaries.[2] This prompted Hugo Slim to argue that

Humanitarian aid obviously does have a dark side. Misapplied or not, the provision of help may well have negative repercussions beyond its original intention. The challenge for relief agencies is to determine the proper limits of their moral responsibility for this dark side, and then make all efforts to mitigate against it in their programmes.[3]

The international community and humanitarian organizations did take this critique very seriously and agonized over how to ensure that aid delivered would not yield unintended consequences by setting up standards, codes of conduct, monitoring and reporting procedures, etc. This became known as the "professionalization of aid."

Another change in the field that affected the humanitarian community directly was the increasing attacks on humanitarian aid workers by terrorist organizations; these became particularly problematic in the post-9/11 wars in Afghanistan and Iraq, which were part of the larger global war on terrorism (GWOT) initialized by the United States of America and its coalition of the willing. The effects of this change in the humanitarian operational space will be discussed in more detail in the next section.[4]

In summary, the field of humanitarian action is under constant influence from a variety of factors that in part determine analysis requirements of rapid needs assessment (RNA) teams, security experts, project design teams, and project managers. The times in which it was considered to be sufficient to deliver some food and makeshift shelter are past. Today, humanitarian action is a huge industry, and states as well as international organizations are willing to spend massive amounts of money and provide in-kind aid to help disaster- and conflict-stricken populations, which in turn attracts not-for-profit and profit-oriented organizations and faith-based and secular organizations alike.

Moreover, foreign aid spending forms an important part of foreign policy strategies. These strategies, particularly when trying to utilize aid to achieve political goals rather than simply providing relief aid to a population, can put further pressure on aid organizations in the form of donor-driven political priorities. At the same time, humanitarians increasingly face safety and security risks, are required to provide better aid standards, and have to comply with counterterrorism legislation.[5]

Among the most important factors affecting humanitarian space and analysis needs are:

- humanitarian principles and humanitarian space;
- effects of local organized crime, terrorism, and counterterrorism;
- professionalization of humanitarian aid (standards of accountability); and
- coordination challenges among humanitarian stakeholders.

1.2 HUMANITARIAN SPACE AND HUMANITARIAN PRINCIPLES

Humanitarian space can entail several definitions and understandings. It can be: (1) the operational space of humanitarian agencies necessary to meet humanitarian needs in accordance with humanitarian principles; (2) the space within which beneficiaries are able to uphold their rights to relief and protection; (3) a sphere in which international humanitarian law is respected, allowing for unhampered relief aid; or (4) humanitarian space as "a product of the dynamic and complex interplay of political, military and legal actors, interests, institutions and processes."[6] Most commonly, it simply denotes the "humanitarian operating environment." There are several approaches to achieving this operational space, generally distinguished by whether they rely on military protection of aid workers or on the concept of humanitarian legitimacy (also called "acceptance"). The latter depends, according to the ICRC, on the upholding of the humanitarian principles. Accordingly Thürer explains:

> The first issue is the subjective impartiality of the people who represent the organizations, the second being that of the structural characteristics of the organizations themselves—they must have room for manoeuvre with respect to the government and/or the parties to the conflict; independence and impartiality must be integral characteristics of the organization, and these characteristics must be guaranteed. Furthermore, their impartiality and independence must not only exist objectively, but must also be experienced and perceived by the outside world.[7]

Since their establishment in international humanitarian law, the humanitarian principles have become somewhat of a sacred vow to humanitarian aid agencies, the UN humanitarian system, European Commission's Humanitarian Aid and Civil Protection department (ECHO), etc. To them, these principles are the all-encompassing norms that are or should be present in all humanitarian operations; although it has to be mentioned that not all actors adhere to them or interpret them equally. The four universally applicable principles (of the seven obligatory to the Red Cross established at the XX International Conference of the Red Cross Vienna, 1965) are:

- *Humanity*: to prevent and alleviate human suffering wherever it may be found.
- *Impartiality*: no discrimination as to nationality, race, religious beliefs, class or political opinions; to relieve suffering, giving priority to the most urgent cases of distress.
- *Neutrality*: to not take sides in hostilities or engage at any time in controversies of a political, racial, religious or ideological nature.

• *Independence*: to be autonomous with regard to states, international organizations and other authorities.[8]

Humanity is the overall objective, the reason for all humanitarian work. It also gives guidance as to what should always be the prime directive when one is faced with difficult situations that require a decision (so-called hard cases). Impartiality, neutrality, and independence are principles that guide the modus operandi of humanitarian operations. They determine the way in which humanity is to be achieved in external relations with beneficiaries, donors, and warring factions. This means that it requires the humanitarian actor to set deliberate actions toward beneficiaries, donors, and other stakeholders in order to create the perception of being a legitimate actor, which in turn is thought to achieve what is referred to as "humanitarian space."

Impartiality is the operational instrument in the field ensuring that nobody is being discriminated against. It is a principle that bridges the donor and the beneficiary sphere and prohibits an organization's ideology from interfering with the principle of humanity, which posits the need of people as the sole determinant measure of aid distribution. *Neutrality* refers to not choosing sides between the opposing goals of parties in a conflict (this includes the international community and donor perspectives). As a principle located in the beneficiary or local sphere it ensures that parties to the conflict do not oppose the delivery of aid to each other because both can benefit from the same advantage. In order to ensure this picture of an aid agency to be truly impartial, it also needs to be seen as independent from donor and state interests (e.g., concerning democratization and regime change agendas of states). In other words, *independence* serves to create an image of detachment from political goals present in the donor sphere. All four principles together form the humanitarian space as one determined by how different stakeholders view the humanitarian organization (see Figure 1.1).

A violation of any of these principles can lead to stakeholders perceiving the humanitarian organization as being less neutral, and it can thus give cause to attacks, denial of access, and other hindrances that limit the operational space. Of course, this concept of humanitarian space that considers principles would suffice to protect humanitarian aid workers assumes (sometimes wrongly) that these principles have just as much effect on criminal entities. To cope with the threat of criminal actors, which simply aim to profit from aid and relief organizations, for example, through kidnapping, carjacking, theft, or sexual assault, often requires different measure in addition to acceptance-creating measures. In particular, kidnapping, the average global rate of which has risen by 28 percent in the three years prior to 2014,[9] increases the call for military protection or security details. "The challenge with a more protection-based approach, however, is that such measures must be carefully designed so as not to limit contact, and alienate the host community."[10] With regard to

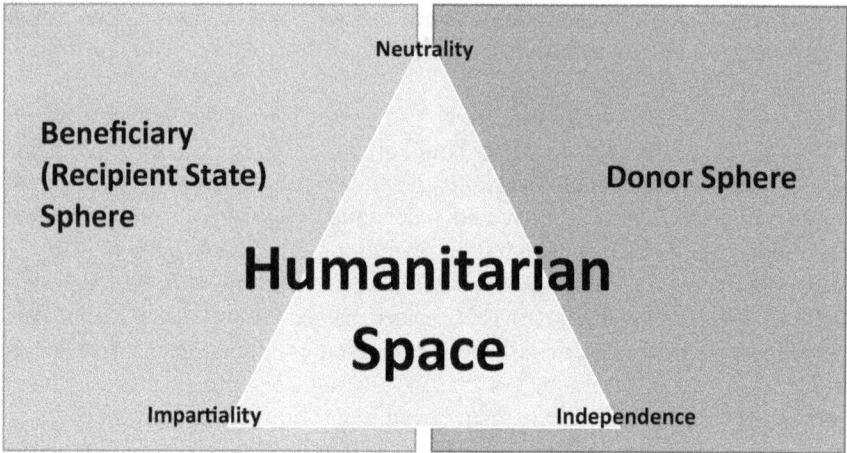

Figure 1.1   Humanitarian Space as Consisting of Humanitarian Principles

these criminal security issues, acceptance-based security might work only to a limited degree, and humanitarian organizations might have to resort to other means of protection, which require a much more in-depth analysis of the local context and its stakeholders. Of course, the challenge is to continue to operate on the basis of humanitarian principles, while ensuring staff security, and to work closely together with the local population.

1.3   EFFECTS OF TERRORISM AND COUNTERTERRORISM

The attacks on the World Trade Centre and the Pentagon on September 11, 2001, had a profound effect on world politics. It eventually led to interventions in Afghanistan and Iraq. Also, the consequences of the politics of GWOT did not halt before the humanitarian principles and the misuse of "hearts and mind" practices by the invading forces. Intelligence agencies on the ground further blurred the lines between humanitarian organizations and enemy combatants.

Initially, after the first terrorist attacks hit the United Nations Office for the Coordination of Humanitarian Affairs (UN-OCHA) in Baghdad in August 2003, which killed 22 people including UN envoy Sergio Vieira de Mello, the humanitarian community hardly responded. It was only a year later, when NGOs themselves became the target, starting with the kidnapping of two Italian aid workers (the "two Simonas incident" as it was referred to in the NGO community), that the humanitarian community became aware of its own vulnerability and decided to respond by either going low-profile or leaving the country altogether.[11] To illustrate the seriousness of the situation in numbers, during the year 2008, UN secretary general Ban Ki-Moon reported the following (the numbers refer to UN staff and in the brackets to NGO staff): 25 (63) deaths from attacks; 490 (236) attacks; 160 (70) cases of detention by state authorities; 39 (103) incidents of unlawful detention by nonstate actors; 263 (41) cases of assault; 546 (132) incidents of harassment; 578 (113) armed robberies; 119 (50) incidents of vehicle hijacking, etc.[12]

The effect of terrorism and counterterrorism on humanitarian action cannot be underestimated. The United States, as one of the world's biggest humanitarian donors, is particularly concerned that money dedicated for aid will reach terrorist organizations. International and regional organizations have their own concerns when it comes to the dual role they play with regards to the political nature of development aid, which conflicts with the neutral and impartial nature of humanitarian aid. These concerns and strategies to resolve them often do not match the NGOs' perception of the situation and their concerns for safety and security in the field. The local beneficiaries, in the meantime, are addressees of terrorist and counterterrorist operations and hearts and minds tactics and recipients of humanitarian aid.

In the years after 9/11 the impact of donor policies, encouraging the militarization of aid, on humanitarian actors increasingly affected the image of humanitarian actors as not being impartial and neutral in conflicts. There are, however, also important arguments in favor of the use of military support in humanitarian action, as, for example, concerning the provision with the necessary transport and logistics, or by protecting civilians and aid workers from violence by state and nonstate actors. In this regard, the military can often also be seen as a humanitarian actor itself and is present in civil and military cooperation (CIMIC) together with other stakeholders such as UN agencies.

The two most common arguments for and against military protection of humanitarian aid workers are either diametrically opposed or constitute a vicious cycle: (1) humanitarian assistance needs military protection/involvement because they are being attacked and (2) military involvement is a cause of the attack against humanitarian aid workers. Advocates of argument (2) usually demand a strict separation of the military and humanitarian organizations. A common alternative strategy to a hardening of the targets by military protection is the creation of humanitarian space through acceptance.

The GWOT, even if the term has disappeared from public discourse, is continuing to affect the operation of humanitarian organizations in various ways. Regarding funding of humanitarian actors, NGOs increasingly try to keep their origins secret and to steer free from implicit or explicit political agendas of donor states. This relates strongly to how NGOs position themselves vis-à-vis beneficiaries and the wider public. GWOT has also had an impact on programs and projects: it led to the reduction of proximity of international NGOs to the field by the increasing use of implementing partners and steering of projects from save locations (remote controlling); furthermore, NGOs tend to reduce their visibility in areas with hostile stakeholders. The United States has introduced the Partner Vetting System (PVS) for all organizations that apply for funding from United States Agency for International Development (USAID), which has staff details and details of implementing partners screened through CIA, FBI, and NSA. This system raised concerns with regards to being at best a big administrative burden to NGOs and at worst an infringement on privacy with the potential of even being a security risk.[13] The PVS, together with terror lists of intergovernmental organizations and states, might help to monitor suspect entities, but in the eyes of many humanitarian organizations it reduced humanitarian operational space and put humanitarians at risk of legal prosecution if they happened to be viewed as cooperating in any way with terrorist organizations, be it through direct assistance of people in need or in cases of negotiation for access to certain regions.

1.4   PROFESSIONALIZATION OF HUMANITARIAN AID

The trend toward professionalization of aid can be attributed to an increasing awareness among the humanitarian community and other stakeholders that aid is not intrinsically good because of the good intention behind it, but that when conducted unprofessionally it can lead to bad (unintended) consequences. Humanitarian organizations are increasingly under pressure to perform better, to uphold standards, and to be accountable toward different stakeholders for their local projects, their funding, their mandates, and their overall mission.

For one, governmental and private donors expect their implementing partners to show results for the investment ("Did the organization do what it promised to do for obtaining the funding?")—this is in most cases a question of accounting. Beyond that, the academic community has an important role in assessing and evaluating the successes and failures of aid organizations in disaster situations. This most often goes beyond the mere accounting and asks questions of add-on "collateral damage" (unintended consequences such as destruction of the local market), the longterm impact (such as aid dependency), or questions about cultural appropriateness, gender equality, beneficiary participation, and ethics. The peer group of established humanitarian agencies, newcomers, commercial relief contractors, such as DHL services of the German Post or Development Alternatives Inc., and the military further increase the pressure on humanitarian organizations to professionalize (Figure 1.2).[14] Most importantly, however, a push originating from academics and donors for a greater accountability toward the inclusion of beneficiaries in all stages of a relief project (planning, implementation, evaluation) raised the bar even higher. All these stakeholders put pressure on aid organizations

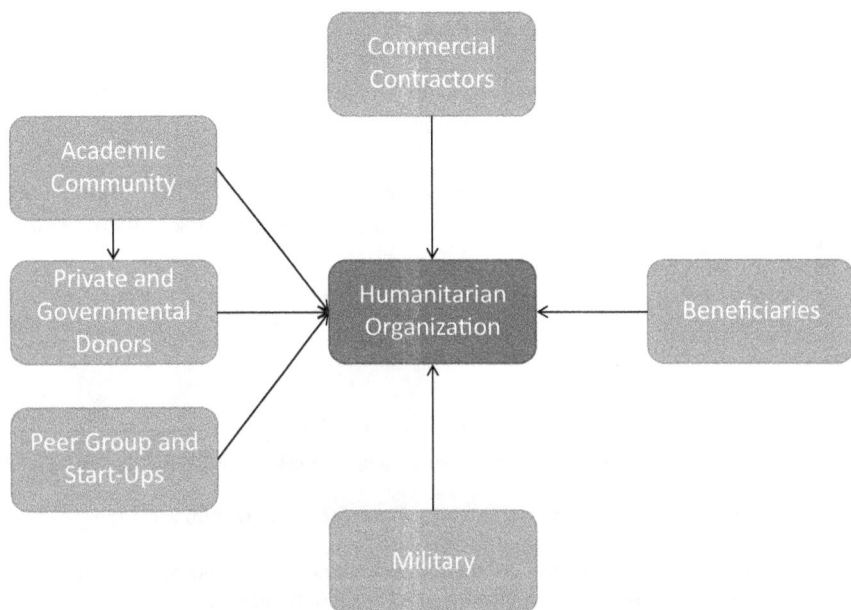

Figure 1.2   Pressure Exerting Stakeholders for Professionalization. *Note*: Adapted from: Warren Lancaster, "The Code of Conduct: Whose Code, Whose Conduct?," *Journal of Humanitarian Assistance*, April 18, 1998, http://jha.ac/1998/04/18/the-code-of-conduct-whose-code-whose-conduct/.

to improve their performance, to be transparent in their actions, and to almost volunteer accountability to all interested parties.

At the beginning of the 1990s there were almost no common standards besides international humanitarian law. The failure of many humanitarian projects during that time was in part attributed to the lack of standards of performance and accountability. Therefore, starting with initiatives of the International Federation of the Red Cross and Red Crescent and the UN-OCHA, today there are several important standards and codes. These are important as they set the parameters of operations. Among others, important codes and standards to be mentioned are:

- *Code of Conduct for the International Red Cross and Red Crescent Movement and NGOs in Disaster Relief*: this voluntary code of conduct was set up in 1994 and is a yardstick for self-governance of humanitarian organizations. It is assumed to be a minimum standard of professional conduct containing among other elements the humanitarian principles.[15]
- *Sphere Standards (Humanitarian Charter and Minimum Standards in Disaster Response)*: it comprises widely recognized sets of common

principles and universal minimum standards for disaster relief. The minimum standards are performance benchmarks in the following areas: water, sanitation and hygiene promotion (WASH), food security, nutrition, and food aid; shelter, settlements, and nonfood items; health services.[16]

* *Core Humanitarian Standards (CHS)*: launched in December 2014, it replaces the HAP 2010 Standards, the People in Aid Code of Good Practice, and the Core Standards section of the Sphere Handbook.[17] It covers the commitments in Table 1.1.
* *Quality COMPAS reference framework*: this is a method of quality assurance developed on the basis of a six-year research project. It uses its own

Table 1.1   Core Humanitarian Standards – Commitments

1. Communities and people affected by crisis receive assistance appropriate and relevant to their needs.
2. Communities and people affected by crisis have access to the humanitarian assistance they need at the right time.
3. Communities and people affected by crisis are not negatively affected and are more prepared, resilient, and less at-risk as a result of humanitarian action.
4. Communities and people affected by crisis know their rights and entitlements, have access to information, and participate in decisions that affect them.
5. Communities and people affected by crisis have access to safe and responsive mechanisms to handle complaints.
6. Communities and people affected by crisis receive coordinated, complementary assistance.
7. Communities and people affected by crisis can expect delivery of improved assistance as organizations learn from experience and reflection.
8. Communities and people affected by crisis receive the assistance they require from competent and well-managed staff and volunteers.
9. Communities and people affected by crisis can expect that the organizations assisting them are managing resources effectively, efficiently, and ethically.

Table 1.2   COMPAS Criteria and Key Processes

A. The project responds to a demonstrated need	B. The project achieves its objectives
C. The project removes or reduces the risk of negative impacts	D. The project aims for positive impacts beyond implementation
E. The project is consistent with the agency's mandate and principles	F. The project respects the population
G. The project is flexible	H. The project is integrated in its institutional context in an optimal manner
I. The agency has the necessary resources and expertise	J. The agency has the appropriate management capacity
K. The agency makes optimal use of resources	L. The agency uses lessons drawn from experience

set of tools and offers training modules and consultancy services.[18] The COMPAS criteria and key processes are worth mentioning as they can be considered minimum quality criteria similar to the Core Standards (Table 1.2).[19]

1.5 COORDINATION CHALLENGES AMONG HUMANITARIAN STAKEHOLDERS

Humanitarian action on the level of the UN dates back until and even before the inception of the UN itself. In November 1943, a predecessor of the UN, the United Nations Relief and Rehabilitation Administration (UNRRA), was established. It was set up to provide aid to freed areas and to refugees. Out of this organization grew, after the end of World War II, the first two UN aid agencies, known today as UN High Commissioner for Refugees (UNHCR) and United Nations International Children's Emergency Fund (UNICEF). During the Cold War several funds and programs followed, such as the World Food Programme (WFP, 1961) and the United Nations Development Programme (UNDP, 1965), to cater to humanitarian needs.[20]

The proliferation of agencies within the UN with mandates relating to relief aid led to the need to coordinate and restructure the UN's humanitarian system in organizational and operational terms. In 1991, the UN General Assembly (UN-GA) responded to this need with its landmark resolution 46/182,[21] which aimed at a consolidation of the overall UN system of humanitarian aid. First of all, it established the operational principles, which from now on would be binding to all UN agencies delivering humanitarian aid: humanity, neutrality, and impartiality. Furthermore, it established in accordance with general principles of international law (specifically the sovereignty of states) that the primary responsibility for initiation, organization, coordination, and implementation of humanitarian assistance lies with the state concerned. In terms of operational principles, the UN-GA further added that linking relief, rehabilitation, and development (LRRD) should be implemented as a fundamental principle within the UN humanitarian system as a whole. In structural terms the resolution established coordination mechanisms for the organization of actors, the consolidation of appeals processes for funding, and overall strategy development:

- Inter-Agency Standing Committee (IASC),
- Emergency Relief Coordinator (ERC) as Under-Secretary General,
- Central Emergency Response Fund (CERF),
- Consolidated Appeals Process (CAP), and
- Department of Humanitarian Affairs (DHA).

In 1998, the DHA was restructured by the Secretary General into the OCHA with an expanded mandate to include the coordination of all humanitarian response on UN level, policy development, and humanitarian advocacy.[22]

The failures of responding to the 2004 Darfur crisis prompted the ERC to launch the *Inter-Agency Real-Time Evaluation of the Humanitarian Response to the Darfur Crisis* to develop lessons learned. It concluded that the humanitarian response to the Darfur crisis was "delayed and inadequate, primarily due to the inability of agencies to mobilize capacity and resources."[23] Further frustration mounted with the response to the 2004/5 Indian Ocean tsunami, which eventually led the ERC to commission the Humanitarian Response Review (HRR). This report concluded that the overall system of humanitarian action (including the UN, Red Cross Movements, ICRC, and NGOs) was in need of a better humanitarian leadership for developing an overall strategy and of a clustering of agencies into a sectoral coordination in order to improve strategies on this level as well.[24]

This reform process led the IASC to develop the Cluster Approach with the following aims:

> At the global level, the aim of the Cluster Approach is to strengthen system-wide preparedness and technical capacity to respond to humanitarian emergencies by ensuring that there is predictable leadership and accountability in all the main sectors or areas of humanitarian response.
>
> Similarly, at the country level the aim is to strengthen humanitarian response by demanding high standards of predictability, accountability and partnership in all sectors or areas of activity.[25]

The Cluster Approach assigns leadership in different sectors of humanitarian aid to different organizations that are particularly well versed in the specific area. These cluster leads coordinate the overall cluster strategy, develop preparedness, and eventually are providers of last resort in case implementing partners fail to perform (with exception of the ICRC). On a local level these responsibilities contain more specifically: establishment and maintenance of appropriate humanitarian coordination mechanisms; coordination with national/local authorities, state institutions, local civil society, and other relevant actors; participatory and community-based approaches; needs assessment and analysis; emergency preparedness; planning and strategy development; application of standards; monitoring and reporting, etc.[26] Figure 1.3 illustrates the Cluster Approach as it is presently implemented.

As became evident from the earlier elaborations, the humanitarian community has invested much time to improve relief efforts and aid provision over the past decades. In this sense, standards and coordination mechanisms represent important elements that guide operations planning and need to be taken into account by humanitarian agencies.

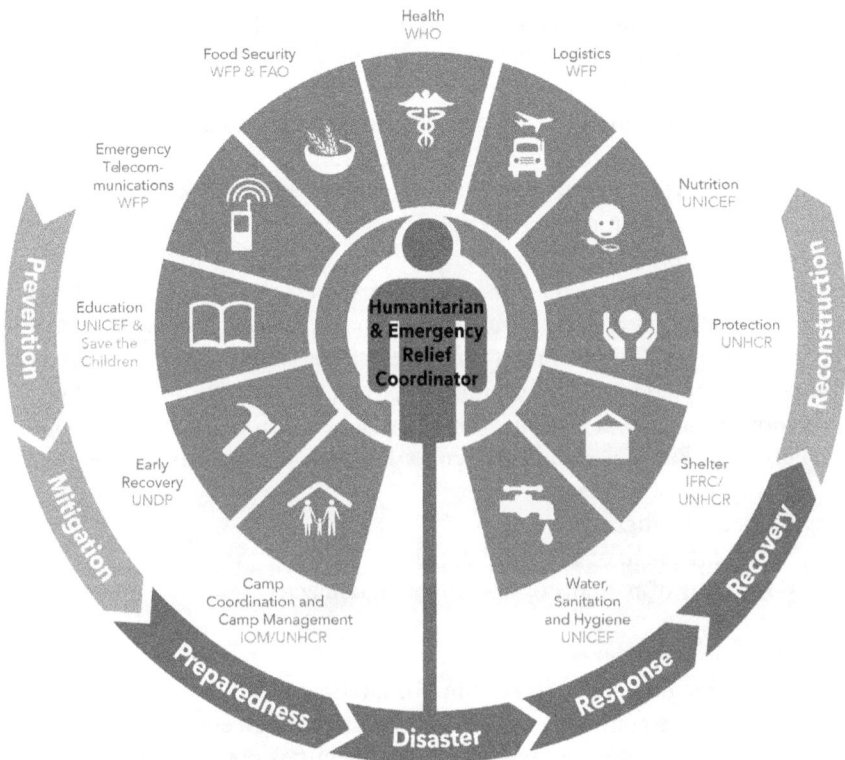

Figure 1.3 Cluster Approach. *Note*: UN OCHA, "What Is the Cluster Approach? | Humanitarian Response," accessed February 3, 2015, http://www.humanitarianresponse. info/coordination/clusters/what-cluster-approach.

1.6 DEFINING HUMANITARIAN INTELLIGENCE

Helmuth von Moltke famously stated, "In war you will generally find that the enemy has at any time three courses of action open to him. Of those three, he will invariably choose the fourth."[27] As in other areas of intelligence analysis, humanitarian intelligence aims to reduce uncertainty and risk by providing the basis of informed decision-making. In general, intelligence analysis employs research methods similar to those used in market research or academic research, but three key distinctions exist between them and humanitarian and security intelligence. First, accurate information is not readily available and a wide range of methods and techniques must be deployed for data collection to compensate for that fact. Second, concealment, deception, and denial are routinely encountered. Actors doubtful to new third parties with potentially diametrically opposed agendas are encountered with suspicion, secrecy, or even hostility. Third, biases with regards to anticipated deception and negative expectations regarding adversary actors tend to affect analytic interpretations. The fear that no information can be fully trusted (as it might be fed by counterintelligence) can lead even to a point where analytical assessments have to yield to ad hoc intuitive decisions. Humanitarian intelligence has these three elements in common with traditional intelligence analysis. However, in many respects the tools and methods are quite different from traditional intelligence tradecraft. In art, this has to do with limited capacities of humanitarian actors regarding signal intelligence, in part it has to do with different normative and operational standards specific to humanitarian action (e.g., humanitarian principles). This is particularly true when it comes to accepted tools of recruiting informants and acquiring information.

In terms of a general classification of intelligence, the following taxonomy of Hank Prunckun is very useful even for humanitarian intelligence purposes:

Tactical Intelligence:
- Is short-range or time limited; and
- Consists of patterns or operational mode activities.

Strategic Intelligence:
- Considered to be a higher form of intelligence;
- Provides a comprehensive view of a target or an activity;
- Comments on future possibilities or identifies potential issues;
- Provides advice on threats, risks, and vulnerabilities;
- Provides options for planning and policy development;
- Assists in allocating resources; and
- Requires extensive knowledge of the target or the area of activity.

Operational Intelligence:
- Provides immediate insight that supports an operation; and
- Oriented toward a specific target or an activity.[28]

To define "humanitarian intelligence" is a matter of capturing the varieties of practices of humanitarian actors, trying to assess the status quo in a humanitarian crisis, the impact of humanitarian projects and program, as well as the underlying causes of persistent and complex emergencies. "Humanitarian intelligence" is then defined as:

the use of investigative and analytical techniques in service of rapid and continuous assessment, project and program development, impact evaluation and learning.

In terms of this taxonomy, the intelligence needs regarding policymaking and program development are best comparable with strategic intelligence; project development requires the skills of the domain of tactical intelligence, and the skills and information necessary for the daily work of the security officer in the context of the humanitarian operation would broadly fall into the area of operational intelligence.

In order to achieve consistency and interorganizational compatibility of intelligence, coordinating bodies, such as the UN-OCHA, have devised a variety of assessment tools and standards. This demand for mainstreaming of intelligence gathering and analysis is a consequence of the strong needs for coordination among different international, regional, and local governmental organizations and NGOs, and to some extent their common financing through centralized donor organizations such as the European Commission (DG-ECHO) and USAID. Mainstreaming, however, remains difficult in part due to the diversity of specializations (food, health, shelter, WASH, etc.), the different needs (project, program, rapid needs, or impact assessment), the different standards applied (rights- vs. needs- based approaches), and many other factors.

Distinct from other analytical techniques humanitarian intelligence operates on specific key assumptions regarding security and safety:

1. Increased risks: routinely operating in volatile or hostile environments
2. Higher threat acceptance threshold, for example: negotiating access with potential hostiles
3. Operational security: providing humanitarian space
4. Including threats to physical and mental health of staff
5. Different clients (ECHO, diplomats, aid agencies, etc.) need different tools and reporting formats
6. Target centric: staff safety and security are as much of concern as livelihood of beneficiaries
7. Sociocultural intelligence needs for stakeholder interaction

Humanitarian intelligence therefore focuses just as much on how to use humanitarian early warning indicators to assess risks, evaluate trends, and write early warning analyses as it does on how to provide guidance on the operational design of humanitarian relief efforts. Another important aspect of humanitarian intelligence is that operational security depends on intelligence analysis. This operational security is not simply an augmentation of an operation by adding a security feature, but in fact it means that the whole operation needs to be designed in such a way that operational security is ensured intrinsically through every aspect of the project design. Humanitarian intelligence then goes beyond just giving advice on decision-making, but it requires the analyst to bridge analysis and project design by informing every single project design decision with the necessary piece of intelligence.

Since unlike governments, NGOs' resources are very limited, often the same group of people usually conducts humanitarian intelligence analysis and operations planning. That means that the intelligence analyst is often also the project designer. Familiarity with the organizational capacities is in most cases a plus; it can, however, also lead to biases concerning the evaluation of data and the needs for operations to succeed. Humanitarian intelligence analysis, therefore, is specifically under pressure to link all analytical steps as closely as possible to the project design process within the LogFrame. In the end, it has to tie neatly into the project management cycle as intertwining with the intelligence cycle.

Operational humanitarian intelligence consists of RNA and field awareness intelligence for rapid relief aid (i.e., in military terms called the battlefield awareness, e.g., about accessibility of roads, mobility of beneficiaries, presence of criminal entities). Tactical humanitarian intelligence goes beyond that and is necessary in full-fledged projects; it includes among other information particularly a stakeholder analysis that informs about the intentions of actors. Strategic humanitarian intelligence is mostly a policy tool or relevant for aid projects and programs with a longer time horizon than a two-week quick impact operation. The latter interacts however with tactical humanitarian intelligence due to the ongoing trend toward LRRD.

One can conclude that humanitarian intelligence is closely related to traditional intelligence analysis. However, while it shares common characteristics with military and security intelligence, it differs very much from it when it comes to humanitarian principles, operational parameters, and the need to create a positive local perception, as well as the potential to engage with beneficiaries in a long-lasting collaboration. Humanitarian intelligence then must be particularly wary about the clandestine element that often accompanies the field of intelligence, since trust by all stakeholders involved is one of the foremost elements that contribute to success and future collaboration. This trust element is particularly expressed in the concept of accountability.

REVIEW QUESTIONS

- What is humanitarian space, and how do we achieve it?
- What was the effect of terrorism and GWOT-related policies and counterterrorism tactics on the humanitarian system?
- Which factors lead to an increasing professionalization of aid?

- How do norms and standards ensure professionalization of aid?
- What is the global UN coordination system for humanitarian aid, and how does it work?
- What are the key assumptions that humanitarian intelligence operates on?

NOTES

1. Walter Clarke and Jeffrey Herbst, "Somalia and the Future of Humanitarian Intervention," *Foreign Affairs* 75, no. 2 (April 1996): 70.

2. Mary B. Anderson, *Do No Harm: How Aid Can Support Peace or War* (London: Lynne Rienner Publishers, 1999).

3. Hugo Slim, "Doing the Right Thing: Relief Agencies, Moral Dilemmas and Moral Responsibility in Political Emergencies and War," *Disasters* 21, no. 3 (September 1997): 244–57.

4. Andrej Zwitter, "Humanitarian Action on the Battlefields of the Global War on Terror," *The Journal of Humanitarian Assistance (online Journal)*, October 25, 2008, http://sites.tufts.edu/jha/archives/223; Joanna Macrae and Adele Harmer, "Humanitarian Action and the 'Global War on Terror': A Review of Trends and Issues," HPG Report (London: Overseas Development Institute—Humanitarian Policy Group, July 2003).

5. For a detailed legal review on EU and US counterterrorism legislation concerning humanitarian and development aid, see: Andrej Zwitter, "Humanitarian Action, Development and Terrorism," in *Research Handbook on International Law and Terrorism*, ed. Ben Saul (Cheltenham: Edward Elgar, 2014), 315–32.

6. Sarah Collinson and Samir Elhawary, "Humanitarian Space: A Review of Trends and Issues" (London: Overseas Development Institute—Humanitarian Policy Group, April 2012), 1, http://www.odi.org/sites/odi.org.uk/files/odi-assets/publications-opinion-files/7643.pdf.

7. Daniel Thürer, "Dunant's Pyramid: Thoughts on the 'Humanitarian Space,'" *International Review of the Red Cross* 89, no. 865 (March 2007): 60.

8. Jean Pictet, "The Fundamental Principles of the Red Cross: Commentary," *ICRC*, January 1, 1979, https://www.icrc.org/eng/resources/documents/misc/fundamental-principles-commentary-010179.htm.

9. "Aid Worker Security Report 2013—The New Normal: Coping with the Kidnapping Threat," Aid Worker Security Database (AWSD) (Humanitarian Outcomes, 2013), 4, https://aidworkersecurity.org/sites/default/files/AidWorkerSecurityReport_2013_web.pdf.

10. Ibid., 7.

11. Zwitter, "Humanitarian Action on the Battlefields of the Global War on Terror."

12. Ban Ki-Moon, "Safety and Security of Humanitarian Personnel and Protection of United Nations Personnel," Report of the Secretary-General to the General Assembly (August 18, 2008).

13. Zwitter, "Humanitarian Action, Development and Terrorism."

14. Abby Stoddard, "Humanitarian Firms: Commercial Business Engagement in Emergency Response," in *Humanitarian Assistance: Improving U.S.–European Cooperation*, ed. Julia Steets and Daniel S. Hamilton (Washington, DC: Center for Transatlantic Relations, The Johns Hopkins University/Global Public Policy Institute, 2009), 246–66.

15. http://www.ifrc.org/en/publications-and-reports/code-of-conduct/#sthash. M46QiRp2.dpuf.

16. http://www.sphereproject.org.

17. http://www.corehumanitarianstandard.org.

18. http://www.compasqualite.org.

19. Groupe URD, "Quality COMPAS Companion Book," Version 9.06-EN (Plaisians (France): Group Urgence Réhabilitation Développment, 2009), 8, http://www.compasqualite.org/Setup/en/V9.06-EN_Quality_COMPAS_companion_book.pdf.

20. Andrej Zwitter, "The United Nations Legal Framework of Humanitarian Assistance," in *International Law and Humanitarian Assistance: A Crosscut through Legal Issues Pertaining to Humanitarianism*, ed. Hans-Joachim Heintze and Andrej Zwitter (Berlin, Heidelberg: Springer Verlag, 2011), 53–55.

21. UN General Assembly, Strengthening of the Coordination of Humanitarian Emergency Assistance of the United Nations, December 19, 1991, UN Doc. A/RES/46/182.

22. OCHA, History of OCHA, http://www.unocha.org/about-us/who-we-are/history.

23. Vanessa Humphries, "Improving Humanitarian Coordination: Common Challenges and Lessons Learned from the Cluster Approach," *Journal of Humanitarian Assistance*, April 30, 2013, http://sites.tufts.edu/jha/archives/1976.

24. Costanza Adlnolfi et al., "Humanitarian Response Review," Independent Report Commissioned by the Under-Secretary-General for Humanitarian Affairs (New York and Geneva: Office for the Coordination of Humanitarian Affairs (OCHA), August 2005), 9–12.

25. "Guidance Note on Using the Cluster Approach to Strengthen Humanitarian Response" (New York, Geneva: Interagency Standing Committee (IASC), November 24, 2006), 2, http://www.humanitarianresponse.info/system/files/documents/files/IASC%20Guidance%20Note%20on%20using%20the%20Cluster%20Approach%20to%20Strengthen%20Humanitarian%20Response%20(November%202006).pdf.

26 Ibid., 7.

27. Clint Watts and John E. Brennan, "Capturing the Potential of Outlier Ideas in the Intelligence Community," *Studies in Intelligence* 55, no. 4 (Extracts, December 2011): 1; https://www.cia.gov/library/center-for-the-study-of-intelligence/csi-publications/csi-studies/studies/vol.-55-no.-4/pdfs-vol.-55-no.-4/Brennan-Reflections%20on%20Outliers-13Jan.pdf.

28. Hank Prunckun, *Handbook of Scientific Methods of Inquiry for Intelligence Analysis* (Scarecrow Press, 2010), 7–8.

Chapter 2

Humanitarian Intelligence in Project Cycle Management

2.1 INTELLIGENCE CYCLE

All intelligence work starts from two premises: (1) a need to know in order to act and (2) an operational environment that contains the data required. Intelligence is built around these two premises. The term "intelligence cycle" describes the traditional process of phases starting from the need to know and arriving at the actionable knowledge; it eventually closes the cycle by feeding this knowledge back into the analysis. One typically distinguishes between six phases:[1]

1. *Direction*: In this phase the decision-maker identifies her intelligence requirements and directs the intelligence staff toward the area of her interest.
2. *Collection*: The collection phase is characterized by gathering data from the operational environment through HUMINT (human intelligence), OSINT (open source intelligence), IMINT (imagery intelligence), ELINT (electronic intelligence), SIGINT (signals intelligence), etc.
3. *Processing*: Before it can be useful to the analyst, the data needs to be processed and sorted in terms of format, language, reliability and validity, and level of analysis in order to become information.
4. *Analysis*: Information, in order to become actionable, requires a further step that integrates separate parts of information, interprets the significance of the information, and aggregates all information into conclusions, or so-called intelligence. These conclusions should be prepared in a way that they are a response to the direction phase and provide a solid basis for further action.
5. *Dissemination*: Depending on the need of the decision-maker, the dissemination can take various forms, for example, reports, oral presentations

or consultations. Furthermore, the preparation of the intelligence depends on the purpose of the analysis (strategic intelligence, tactical intelligence, indicators and warning, etc.).

6. *Feedback*: Ideally the decision-maker then provides feedback to the intelligence team and provides guidance on how to revise and/or deepen the analysis. This feedback can be based on the fact that the decision-maker now understands the situation better or on actions already taken on the basis of the intelligence provided.

The traditional intelligence cycle (see Figure 2.1), thus, describes the process from needing actionable knowledge to acting on the basis of knowledge.

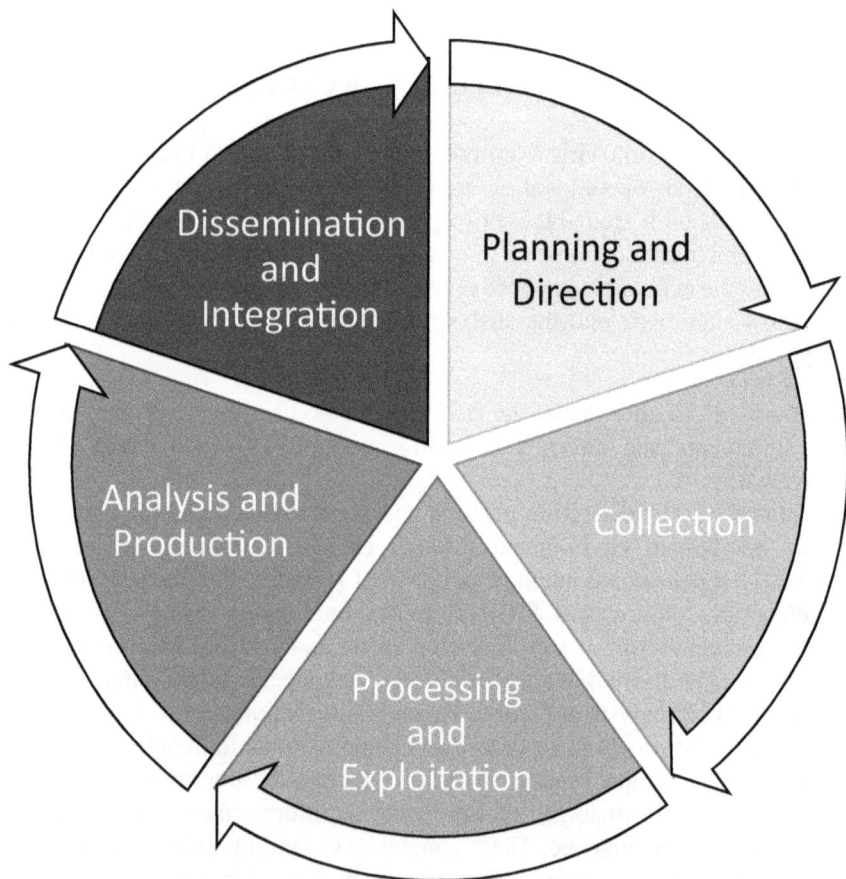

Figure 2.1 Traditional Intelligence Cycle. *Note:* Joint Chiefs of Staff, Joint Intelligence, Joint Publication 2-0 (Defense Technical Information Center (DTIC), 2013), 1–6; http://www.dtic.mil/doctrine/news_pubs/jp2_0.pdf.

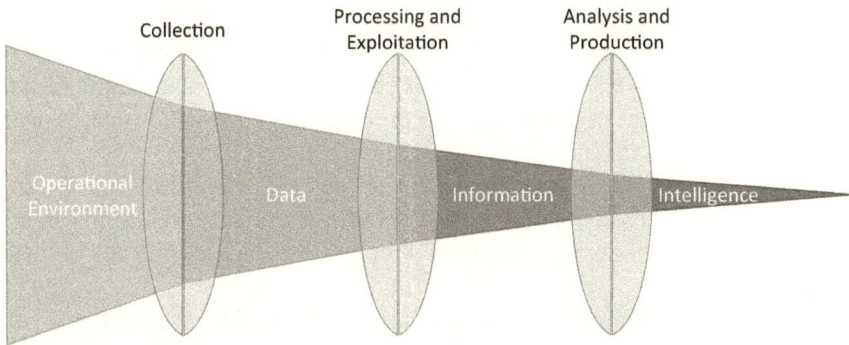

Figure 2.2 **Relationship of Data, Information and Intelligence.** *Note*: Joint Chiefs of Staff, Joint Intelligence, Joint Publication 2-0 (Defense Technical Information Center (DTIC), 2013), 1–2; http://www.dtic.mil/doctrine/news_pubs/jp2_0.pdf.

In the steps that come between direction and dissemination, the data for this purpose is collected and funneled, processed into information, and analyzed to form intelligence (see Figure 2.2).

The intelligence cycle has not been without critique. Particularly, Robert M. Clark discusses the irrelevance of the intelligence cycle and proposes alternatively a "target centric approach."[2] When one looks at the practice of intelligence analysis, one notices an intermingling between the different phases. For example, intelligence analysts correspond with the decision-maker to narrow, widen, or redefine the scope of the question. Also, the mind does not work in this linear fashion, but jumps back and forth between problem, data requirements, analysis, and so on. Furthermore, informal networks are simultaneously forming to solve an intelligence problem in the different "phases" of the cycle. Ideally, all stakeholders in the intelligence process should be part of coming to the conclusion. "In summary, the traditional cycle may adequately describe the structure and function of an intelligence community, but it does not describe the intelligence process. In the evolving world of information technology, the traditional cycle may be even less relevant."[3]

Despite the valid critique, the intelligence cycle is useful because it helps to construct the different phases into logical steps, indicating where failures can sneak into the intelligence process:

1. *Direction*: Failures in this first phase can happened on both sides, the intelligence consumer and the producer. The consumer, on the one hand, might

not know the topic or her intelligence needs well enough to formulate good intelligence requirements, that is, they might be too broad, too narrow, or misdirected. The intelligence producer, on the other hand, might not understand the consumer's intelligence needs or her action capabilities or simply misunderstand the requirements.

2. *Collection*: Typical problems in the collection phase are issues of data accessibility, validity, and reliability. Furthermore, data collection can be subject to biases of the analysts or simply the ability to collect the right data.

3. *Processing*: In the processing phase one needs to address the question of reliability and validity specifically. At this stage the analyst decides what information is important or can be neglected, which data (source) can be trusted and which not. In this process, it becomes evident whether enough data has been collected to advise decision-making, or even if there is too much data.

4. *Analysis*: This phase is most prone to failures and mistakes. Many textbooks on intelligence analysis are dedicated to improving the analysis stage. Most problematic are cognitive biases. Furthermore, cultural and organizational biases, as well as pressure from the consumer, members of the analytic team, or other stakeholders, can influence the accuracy of the analysis.[4]

5. *Dissemination*: Failures in the dissemination process most commonly relate to the ability of the analyst to bring across the most important information to the consumer. This happens, for example, when the dissemination format is not appropriate to the needs of the consumer, the analysis presentation is messy, or the intelligence and/or the recommendations are ambiguous. It can also happen that only in the dissemination phase both intelligence consumer and producer realize that the initial direction has been unclear. In addition, sometimes simply a lack of a standardized vocabulary (e.g., regarding terms expressing confidence in analytic judgments—possible, likely, certainly) can lead to misunderstandings.[5]

6. *Feedback*: When the consumer does not [in time] get back to the intelligence producer with regard to revisions for further analyses or the producer is not receptive to the feedback, then miscommunication perpetuates across the intelligence cycle and is fed back into phases 1 and 2.

For humanitarian intelligence the processes described by the intelligence cycle are not necessarily identical. For larger NGOs, consortia, local clusters within the cluster approach, and international or regional organizations, the intelligence cycle might be applicable. In fact, we will see that the project management cycle is quite similar to the intelligence cycle. The differences emerge from the fact that many small NGOs are consumer, data collector, and analysts at the same time. Particularly in this case, Robert Clark's critique applies as the intelligence production is much more comparable to a networked process among all stakeholders. Without any limitation, however, the typical failures as just discussed hold also true for smaller NGOs and for humanitarian intelligence in general.

2.2   POLICY, PROGRAMS, AND PROJECT CYCLE MANAGEMENT

2.2.1   From Policy to Action

In the humanitarian field one commonly differentiates between projects and programs. Projects are short-term operations at local level, whereas programs usually encompass more projects within a regional strategic focus. Projects that are embedded in a program aim to fulfill with their objectives constitutive parts of higher-level program objectives. In this way, a regional-level coordination with targeted goals can be implemented through a set of projects. This allows for the appropriate allocation of resources among different stakeholders. One of the institutionalized planning tools is the *Humanitarian Action Plans*; these are strategic frameworks enacted by the IASC (Inter-Agency Standing Committee of the United Nations Office for the Coordination of Humanitarian Affairs (UN-OCHA)) and its associated implementation framework, the Cluster Approach.

Projects and programs require strategic, tactical, and logistic planning. But the thought process is not at an end when the project proposal is in a final version. The situation on the ground, assumptions in the Logical Framework, the organization-internal elements, and other humanitarian actors and implementing partners are subject to change. Furthermore, donors require organizations to regularly report on their progress and to show that they are adequately addressing the humanitarian situation as it factually presents itself rather than how it was thought to be at the initial proposal phase, based mostly on second-hand information. In order to place all these requirements in a conceptual framework, business studies devised the so-called project management cycle and on a higher level the program management cycle.

The format of accountability that humanitarian organizations are obliged to fulfill depends very much on the stakeholder to which they owe it. Donors will expect an accounting-based format for monitoring purposes as well as independent evaluations during and after the conclusion of the project or program. The public might want to get insights on websites and the social media into the projects, the people helped, and the direct impact created. The beneficiaries might expect a priori and a posteriori consultations, reporting in accessible language and/or format, as well as involvement in the overall

Policy Level	Program Level	Project Level
• Objectives	• Sub-Objectives	• Sub-Objectives
• Assumptions	• Assumptions	• Assumptions
• Activities	• Sub-Activities	• Sub-Activities
• Results	• Sub-Results	• Sub-Results

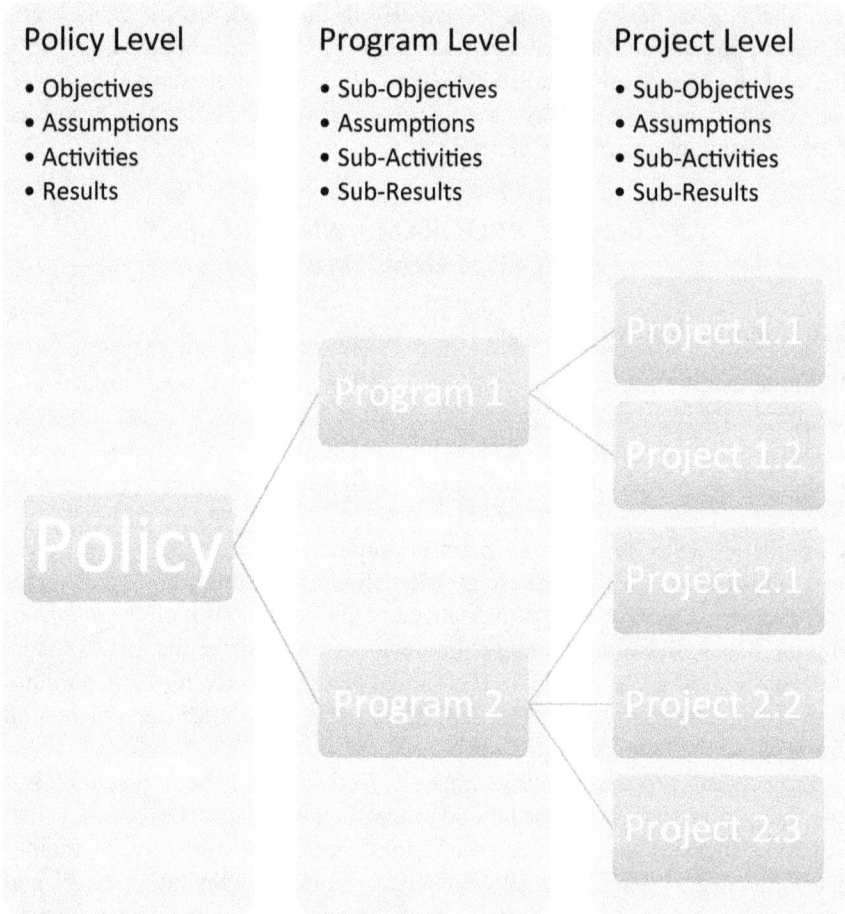

Figure 2.3 From Policy to Project

project. Finally, the organization itself might also wish to improve its future performance. This will usually be achieved by a postmortem analysis of the project and comparison with other projects (by the same or another organization) to determine the variables that contributed to success or failure of the operation.

First of all, it is worthwhile to distinguish between different levels of planning and operation. Although in practice there can be overlaps and fluid transitions, one can generally hierarchically distinguish between: policy level, program level, and project level. The project level can be further structured into components and results. All together ideally form a nested structure where each level contains overall objectives, assumptions, activities, and results. Figure 2.3 illustrates this.

Ideally, the overall objective of a policy would translate into activities based on assumptions about the effect the activities should achieve and projected results. This would be implemented through one or more programs with subobjectives that aim to fulfill the overall objective of the policy. Subactivities on program level then relate to several projects, which on the lowest level of implementation (the operational level of humanitarian organizations working in the field) would be realized again in turn through setting project level sub-objectives. These derive directly from the program-level subobjectives and are based on qualified assumptions about why the activities on project level fulfill these programme level sub-objectives. Furthermore, all levels will ideally establish indicators measuring the results.

2.2.2 Project Cycle Management

Project cycle management is one of the most commonly used concepts in humanitarian action. Similarly to the intelligence cycle, the project cycle is divided into phases. These vary depending on the actor. For example, the Food and Agricultural Organization (FAO) refers to: (1) identification, (2) formulation, (3) appraisal and approval, (4) implementation and monitoring, (5) evaluation, and (6) closure.[6] Again, others simply use four, five, or more than six phases.

Let us define the most important ones:

1. *Identification*: This first phase combines data collection and analysis in one step. It is usually initiated by the onset of a disaster or by appeal of a governmental organization or a government. Several analytical steps belong to this phase, among others the needs assessment.
2. *Planning (Formulation)*: The planning stage in humanitarian action and development aid frequently utilizes the Logical Framework. In this phase, the identified needs, questions of access and logistics, mandate and expertise of the organization, etc. feed into the planning of the project. Furthermore, the planning includes a compilation of costs and the setting up of benchmarks and indicators of success. The explication of assumptions guiding the project is important at this stage.
3. *Appraisal and Approval*: These two steps happen in the sphere of the donor, who decides whether the project is feasible, the costs are realistic, and other criteria (e.g., gender mainstreaming, human rights, integration of beneficiaries in planning and execution) have been met.
4. *Implementation and Monitoring*: This is the operational phase. It encompasses the implementation of the project and the monitoring of the indicators that have been selected to determine whether the project has reached its goals.

5. *Evaluation*: After the completion of the project follows the evaluation phase. Depending on internal policies or donor requirements, the organization conducts an internal evaluation or hires an external evaluator. The purpose of the evaluation can be manifold: financial auditing, lessons learned, reporting toward beneficiaries, etc.

Ideally, the information collected during phase 4 (implementation and monitoring) and phase 5 (evaluation) eventually feed back into the first two phases (identification and planning) of a follow-up project. This would make the project management cycle complete. The purpose of the feedback loop is to ensure that lessons learned are implemented and mistakes are not repeated.

2.2.3 Analysis Elements

Before one can start the project planning for humanitarian operations, one needs to conduct a set of analyses to determine the contextual parameters and the stakeholder field. Only then is it possible to plan operations that show context awareness in all assumptions that feed into such an operation.

Much of this book is about project assumptions. Establishing valid assumptions, as easy as it looks at a first glance, requires many analytical steps that will determine the validity of the assumptions and eventually the success of the project. Before starting the project planning with the Logical Framework (LogFrame) (which will be elaborated in more detail in section 2.2.4), the ECHO handbook on Project Cycle Management recommends four steps in the analysis phase:[7]

- problem and needs analysis (this will be covered more specifically in chapters 4 and 5);
- stakeholder analysis (this will be covered more specifically in chapters 6 and 7);
- analysis of objectives (what can we realistically achieve/what do we want to achieve?—see chapters 4 and 9); and
- analysis of strategies (comparison of different options to help in a given situation; see chapters 8 and 9).

2.2.4 Planning and Reporting—The LogFrame

On program and project level one of the most common planning and reporting tools, used, for example, in variations by USAID, Department for International Development (DFID), and ECHO, is the LogFrame. The LogFrame establishes the logical connection between the operational parameters, the indicators for the measurement of the progress, and the impact of the project, as well as the project assumptions. Within this framework all elements are seen as a causally linked sequence of events. It can be used not only for the planning of projects, but also for monitoring during the implementation phase to help adjust project assumptions and corresponding activities.[8] Furthermore, it is also useful for the postmortem evaluation of a project to determine successful and unsuccessful activities and the reasons behind achieved result. It would go beyond the scope of this book to provide a detailed introduction to the LogFrame. However, it is worthwhile understanding the general idea behind it as it forms a good basis for project management in general and is applicable to many issues discussed in the subsequent chapters.

The logical sequence that the LogFrame assumes is that certain inputs are required to conduct activities, and that certain activities are necessary to achieve certain outputs (see Figure 2.4). The outputs are determined by the purpose of the project (i.e., the specific effect a successful output would result in). The purpose is in turn dictated by the higher-level objective.

The causal relationship between activities, inputs, and outputs employed by the project is established by assumptions about the operational environment (arrows in Figure 2.4). Likewise, assumptions guide the relationship between outputs and purpose and between purpose and goal. The last assumption that also concludes the project traditionally establishes the condition of

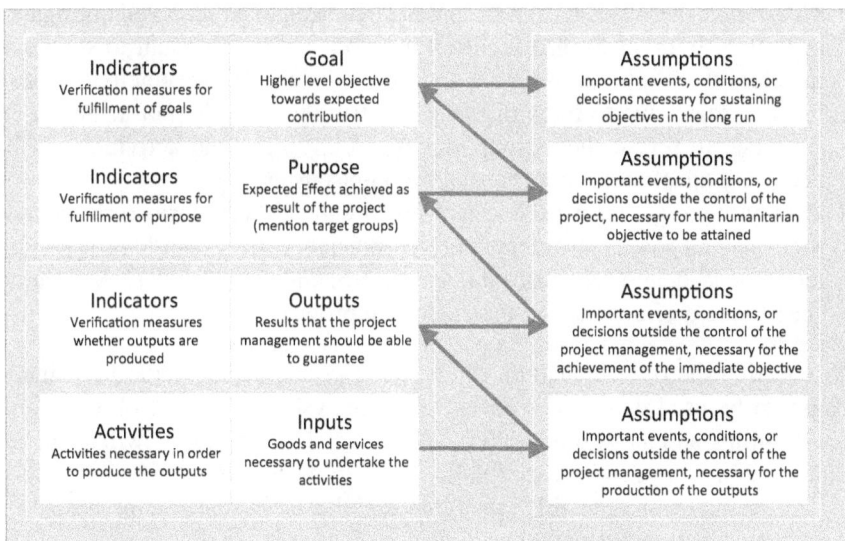

Indicators Verification measures for fulfillment of goals	Goal Higher level objective towards expected contribution	Assumptions Important events, conditions, or decisions necessary for sustaining objectives in the long run
Indicators Verification measures for fulfillment of purpose	Purpose Expected Effect achieved as result of the project (mention target groups)	Assumptions Important events, conditions, or decisions outside the control of the project, necessary for the humanitarian objective to be attained
Indicators Verification measures whether outputs are produced	Outputs Results that the project management should be able to guarantee	Assumptions Important events, conditions, or decisions outside the control of the project management, necessary for the achievement of the immediate objective
Activities Activities necessary in order to produce the outputs	Inputs Goods and services necessary to undertake the activities	Assumptions Important events, conditions, or decisions outside the control of the project management, necessary for the production of the outputs

Figure 2.4 Basic Elements and Description of the LogFrame. *Note*: Adapted from graphs and descriptions in Norwegian Agency for Development Cooperation, *The Logical Framework Approach – Handbook for Objectives-Oriented Planning*, 4th edn (Norwegian Agency for Development Cooperation, 1999), 16–17, http://www.norad.no/en/tools-and-publications/publications/publication?key=109408.

sustainability for the effect of the overall project. For humanitarian projects this is particularly relevant when it comes to the concept of linking relief, rehabilitation, and development (LRRD). This concept was established in part to avoid that humanitarian projects simply end, equipment is unplugged and staff is withdrawn without thinking of the consequences this could have on the beneficiaries and the wider population. This is particularly important in the context of complex political emergencies and is also discussed under the umbrella concept of the relief-development continuum.[9]

In cases in which there are many uncertainties about the contextual environment and the stakeholder field, it is recommendable to establish alternative assumptions for the project logic. These alternative assumptions can then serve for developing a plan B, in case the original project design fails because of faulty assumptions (see specifically section 9.4 on scenario development).

Outputs, purposes, and goals are measured by indicators in order to verify the success of the project and to establish their causal relation with the change of circumstances in the field. The indicators in turn can be further distinguished chronologically in between:[10]

- *Baseline*: this measure presents the conditions measured in indicators before the start of the project. All projects should have baselines in order to be able to determine whether the project had any measurable results.
- *Milestones*: these are steps in the project that need to be achieved during the operation. In order to plan realistic milestones, it is important to set them in achievable dimensions and at appropriate intervals. They help to monitor the project and to track the progress. If milestones are not achieved, it is crucial to revisit the assumptions regarding input and activities and if necessary adapt them to a change of circumstances.
- *Target*: the target measure is determined by the project purpose and represents the end goal measurable in preset indicators. They should be specific, measurable, achievable, relevant, and time bound (SMART). They thereby specify the desired result at the end of the project.

Selecting the right indicators can be quite problematic. The kind of indicators to be used depends on the level of analysis, the unit of observation, accessibility, and many other factors. The topic of the indicators will again be discussed in more detail in section 9.4.1 and in Appendix 5.1.

The example of the DFID in Table 2.1 illustrates the use of baseline, milestone, and target data for the indicator of "training of a number of health professionals" within a hypothetical health project.

Completing the LogFrame should then provide the key parameters of the operational management of a project. For illustration purposes, one can find a hypothetical LogFrame for a project on rice production in Appendix 2.1.

Table 2.1   Use of Indicators for Baseline, Milestone, and Target Measurement

Indicator	Baseline, Year 1	Milestone, Year 2	Milestone, Year 3	Target, Year 4
Number of health professionals at selected central and district hospitals trained on revised curriculum for patient-centred clinical care	0 Doctors 4 Nurses (0 M/4 F)	10 Doctors 15 Nurses (7 M/8 F)	15 Doctors 15 Nurses (7 M/8 F)	25 Doctors 34 Nurses (14 M/20 F)

Source:
NGO training reports (quarterly)
Regional MoH reports (annual).

In order to judge the quality of the project planning with the LogFrame matrix, ECHO suggests the following check points:[11]

1. The vertical logic is complete and accurate.
2. Indicators and sources of verification are accessible and reliable.
3. The pre-conditions are realistic.
4. The assumptions are realistic and complete.
5. The risks are acceptable.
6. The likelihood of success is reasonably strong.
7. Quality issues have been taken into account and, where appropriate, translated into activities, results or assumptions.
8. The benefits justify the costs.

It is evident that the LogFrame requires a lot of intelligence about the operational context and the stakeholder field, knowledge about trends, and predictions about future scenarios. In order to successfully prepare such a project on the basis of a LogFrame or otherwise, the humanitarian analyst essentially has to follow the intelligence cycle from phase 1 (Planning and direction) to phase 5 (Dissemination and integration). The following chapters provide the theoretical foundation and the tools necessary to come from data to information and finally to intelligence.

REVIEW QUESTIONS

- How does data differ from intelligence?
- What are the phases of the intelligence cycle?
- What are the potential failures in the different phases of the intelligence cycle?

- What is the logic of coming from policy to project?
- What are the phases and what is the purpose of the project management cycle?
- What is the purpose of the LogFrame?
- Explain the logical connection between inputs, outputs, purpose, and goal in the LogFrame.

NOTES

1. See generally: Joint Chiefs of Staff, *Joint Intelligence*, Joint Publication 2-0 (Defense Technical Information Center (DTIC), 2013), http://www.dtic.mil/doctrine/new_pubs/jp2_0.pdf.

2. Robert M. Clark, *Intelligence Analysis: A Target-Centric Approach* (Washington, DC; London: CQ; SAGE [distributor], 2013).

3. Ibid., 7.

4. See particularly this groundbreaking contribution that defined much of the contemporary work on intelligence analysis: Richards J. Heuer, *Psychology of Intelligence Analysis* (Center for the Study of Intelligence—Central Intelligence Agency, 1999), https://www.cia.gov/library/center-for-the-study-of-intelligence/csi-publications/books-and-monographs/psychology-of-intelligence-analysis/index.html.

5. This will be discussed in section 3.6.

6. Office of Knowledge Exchange, Research and Extension, "Guide to the Project Cycle—Quality for Results" (Rome: Food and Agricultural Organization, 2012), 6–7, http://www.fao.org/docrep/016/ap105e/ap105e.pdf. DG-ECHO refers to these six phases: (1) programming, (2) identification, (3) appraisal, (4) financing, (5) implementation, (6) evaluation.

7. ECHO, "ECHO Manual: Project Cycle Management" (Brussels: European Commission Directorate-General for Humanitarian Aid—ECHO, June 2005), 8, http://ec.europa.eu/echo/files/partners/humanitarian_aid/fpa/2003/guidelines/project_cycle_mngmt_en.pdf.

8. Norwegian Agency for Development Cooperation, *The Logical Framework Approach—Handbook for Objectives-Oriented Planning*, 4th edition (Norwegian Agency for Development Cooperation, 1999), 10–12, http://www.norad.no/en/tools-and-publications/publications/publication?key=109408.

9. Joanna Macrae et al., "Conflict, the Continuum and Chronic Emergencies: A Critical Analysis of the Scope for Linking Relief, Rehabilitation and Development Planning in Sudan," *Disasters* 21, no. 3 (1997): 223–43, doi:10.1111/1467-7717.00058.

10. Value for Money Department, FCPD, "Guidance on Using the Revised Logical Framework," How to note—DFID Practice Paper (Department for International Development, February 2009), http://mande.co.uk/blog/wp-content/uploads/2009/06/logical-framework.pdf.

11. ECHO, "ECHO Manual: Project Cycle Management," 15.

Part II

FROM DATA TO CONTEXT

Chapter 3

Information Collection, Reliability, and Probability

3.1 INFORMATION COLLECTION

Information collection serves only one goal—to establish as solid and as unbiased an understanding of a given context as possible. More precisely, information collection is only one among a series of steps necessary to successfully conduct any kind of analysis. It is, however, important for information collection to understand the purpose of further analytical steps with regard to humanitarian action first: to contribute to a more effective assessment, anticipation, and monitoring of vulnerable people's assistance and protection needs.[1]

Effective assessment requires selecting the right indicators for your context analysis. This will be dealt with in the chapters concerning the sectoral assessments (specifically chapters 5 and 9). Effectiveness means, more precisely, to collect not too much and not too little information. It will be hard to quickly assess and sift through too much information. Too little information will be missing the relevant data and make the conclusions susceptible to unavoidable biases in the base data. In other words, one needs enough data to check on uncertain sources. The sources (reliability) as well as the validity of the data (i.e., how well the data describes what the analyst wants to know) determine how much data one needs. The lower the reliability and validity rates, the less confidence the analyst will have in the assessment (this is discussed in more detail in section 5.2 under the term "confidence margin"). Analysts need to seek for a high measure of validity and reliability in order to:

- correctly diagnose the type and degree of humanitarian problems and how they are interrelated,
- correctly analyze and understand stakeholder dynamics of humanitarian crises,

- confidently identify core causes of these problems, and
- precisely reveal inconsistencies and gaps in humanitarian projects and programs (i.e., unravel project assumptions and juxtapose them to context and stakeholder field).

3.2   INFORMATION SOURCES

Intelligence usually relies on five traditional intelligences collection disciplines: (1) human intelligence (HUMINT), (2) signals intelligence (SIGINT), (3) imagery intelligence (IMINT), (4) measurement and signatures intelligence (MASINT), (5) open-source intelligence (OSINT). Not all these different collection disciplines are equally available to humanitarian analysts. This has in part to do with the difference in resources and access between humanitarians and states; for example, for a long time satellite imagery was the almost exclusive domain of state intelligence. This is, however, slowly changing with the advancement of technological resources available to humanitarian analysts. In the following, I will describe how the traditional intelligence collection disciplines are increasingly relevant to humanitarian analysts.

Human Intelligence: Collecting information directly from the ground through observation, surveys, interviews, and focus groups belongs to the traditional tradecraft of humanitarian intelligence and has been practiced since the beginning of humanitarian action. Innovation in this domain is mostly facilitated by the increasing availability of cell phone technology, which increases both the speed and the reach of HUMINT. Crowd-sourced information gathering through tools such as USHAHIDI,[2] People's Intelligence (PI),[3] or ELVA[4] allow individuals, in part through using low-cost GSM technology, in part through smart-phone technology, to send relevant information to data collection points that can collect and visualize this information in near real-time and make it accessible to humanitarian analysts in various forms (such as by visualizing it on maps with the help of geocoded data). These so-called crisis mappers today belong to the first responders in humanitarian action. This effectively shifts HUMINT further into the domain of SIGINT. However, traditional HUMINT in the form of experts who conduct rapid needs assessments on the ground will probably not be replaced by modern tools any time soon. This, in part, has to do with the fact that the aforementioned tools are vulnerable to manipulation by parties out for their own interests and collection gaps, such as in cases where GSM infrastructure has also been damaged. At the same time rapid needs assessment teams possess the skills and knowledge relevant for the expertise of the humanitarian aid organization and know which data to look for specifically—this enables selected data collection and reduces noise as well as the collection of massive amounts of nonrelevant data. Furthermore, crisis mapping in the form of crowd-sourced geocoded data projected on online maps is highly dependent on open data (i.e., data accessible to everyone for the purpose of uploading and information sharing). Open data, however, bears its own risks. Examples of misuse of open crowd-sourced data are manifold as Raymond, Howarth, and Hutson describe:

> In Syria, protesters paid a brutal price when intelligence teams connected names to faces shown in video footage. In Egypt, social media accounts were traced, and Facebook's anti-pseudonym policy came under fire as a security hazard. These tactics are hardly new—as any human rights advocate in Myanmar can confirm—but they have a clear chilling effect on those in the field and would-be allies from abroad. Mapping the locations of even the most innocuous human actors, such as the World Food Program distribution points or the clinics of Médecins Sans Frontières, can attract the violent attentions of armed actors. Crisis mappers learned that lesson well when Pakistan-based Taliban forces threatened to attack foreign aid workers responding to the 2010 floods and food crisis.[5]

In short, even if crisis mapping has tremendously helped data gathering, intelligence generated through this approach can very easily fall into the hands of criminals preying on aid workers for their valuable resources or for achieving political goals.

Signals Intelligence: This area, traditionally reserved to intelligence agencies, collects data from electronic transmissions. Humanitarian intelligence will increasingly rely on this sort of information. The above-mentioned crowd-sourcing tools, however, are only one element to humanitarian SIGINT. For example, telephone providers are increasingly making their call data available for humanitarian and development purposes.[6] The use of geocoded cell phone data, whether provided by telephone providers or through crowd sourcing, certainly bears promising advantages for the improvement of effectiveness and efficiency of aid, but it also has the potential for extremely negative unintended consequences. These negative effects go far beyond privacy concerns and include risks of misuse of this data for criminal purposes by mal-intended armed actors, as mentioned above.

Imagery Intelligence: The discipline of IMINT is as old as photography. It essentially means the distilling of information from imagery data, whether simple cell phone photos, arial pictures, or satellite imagery. This discipline is increasingly becoming relevant to humanitarian analysts. This has become available to the larger humanitarian community and the layperson very basically with non-real-time satellite imagery, as, for example, Google Earth, and the provision of arial imagery to humanitarian actors by governments and international organizations for humanitarian operational planning. With the availability of increasingly affordable arial drone technology, IMINT will probably be increasingly directly utilized by humanitarian organizations (the keyword here is "humanitarian drones"). This possibility will of course strongly depend on the national legal regulations to allow or forbid the use of drones in the event of emergencies. Unmanned aerial vehicles (UAVs), already in use in the 2013 Typhoon Haiyan disaster in the Philippines, were also employed after the 2014 cyclone that hit Vanuatu. For that purpose "United Nations Office for the Coordination of Humanitarian Affairs (OCHA) activated the Digital Humanitarian Network (DHN), a consortium of volunteer and technical communities, to provide initial damage assessments just hours after Cyclone Pam hit Vanuatu, blocking roads with falling trees and cutting off communications to the outer islands."[7]

Measurement and Signatures Intelligence: This will probably remain for much longer outside the reach of humanitarian intelligence with a few exceptions, such as remote sensing concerning natural disasters such as earthquakes and storms. It includes the collection of telemetric data or electromagnetic emissions and is currently mostly used to assess weapons capabilities and industrial activities.

Open-Source Intelligence: Since the onset of the Internet Age, OSINT has become one of the major disciplines of intelligence collection for aid analysts particularly when it comes to strategic intelligence and the analysis of contexts and stakeholder fields. OSINT refers to the collection of data from open access sources, such as media sources (radio, television, newspapers), academic and think-tank research, openly available statistics and census data, and increasingly social media, such as Twitter and others. While the Internet has pretty much taken the lead in being the major source of OSINT, the evaluation of reliability and validity of the information remains (or increasingly becomes) an issue of concern. This is paired with the sheer masses of data produced, the variety of formats, and the speed of data increase, leading to the term "Big Data."

3.3   COLLECTION TOOLS AND STANDARDS

The intelligence collection and eventual sharing remains an issue of concern. For instance, how to unify the variety of information collected by different agencies within one cluster, for example, WASH (water, sanitation, and hygiene), and to ensure that the indicators are comparable and valid? In order to come to common standards of measurement for rapid needs assessment and other forms of humanitarian intelligence international efforts have tried to introduce common approaches.

The Multi-Cluster/Sector Initial Rapid Assessment (MIRA) developed by IASC Needs Assessment Task Force (NATF) is one of these efforts. MIRA is a toolbox, based on the cluster approach, that aims to provide a preliminary scenario definition (PSD) within the first 72 hours after the onset of a disaster and an in-depth sectoral assessment report, released after 2 weeks. MIRA distinguishes different phases of the rapid needs assessment and distributes the responsibility of data collection, aggregation, and analysis based on a generic timeline over different actors, such as OCHA, the government, cluster leads, humanitarian coordinators (HC), and humanitarian country teams (HTC) (see Figure 3.1).

The assessment is based on a report template consisting of key questions designed to focus the data gathering and collection process, which then is fed into the overall needs assessment report per sector. MIRA is particularly useful as it streamlines the humanitarian intelligence process to fit to the cluster approach.[8] The PSD, which should be ready after 72 hours, provides the most pressing information (see Table 3.1).

In this initial phase of needs assessment, much of the data might have to rely on secondary sources, as access to the disaster site is often very limited. The form for the PSD aims to feed into resource mobilization tools, such as the Flash Appeal.[9]

The secondary analysis similarly requires the answering of key questions aimed at focusing the data collection and assessment process in the form of a template.[10] The purpose of this second phase report is to help decision-makers at local, national, and international levels to assess the situation in detail. Furthermore, the MIRA report communicates key findings regarding the nature and dynamics of the crisis and helps in further defining strategic humanitarian priorities. This phase requires the humanitarian analyst to have sector-specific knowledge and skills, emergency programming skills (see program and project management cycle), and an extensive knowledge of the geographic areas concerned.[11]

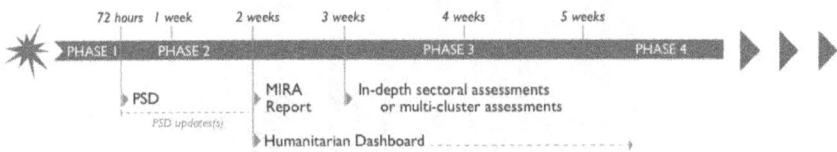

Figure 3.1 MIRA Phases and Products. *Note*: Needs Assessment Task Force (NATF), "Multi-Cluster/Sector Initial Rapid Assessment (MIRA)" (Geneva: Inter-Agency Standing Committee (IASC), March 2012), 5, https://docs.unocha.org/sites/dms/Documents/mira_final_version2012.pdf.

Table 3.1 Key Information for Preliminary Scenario Definition*

– Drivers of the crisis and underlying factors	– International capacities and response
– Scope of the crisis and humanitarian profile	– Humanitarian access
– Status of populations living in affected areas	– Coverage and gaps
– National capacities and response	– Strategic humanitarian priorities

* Needs Assessment Task Force (NATF), "Multi-Cluster/Sector Initial Rapid Assessment (MIRA)," 18–19.

Table 3.2 Indicators for Health Cluster, Subdomain H1 General Clinical Services and Essential Trauma Care

Title	Description	Unit of Measurement	Denominator
Number of functional basic health units/10,000 population	Proxy indicator of geographical accessibility, and of equity in availability of health facilities across different administrative units	Facility	The total population for the same administrative or health area, at the same point in time
Number of functional health centers/50,000 population	Proxy indicator of geographical accessibility, and of equity in availability of health facilities across different administrative units	Facility	The total population for the same administrative or health area, at the same point in time
Number of functional district-rural hospitals/250,000 population	Proxy indicator of geographical accessibility, and of equity in availability of health facilities across different administrative units	Facility	The total population for the same administrative or health area, at the same point in time
Number of inpatient beds/10,000 population	Indicator for the availability of hospital beds across crisis areas and proxy indicator of equity in the allocation of resources	Bed	The total population for the same administrative or health area, at the same point in time
Number of community health workers/10,000 population	Indicator monitoring the availability of human resources key to delivering community-based intervention	Individual	The total population for the same administrative or health area, at the same point in time
Number and percentage of functional health facilities providing selected relevant services	Proxy indicator for the physical availability and geographical accessibility of selected services relevant to the local context	Facility	The total population for the same administrative or health area, at the same point in time

Another effort to mainstream data collection and coherence of the indicators used across agencies is the Humanitarian Indicators Registry of OCHA. This registry works in conjunction with the IASCs Humanitarian Programme Cycle (HPC) reference module. The listed indicators have been developed by the global cluster leads to standardize key indicators across sectors and countries to allow for comparison, response monitoring, and data sharing. While using common indicators has definitive advantages, there are of course limitations regarding the universalizability of indicators.[12] These indicator lists, which are regularly updated, are sortable by cluster and subdomain and provide detailed information regarding their correct use and application across sectors. The indicator lists can be downloaded as Excel files. Table 3.2 provides a sample of indicators for the health cluster (subdomain H1 general clinical services and essential trauma care).

3.4 VALIDITY AND DATA SELECTION

Information and evidence can be called valid if the information generated is relevant to the situation at hand and represents what one wants to know. In other words, evidence is valid if one collects information that correctly represents the dimensions of study in a particular context. This is related to a correct and precise translation of these dimensions into particular indicators, or other forms of operationalization. For example, if one decides that food access is an important dimension to analyze needs of people struck by drought, then there might be different ways to measure this. For example, one could measure household income and food prices on the market. One question is whether it is sufficient to choose one type of indicator or focus on a set of indicators (in this case: both on household income and food prices). A second question is of how to measure these dimensions exactly. For example, if income is measured in monetary terms, how to translate "in-kind" income (such as crops harvested on own land) in monetary terms? The third question is when one can speak of problems in food access. In other words, what is the threshold: how low should the income and how high should the prices be to speak of hampered food access? These are all elements that contribute to the generation of valid evidence and that a humanitarian crisis analysis framework should provide guidance on. It is recommended to use two sets of criteria relating to validity: (a) validity regarding levels of analysis, and (b) validity of indicators for contextual dimensions.

Point (a), as mentioned above, aims to increase validity in terms of reaching completeness regarding intervening factors that might prevent success of a project or cause unintended consequences in one specific context and defined geographic or organizational area. It is necessary to assess the information one has with regard to the levels of analysis to which the data pertain. For example, does the information refer to a nation, a region, or a subgroup in a city, and to what extent is this useful information for the particular humanitarian problem at hand? This means, for example, information collected about the gross domestic product (GDP) at a national level will inform little about the financial situation at the local level. It might even be completely misleading. In short, the data needs to represent the right level of analysis. Another necessary element in (b) is the assessment of indicators for context dimensions (see chapter 5 and Appendix 5.1). One should be aware that lists of indicators are always limiting; this means that they restrict one's thinking about other possible indicators, or proxy indicators in case a direct measurement is not possible. Furthermore, some indicators are better than others in describing the state of a context dimension. Indicator lists are never complete and not applicable to all times and places; this depends on the situation that is assessed, as well as on the availability and reliability of information. Point (b) furthermore relates to the validity of the data in terms of having the right data for the right purpose. For example, knowing the average nutritional levels of a region does not tell me how many people in a village are in need of what kind of nutrition. Hence, each time one has to critically assess what indicators to use and what information is available, at what level. What does one know, and what information is still needed?

3.5   RELIABILITY OF DATA

Reliability of the data and the sources of the data need to be taken very seriously. Faulty, misleading, or plainly wrong information can jeopardize the success of a project and the reputation of an organization. Sometimes, deception is exactly the aim of the data provider, sometimes wrong information is simply the result of human error, and at other times it is the result of a bias in the data provider. When assessing the comprehensive context in a specific case, one is often confronted with data in different formats and of different quality. How to use the available data in such a way that a reliable and valid analysis can be made? The steps in Box 3.1 facilitate the correct selection of information to be used for any data.

The aim of this quick assessment is to categorize your sources from most reliable to least reliable sources. For example, data coming from an authoritarian government denying the outbreak of cholera in its own country (maybe to avoid an influx of foreign agencies) are of much less value than data presented by an IGO or independent academic institute that claims that there is an outbreak of cholera. Categorizing your sources in this way helps you to deal with such inconsistent or conflicting information. In the ideal situation

Box 3.1   Data and Source Reliability Check

Step 1: collect data from a number of information sources.

Step 2: do a quick assessment about their reliability. The following questions could help the analyst in this regard:

- Is the source generally reliable? For example, are the authors transparent in how they collected the information (method), what their sources were, who their respondents were, and so on?
- Is the source independent from partial stakeholders?
- Are the data and/or intelligence presented coherently with other assessments?
- Is the way the data is presented emotionalized or in any other ways biased?

Step 3: rank your sources from most reliable to least reliable.

Step 4: if data is lacking search for other sources to replace least reliable and conduct Step 2 for the new sources.

[*Step 5*: if time permits, apply the rating scales for source and data reliability in Table 3.3.]

one only works with the most reliable sources; however, if certain information is needed, then one could work with less reliable sources if absolutely necessary. However, one then needs to carefully assess the potential bias in the information presented and to account for this bias in the analysis.

If one aims to assess the context of a specific group or set of actors, then one is confronted with a multitude of information and data about the relevant sectors, the majority of which are reports of various actors in the field giving qualitative data and more rarely quantitative data. In order to answer these questions, one has to collect a number of information sources, and one has to run through a quick assessment about its reliability. The following verification techniques can help the analyst in this regard:

- background check of the data provider;
- cross-checking the information with the same data of a different source (A1 = A2); and
- cross-checking the information with different data of a different source (A1 ~ B1).

Intelligence analysts routinely check the reliability of information. For example, Table 3.3 illustrates a quite detailed reliability check employed by the Canadian government.

Table 3.3 Source Reliability and Data Accuracy Rating Matrix Based on Work of the Canadian Intelligence

Source Rating Scale	Source Reliability Rating	History of Reliability	Source Authenticity	Source Objectivity	Source Access to Information	Source NOT Vulnerable to Manipulation	Meets Number of Criteria
A	Reliable	Yes	Yes	Yes	Yes	Yes	All 5
B	Usually reliable	Yes	Yes or No	Yes or No	Yes or No	Yes or No	History, plus 3
C	Fairly reliable	Yes	Yes or No	Yes or No	Yes or No	Yes or No	History, plus 2
D	Not usually reliable	Yes or No	Yes or No	Yes or No	Yes or No	Yes or No	2 of 5
E	Unreliable	No	Yes or No	Yes or No	Yes or No	Yes or No	N/A
F	Cannot be judged	No basis for evaluating the reliability of the source					

Note:

1. To be rated "A," the source's authenticity must be verifiable, and the source's history of reliability must be verifiable post-factum or by independent verifiable means.
2. To be rated "A" or "B," the source's reporting must always be reliable with no significant errors.
3. To be rated "C," the majority of the source's reporting must be accurate and actionable.
4. To be rated "D," a minority of the source's reporting must still be accurate and actionable.

Data Rating Scale	Information Accuracy Rating	Independent Verifiable Means	Source Subject Competency	Logical	Practical and Plausible	Consistent	Meets Number of Criteria
1	Confirmed	Yes	Yes	Yes	Yes	Yes	All 5
2	Probably true	No	Yes	Yes	Yes	Yes	4
3	Possibly true	No	Yes or No	Yes or No	Yes or No	Yes or No	3
4	Doubtfully true	No	Yes or No	Yes or No	Yes or No	Yes or No	2
5	Improbable	No	Yes or No	Yes or No	Yes or No	Yes or No	0 or 1
6	Cannot be judged	No basis for evaluating the validity of the information					

3.6 ESTIMATIVE PROBABILITY

Closely linked to data collection and analysis as well as to the way estimations are presented are so-called terms or words of estimative probabilities. Words of estimative probability (WEPs) are terms used to describe how likely it is that a certain event will happen. For example, an experienced reader of intelligence reports might equate "there is a *very good chance* that we will encounter roadblocks" with a *70–80 percent probability*. A small study of 23 NATO officers accustomed to reading intelligence reports showed that there is a general (albeit vague) common understanding of the terms used in intelligence reports (see Figure 3.2).

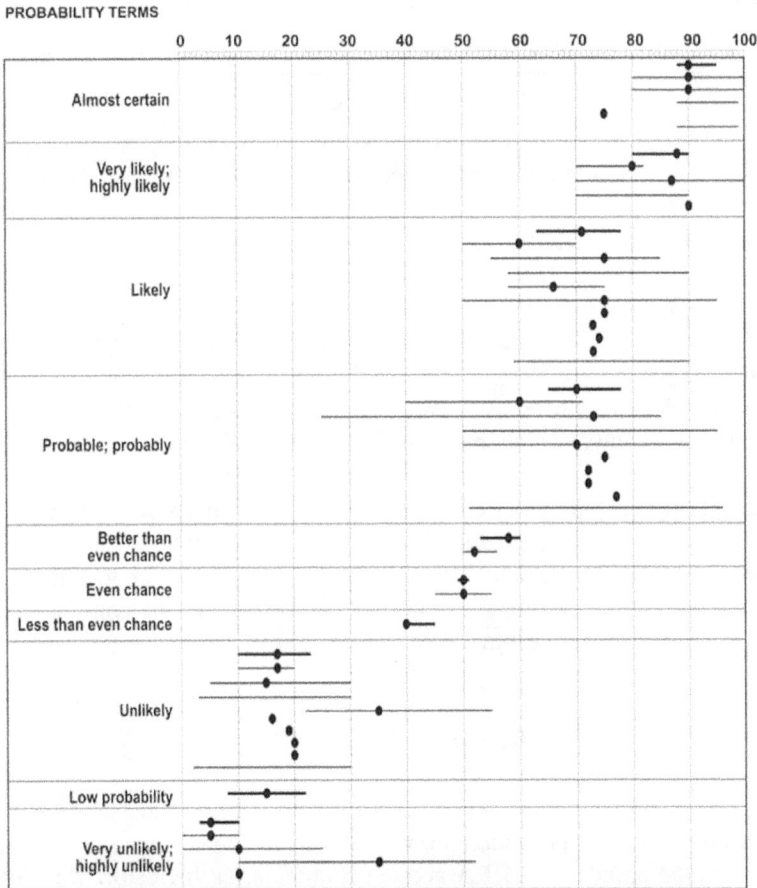

Figure 3.2 Perceptions of Uncertainty. *Note*: Barnes, Making Intelligence Analysis More Intelligent: Using Numeric Probabilities, *Intelligence and National Security*, 334.

Table 3.4   Expressing Confidence in Analytic Judgments*

Low	Moderate	High
Uncorroborated information from good or marginal sources	Partially corroborated information from good sources	Well-corroborated information from proven sources
Many assumptions	Several assumptions	Minimal assumptions
Mostly weak logical inferences, minimal methods application	Mix of strong and weak inferences and methods	Strong logical inferences and methods
Glaring intelligence gaps exist	Minimum intelligence gaps exist	No or minor intelligence gaps exist
Terms/expressions	*Terms/expressions*	*Terms/expressions*
Possible	Likely, unlikely	Will, will not
Could, may, might	Probable, improbable	Almost certainly, remote
Cannot judge, unclear	Anticipate, appear	Highly likely, highly unlikely
		Expect, assert, affirm

*Joint Chiefs of Staff, Joint Intelligence, A–2 (114).

There is an important difference between risk and uncertainty. Risk means that in a scenario the probabilities are exactly known (e.g., in tossing a coin or roulette). Intelligence analysts, however, rarely encounter risk but rather situations of uncertainty, that is, situations where probabilities can at best be estimated. In cases of uncertainty, the statement "there is an 80% chance" does not mean to convey that in eight out of ten cases X will happen, but rather that the analyst is fairly certain that X will happen given the evidence.[13] Most of the time WEPs are used to convey that the evidence at hand is of uncertain reliability or validity, which in turn results in uncertain probabilities. In short, WEPs express confidence in the analytic judgment based on key assumptions, the credibility and diversity of sources, and the strength of argumentation. Since there is some ambivalence in the words used it makes sense to either preassign words of estimative probability to percentages or to simply use percentages in the reporting. Another way is to simplify the confidence sets to three categories (see Table 3.4): Low, Moderate, High.

REVIEW QUESTIONS

- Which of the five intelligence collection disciplines can be utilized for humanitarian intelligence and how?
- What is the purpose of MIRA and the Humanitarian Indicators Registry?
- Explain the difference between (a) validity regarding levels of analysis and (b) validity of indicators for contextual dimensions.

- What is reliability, and how do we assess it?
- What is the difference between risk and uncertainty?
- How do WEPs express uncertainty and help in writing intelligence reports?

NOTES

1. Sarah Collinson et al., "Politically Informed Humanitarian Programming Using a Political Economy Approach," Network Papers, HPN Resources (London: Humanitarian Practice Network, Overseas Development Institute, December 2002), 4, http://www.odihpn.org/hpn-resources/network-papers/politically-informed-humanitarian-programming-using-a-political-economy-approach.

2. http://www.ushahidi.com.

3. http://peoples-intelligence.org.

4. http://www.elva.org.

5. Nathaniel Raymond, Caitlin Howarth, and Jonathan Hutson, "Crisis Mapping Needs an Ethical Compass," *Global Brief*, February 6, 2012, http://globalbrief.ca/blog/2012/02/06/crisis-mapping-needs-an-ethical-compass/.

6. See, for example, the Orange projects, Data for Development (D4D), in Senegal or Ivory Coast: http://www.d4d.orange.com/en/home.

7. "Drones and Crisis Mapping—Digital Aid in Vanuatu," Text, *ReliefWeb* (April 14, 2015), http://reliefweb.int/report/world/drones-and-crisis-mapping-digital-aid-vanuatu.

8. An example of the MIRA Report regarding Typhoon Haiyan hitting the Philippines in 2013 can be accessed here: http://reliefweb.int/sites/reliefweb.int/files/resources/MIRA_Report_-_Philippines_Haiyan_FINAL.pdf.

9. The template for the PSD can be downloaded here: http://www.humanitarianresponse.info/programme-cycle/space/document/preliminary-scenario-definitions-psd-template.

10. The template for the MIRA Report can be downloaded here: http://www.humanitarianresponse.info/programme-cycle/space/document/mira-report-template.

11. Needs Assessment Task Force (NATF), "Multi-Cluster/Sector Initial Rapid Assessment (MIRA)," 19–20.

12. OCHA, "Indicators Registry," *Humanitarian Response*, accessed March 25, 2015, http://www.humanitarianresponse.info/applications/ir.

13. Jeffrey A. Friedman and Richard Zeckhauser, "Handling and Mishandling Estimative Probability: Likelihood, Confidence, and the Search for Bin Laden," *Intelligence and National Security* 30, no. 1 (January 2, 2015): 4–6, doi:10.1080/02684527.2014.885202.

Chapter 4

Understanding Complex Contexts

Context matters. It matters not only because it gives a better sense of a situation but because it always informs the analysis in different ways. We can identify the influence of at least three contexts that inform the production of an intelligence report: (1) The actual context (i.e., the reality) of the observed environment will determine the actual processes on the ground, which the analyst can observe. (2) The information regarding the context of the observed process (and the lack of information), that is, the observed reality, will inform the analysis as to how to interpret the processes. (3) The context of the analyst herself will in part also shape how she will interpret an observed process. In this respect, Tilly and Goodin observe:

> Inquiries into democratization and de-democratization, civil and international war, revolution and rebellion, nationalism, ethnic mobilization, political participation, parliamentary behavior, and effective government all raise contextual questions: when, where, in what settings, on what premises, with what understandings of the processes under investigation? Viable answers to questions of this sort require serious attention to the contexts in which the crucial political processes operate.[1]

A good context analysis makes the context of an observed process explicit. Thereby, it reduces the implicit contextual assumptions that can introduce biases into the analyst's interpretation and which stem from the analyst's own background. A simple example can illustrate this:

Process: trial for the theft of a cow
Analyst: property was stolen; a fair trial would assign a fair sentence
Result: the sentence—the thief's hands will be cut off

Analyst's context: laws forbid invasive punishments; a cow does not warrant
   the cutting off of limbs

Process context: cows are prime objects of livelihood; the stealing of a cow
   directly and pervasively threatens the ability of a herding community to
   survive; furthermore, it destabilizes the social bonds on which the herding
   community depends.

   If the analyst was to interpret the process and predict the result on the basis
of his or her own context, the introduced bias would grossly misrepresent the
actual process and lead to wrong conclusions. By understanding the context,
the analyst can adjust the analysis to the context that surrounds the observed
process, while reducing biases resulting from underlying value judgments of
his or her own context.

   While the term "context analysis" is common parlance in humanitarian and
development aid and even funding institutions require a context analysis, there
is no common agreement of how to develop such a context analysis, what it
needs to entail, and what conclusions to draw from it. Many analysts treat it
as an annoying but necessary step (be it out of awareness of its relevance or
because of requirements by funding agencies) before they can employ their
tools of choice. Nevertheless, a good context analysis is indispensable for a
good intelligence report, since it is the context that shapes the interpretation of
all specific findings thereafter. Furthermore, a good context analysis will not
only answer general questions, such as about historical, economic, or social
contextual elements, but also (help to) raise specific questions regarding the
case that one did not even know to ask before. It might even provide novel
approaches to solving humanitarian crisis utilizing social mechanisms one
has learned of in context analysis. For example, during the volcano eruption
of Mount Merapi near Yogyakarta, the first organized response did not come
from international aid agencies but from social communities, particularly
the *Gotong Royong* (a strong organized form of neighborhood community).[2]
Being able to use these preexisting social networks does not only improve a
speedy coordination and aid provision but also improves local ownership of
the aid process.

   It has already been mentioned that evidence-based programming and project planning have become the standard of professional humanitarian action.
This evidence base has to include:

- the benchmark against which the humanitarian operation's success can be
  judged (a priori assessment);
- the analysis of the operational environment and factors to be reckoned with
  regarding humanitarian analysis;

- ongoing assessments regarding the humanitarian operation itself, the stakeholder field, and changes in the humanitarian operation space (monitoring); and
- an ex-post analysis for assessing the actual impact of the operation (evaluation).

This chapter will specifically introduce different tools to analyze complex contexts. It will discuss benchmark indicators, visualization, and interpretation strategies. Visualization is an important part of context analysis for several reasons. First, good visual aids allow reducing large amounts of data to a single or a few graphs, thereby facilitating understanding and interpretation. Second, figures and graphs can have much value added for effective communication, because they structure the available information in a relational form. Third, though any data-reduction step always bears the risk of oversimplification, graphical representations force the analyst to explicate the assumptions underlying the analysis, thereby facilitating a critical dialogue with the intelligence consumer. First of all, however, the next section will introduce the reader to the nature of complex contexts as a crucial theoretical foundation to data interpretation. As a special feature and in addition to other assessment tools, the subsequent chapter will introduce the humanitarian analysis and intervention design (H-AID) framework for context analysis and expand on its applications.[3]

4.1 CONTEXT ANALYSIS AND THE NATURE OF COMPLEX CONTEXTS

Context analysis aims to contribute to a more effective assessment, anticipation, and monitoring of vulnerable people's assistance and protection needs.[4] In order to achieve this, it needs to be able to capture the complexities that an operational environment can entail, the wider impact (including the political economy) of the planned intervention, and the prospects for success and possible failure.

Hall and Citrenbaum provide a very useful account of the nature of complex contexts:[5]

Nonlinearity means that a problem has effects, which are disproportional to its causes. In a complex context with political volatility even a political speech can result in violent protests. For instance, the self-immolation of Mohammed Bouazizi, which in combination with the present tensions and facilitated by social media functioned as a catalyst for the Arab Spring and the fleeing of President Ben Ali; this further led to a spreading of protests across North Africa and the Middle East. These nonlinear variables in a complex context are *difficult to solve* and often *impossible to predict* with any degree of preciseness. Hardly anyone would have predicted that the fall of the Egyptian president Mubarak, the Tunisian president Ben Ali, and the Libyan president Gadhafi would have happened in such a short time period and triggered by comparatively minute events.

Chaotic appearance is another characteristic of complex contexts. The complexity is in part a result of the intermingling of people, machines, organizations, religion, and culture, which contributes to the turbulence and appearance of a constantly changing operational environment. In order to make sense of the chaos, context analytical tools should provide categories of analysis to disentangle the many variables of relevance and make them accessible to analysis. Complexity makes it more difficult to discern cause from effect, elements that are necessary for a problem tree analysis and scenario planning.

Complex adaptive systems (CAS) are dynamic stakeholder fields that include individuals, nongovernmental organizations (NGOs), corporations, states, and nonstate armed actors. All these actors act in parallel initiating new events or reacting to the actions of other actors. As every actor is also a rational decision-maker, their possible paths of action can only to some degree be predicted, namely, to the extent to which their goals, resources, and normative decision-making parameters (institutions) are known (see stakeholder analysis in chapter 6). The more the overall control decreases, for example, in cases where state power disintegrates (such as in failed states like Libya, Haiti particularly after the earthquake), the harder it will be to predict the behavior of the CAS and the more the information on the stakeholders required for the analyst to be able to predict future scenarios.

A good context analytical framework for the purpose of humanitarian planning should help the analyst to:

- correctly diagnose the type and degree of humanitarian problems and how they are interrelated;
- analyze and understand stakeholder dynamics of humanitarian crises;
- identify core or root causes of these problems;
- detect inconsistencies and gaps in humanitarian projects and plans (unravel project assumptions); and
- understand, predict, and avoid recurring mistakes in humanitarian operations.

In order to be able to achieve that while taking into account the intricacies of complex contexts, such context analytical tools need to be:

- comprehensive, in order to capture and understand volatile variables and nonlinear cause-effect relationships;

- multidimensional, in order to be able to assess cross-dimensional cause-effect relationships (such as the impact of in-kind food aid on local markets) and reduce unintended consequences;
- targeted and structured, in order to guide the analysts to identify known unknowns and reduce unknown unknowns; and
- flexible, in order to be applicable to a variety of contexts, all of which are per definition unique and constantly changing.

In this regard, it remains crucial to make a final distinction between *needs assessment* and *needs analysis*. Needs assessment is the collection of data pertaining to covered and uncovered needs. This includes actual and potential needs, and the resources currently available to cover them. Needs analysis is the analytic step from knowing what is missing to understanding why it is missing. It requires a comprehensive mapping of the cause-effect relationships and the structural embeddedness of factors that have led to the humanitarian crisis in the first place, that is, of root causes, mitigating variables, and triggers. While still a simplification for the purpose of analyzing the underlying factors of humanitarian crisis through a context analysis, it makes sense to structure data into clusters of causal, moderating, mediating variables. For the purpose of analyzing contexts regarding disaster risk reduction (DRR), Blaikie et al., for example, distinguish on the side of vulnerability between root causes, dynamic pressures, fragile livelihoods, and unsafe locations. On the side of hazards, they consider climatological, geomorphological and geological, biological and ecological, as well as astronomical hazards. Together these clusters of variables determine the disaster risk in one apt formula:[6]

Disaster Risk = Hazard × Vulnerability.

There are of course many models that help to analyze and understand man-made and natural disasters. Some are "quick and dirty" and offer the analyst a rough overview of the situation; others are "slow and thorough" providing deeper insights but also require the analyst to dig deeper and to understand the causal interrelationships between different factors. They might also differ in the extent to which they are generally applicable to a variety of circumstance, and whether or not they give policy and programming advice.[7]

In order to provide the reader with a selection of useful tools to enhance their context analysis skills, this chapter will further elaborate on three generic context analytical tools: omnibus context questions, timelines and chronologies, as well as SWOT analysis. Thereafter, it will provide insight into context-specific tools: the Macro-Micro analysis and the problem tree analysis.

4.2   GENERIC CONTEXT ANALYTICAL TOOLS

4.2.1   Omnibus Context Questions

In order to deal with information more effectively when approaching analytical steps that go more in depth, it is recommendable to first get a general idea about the context. The most general form of context analysis is the omnibus context. Omnibus context questions are applicable to all kinds of contexts and can be formulated generally or specifically for humanitarian crisis. Questions pertaining to all kinds of humanitarian crises would be:

What do we know about the consequences of the crisis? Inquiring about the consequences of a crisis looks at the direct and indirect consequences (first- and second-order effects). These first- and second-order effects are usually those that humanitarian and development aid try to address.
  • The 2014–2015 Ebola crisis resulted in 24,992 infected and 10,365 deceased (first-order effect) in a period until March 2015. In addition, fear of contagion resulted in the breaking down of the market economy on micro and macro levels with long-lasting developmental consequences (second-order effect).[8]

What do we know about the causes of the crisis? This question relates to the causal factors that contribute to the humanitarian crisis and is the second step toward a critical reflection and toward thinking about possible responses regarding the alleviation of direct results, the reduction of vulnerabilities, and the mitigation of second order, indirect effects.
  • The factors that contributed to the wide spread were: the unprecedented outbreak of the virus in a context that previously had never experienced Ebola; high population mobility; badly prepared and ineffective public health infrastructures; cultural beliefs and practices, for example, relying on traditional healers; and ineffective and counterproductive public health information strategies.[9]

What do we know about relevant actors? Knowing the actors that are affected by the crisis and that contribute to the crisis is crucial for planning purposes. The mapping of the stakeholder field might, however, go beyond that, as some actors that are not directly affecting the situation or are affected by it might still be useful for overcoming the crisis. This element will be hard to analyze with generic means of a rapid context analysis and will require the use of specific tools for stakeholder analysis to come to a satisfactory answer (see specifically chapters 6 and 7). However, the

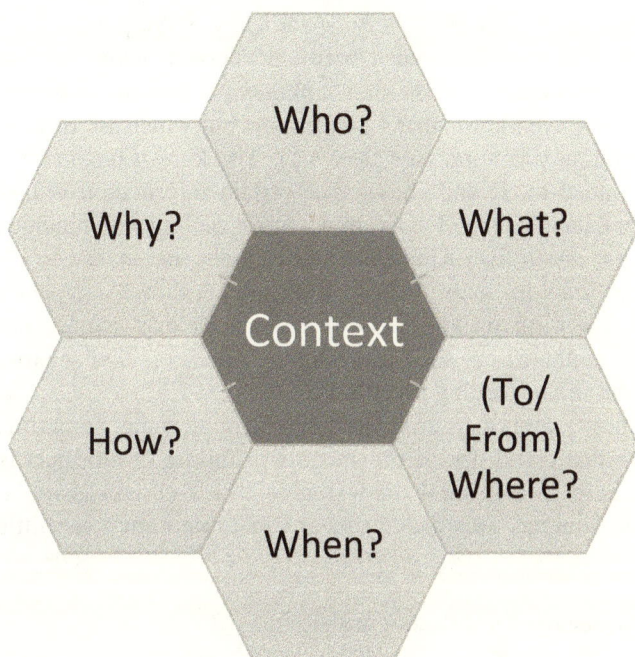

Figure 4.1   W-Questions Technique of Rapid Context Analysis

information already generated helps to ask better questions and to delve deeper into the social mechanisms behind the crisis.

- How did governments initially and down the line respond to the Ebola outbreak? What was the role of the UN and its specialized agencies (specifically the World Health Organization)? Did the declaration of a level 3 emergency result in the desired international cooperation?[10] Which were the populations most affected by the virus?

In intelligence analysis the technique of generic W-questions, used to generate a better understanding of the context, is also called star-bursting.[11] This technique requires the sorting of available information in accordance with generic criteria that are present in all contexts and starts inquiring about actors, modus operandi, time frames, and motives (see Figure 4.1).

In addition, two other important questions to ask are:

- What are the known unknowns?
- What are the unknown unknowns?

These two questions deal very specifically with present and lacking information. One can distinguish between "known unknowns"—pieces of information that I know I need—and "unknown unknowns"—pieces of information I do not even know that I don't know but which are of relevance for the humanitarian operation (see Box 4.1). The known unknowns are quite easily responded to. If one knows that certain information is lacking, one knows what data to collect. For example, when dealing with malnutrition, one can readily access a list of indicators that guides the analyst to looking for the right information, such as direct indicators (calories/day/person), proxy indicators (low birth weight (LBW)) and macro-level factors surrounding the issue of malnutrition, such as droughts, issues of food security, dietary diversity, and infant-feeding practices.[12]

The unknown unknowns are a little more troublesome. Sometimes crucial information that could decide the success or failure of a project is missing simply because of a general unawareness that a certain issue is relevant in the given context. This usually means that one knows too little about a

---

Box 4.1   W-Questions Rapid Context Analysis

Step 1: collect general information about the topic of concern; make sure to collect information that also concerns the general phenomenon to be analyzed, as well as information about actors and the region of concern. Generally helpful are reports by UN agencies, NGOs, and think tanks.

Step 2: conduct an analysis of the reliability of data and information sources according to section 3.5. (This step will be presupposed for subsequent analytic steps.)

Step 3: for each W-Question distil the information relevant from the data. Note that it is not problematic if information in the different questions is overlapping.

Step 4: sort the information for each of the questions and visualize key information in a table (use one column for each W-Question) by summarizing information with keywords.

Step 5: in order to identify the known unknowns, try to detect where information is still lacking from the columns by looking for information gaps.

Step 6: in order to identify the unknown unknowns, try to detect where information is still lacking from the columns and between the columns and the keywords by looking for logical inconsistencies and explanatory gaps.

Step 7: collect the data still missing and apply steps 2–6 as often as necessary to get a relatively complete picture.

given context in order to reasonably predict the effect of an intervention. For example, one might be well aware of all nutritional facts to implement an emergency feeding project, but one might not know enough about the cultural context that might prohibit certain feeding practices or not enough about the security situation in the region to conduct the project safely. The cultural element of feeding practices will generally be a known factor to nutrition experts; that is, it will more likely be a known unknown. However, the relevance of the security element might, due to the focus of expertise, completely escape the expert's awareness of relevance (unknown unknowns). In order to reduce these unknown unknowns, one should generally conduct a thorough analysis of the omnibus context to pick up hints of potentially relevant unknown factors. In addition, as mentioned above, in order to limit the possible unknown unknowns it makes sense to work with issue dependent indicators and to use targeted and structured analytical tools that go beyond the omnibus context and, for example, use security sectors or other even more context-specific categories to guide the research process into domains that a generalist or a specialist in another field would not usually look into.

4.2.2 Timelines and Chronologies

While the queue questions also include the when, they do not specifically utilize the time dimension to generate further insights into the context. For that purpose, timelines and chronologies are a form of omnibus context analysis with a focus on the temporal dimension. Chronologies are the simplest form of time sensitive analysis. They simply present a list of events in chronological order. It is up to the analyst to distil further information from this list, which becomes more difficult by the lack of prioritizing important over less important information and by not visualizing the time dimension to indicate time gaps and the clustering of events, which is inherent to the list-style nature of chronologies, illustrated in Table 4.1.

Box 4.2 Chronology

Step 1: sort the information chronologically.
Step 2: generate a table with two columns; in the left add the time (period), in the right add the information.
Step 3: identify known processes and logical gaps in the information describing the time-bound processes.

Table 4.1 UNHCR's Chronology of Syria's Displacement Crisis 2011–2013*

11 March	Syrian crisis begins with peaceful protests that spread nationwide in April.
11 May	First camps for refugees open in Turkey.
12 March	UNHCR appoints a regional refugee coordinator for Syrian refugees.
12 July	Za'atri Refugee Camp opens in Jordan.
12 September	UNHCR scales up relief operations inside Syria and across the region. UNHCR chief António Guterres and special envoy Angelina Jolie visit refugees in Lebanon, Jordan, and Turkey.
12 October	UNHCR urges European Union states to uphold their asylum principles by ensuring access to their territory and to asylum procedures and harmonizing their approaches in the review and granting of asylum claims.
12 November	UNHCR aid reaches 300,000 displaced people across Syria.
12 December	Neighboring countries host half a million refugees. UNHCR and partners launch a US$1 billion Regional Response Plan for Syrian refugees in Jordan, Iraq, Lebanon, Turkey, and Egypt.
13 March	The number of Syrian refugees reaches 1 million, outpacing projections. UNHCR calls for safe passage of humanitarian convoys inside Syria as needs grow amid intensified civil conflict.
13 April	António Guterres warns the UN Security Council that almost half of Syria's 20.8 million population could be in need of humanitarian help by the end of 2013.
13 June	UN humanitarian agencies, on behalf of dozens of aid organizations, announce the biggest aid appeal in history, totaling some US$4.4 billion. This includes almost US$3 billion for humanitarian relief in the region surrounding Syria (the Regional Response Plan) and US$1.4 billion for the aid response inside Syria (the Syria Humanitarian Assistance Response Plan). On top of this, US$830 million is requested for the governments of Jordan and Lebanon.
13 July	On the first anniversary of its opening, Za'atri camp hosts 120,000 refugees.
13 August	The number of Syrian refugee children passes 1 million. Spike in arrivals of Syrian Kurd refugees in northern Iraq, including almost 50,000 in a two-week period.
13 September	The number of Syrian refugees passes the 2-million mark, compared to 230,000 one year earlier. The number of internally displaced stands at 4.25 million. UNHCR and government ministers from Turkey, Jordan, Lebanon, and Iraq meet in Geneva and pledge joint action to seek greater international help for host countries struggling to cope with the Syrian refugee crisis. Growing numbers of Syrians seek to reach Europe by sea. Germany accepts first group of Syrian refugees for temporary relocation.

*"Fact Sheet: Timeline and Figures/Syria Displacement Crisis" (UNHCR, September 2013), http://www.unhcr.org/5245a72e6.pdf.

In comparison, a timeline is a visualization of events on a time axis. "Timelines are graphical representations people can fill in with details; as visual artifacts, they are more easily processed than other forms of communication. Timelines capitalize on the obviousness provided by their visibility as well as on people's ability to supply narrative structure to static images."[13] In general, timelines serve temporal issues in the management of processes:

1. need for schedules—the reliable prediction of points in time;
2. need for synchronization—coordination of functionally separate but time dependent processes;
3. need for time allocation—distributing activities over time to improve effectiveness and efficiency.[14]

There are a few important things to consider when drawing a timeline: The distance between the events should ideally represent the equivalent time between the events; that is, events are not only chronologically distributed, but the distance between them should also represent the length of the time passed. This is important to identify gaps in knowledge regarding processes and developments initiated in the past of `the plotted data or visibly emerging at a later moment. Furthermore, which events are represented and why? It is possible to use color-coding, or multiple parallel timelines for different kinds of events, in order to distill further information from the data and begin to analyze how different events relate to each other? By projecting events visually on a time axis, the visualization can serve to:

- identify processes and knowledge gaps about processes;
- understand timing;
- identify patterns and correlations;
- distinguish between recurrent and nonrecurrent events;
- discover trends and anomalies; and
- track concurrent events and mutual effects.

One of the most problematic pitfalls when analyzing timelines is to assume a cause–effect relationship between precedent and antecedent events visualized. The relationship that one can deduce is correlational at best. There might, however, also be events on a timeline that are not directly related to each other at all and are simply connected to the issue by thematic or geographical proximity.

The example in Figure 4.2 illustrates the depiction of known processes and key events on a seasonal timeline for a food security update developed for Ethiopia in June 2007. It concluded that due to a lack of *sugum* (major pastoral rains) from March to May, severe water and pasture shortages caused unusual movement of livestock and people. If the *karma* (July–September) rains would not perform exceptionally well, the situation was to deteriorate into a humanitarian emergency.

Similarly, the Famine Early Warning Systems Network used a combination of context-specific, nonrecurring key processes (arrival of Malian refugees, subsidized cereal sales, start of Ramadan, etc.) overlaid on seasonally recurring processes (rainy season, grain harvest, etc.) to illustrate the food security situation in Burkina Faso in the period of April 2012–April 2013 (Figure 4.3).

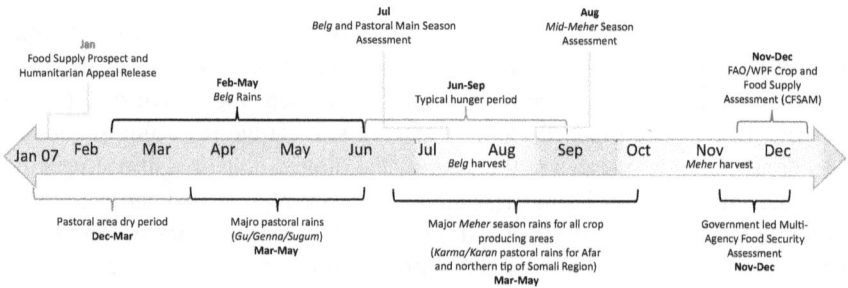

Figure 4.2 Single Timeline for Food Security in Ethiopia for January to December 2007. *Note*: USAID, "Ethiopia Food Security Update Jun 2007: Humanitarian Crisis Possible in Somali Region," Text, Famine Early Warning Systems Network (June 21, 2007), http://reliefweb.int/report/ethiopia/fews-ethiopia-food-security-update-jun-2007-humanitarian-crisis-possible-somali.

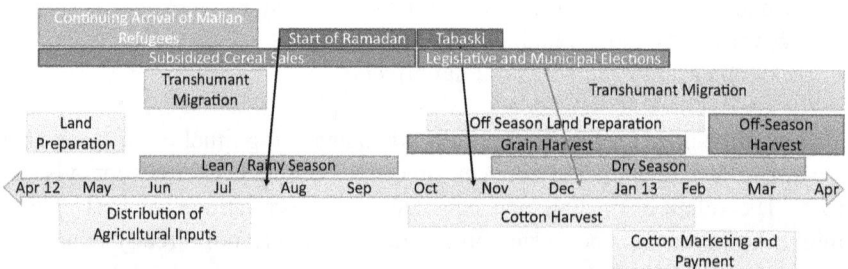

Figure 4.3 Multiple Timelines of Seasonal and Non-recurring Processes Regarding Food Security in Burkina Faso for April 2012 to April 2013. *Note*: "Burkina Faso—Food Security Outlook: Tue, 2012-07-31 to Mon, 2012-12-31," Famine Early Warning Systems Network, accessed April 24, 2015, http://www.fews.net/west-africa/burkina-faso/food-security-outlook/july-2012.

Box 4.3 Timelines

Step 1: draw a line with a specific start and end point and mark the time units in between in accordance with the time scale used.

Step 2: plot the information on the timeline; note that the distance between the events should also represent the length of the time passed.

Step 2a: differentiate reoccurring and nonreoccurring events on either side of the timeline or by using different colors or shapes. Do the same for different categories of event information (e.g., natural phenomena, violent crimes, health hazards, political developments).

Step 2b: if there is too much information, use more parallel timelines; make sure that the time axes and the time intervals are identical.

Step 3: identify known processes and logical gaps in the information describing the time-bound processes.

Step 4: mark events for which information regarding their preceding processes are missing; if known, write down the elements of that process and highlight timespans within which it is likely that these process elements would have occurred.

Step 5: mark event information that reflects possible elements of hidden processes and outcomes in the future (suspected processes); write down the information that if known would solidify the likelihood of the suspected processes being present; check for data regarding these elements.

Step 6: identify reoccurring patterns and correlations (i.e., events that most likely are connected through a logical cause–effect relationship); solidify certainty about patterns and correlations by finding supporting evidence in the data.

This information was then used for scenario building (see also chapter 9) in order to predict growing food security crisis particularly in July. It further predicted tensions regarding food security between August and September, until grain and cotton harvest would start again in October.

Knowing which processes are dependent on the outcomes of other processes or which can be conducted in parallel increases the effectiveness of logistical planning of a humanitarian operation. Multiple timelines are particularly useful in this regard and for planning of humanitarian operations in general. Timelines for planning purposes are called Gantt charts. These charts assign a timeline for each process and may additionally add a percentage for progress and assigned teams (Figure 4.4 provides a hypothetical example of a humanitarian Gantt chart).

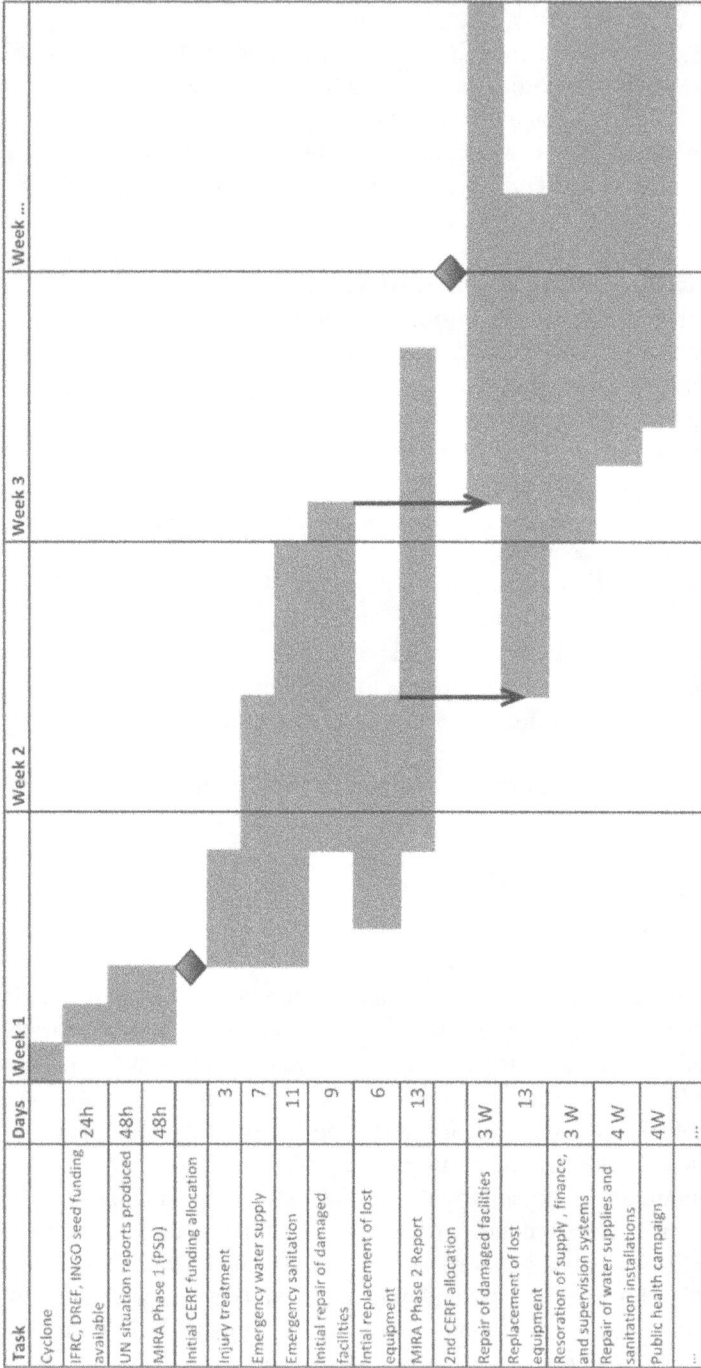

Task	Days	Week 1	Week 2	Week 3	Week ...
Cyclone					
IFRC, DREF, INGO seed funding available	24h				
UN situation reports produced	48h				
MIRA Phase 1 (PSD)	48h				
Initial CERF funding allocation					
Injury treatment	3				
Emergency water supply	7				
Emergency sanitation	11				
Initial repair of damaged facilities	9				
Initial replacement of lost equipment	6				
MIRA Phase 2 Report	13				
2nd CERF allocation					
Repair of damaged facilities	3 W				
Replacement of lost equipment	13				
Restoration of supply , finance, and supervision systems	3 W				
Repair of water supplies and sanitation installations	4 W				
Public health campaign	4W				
...					

Figure 4.4 GANTT Chart of Humanitarian Response after a Cyclone. *Note*: [i] For a timeline of UN disaster response tools and services in medium and large scale emergencies see: http://www.unocha.org/publications/asiadisasterresponse/ToolsAndServicesForDisasterResponse.html; regarding WHO guidelines for health response timelines to different emergency categories see: http://www.who.int/hac/techguidance/tools/manuals/who_field_handbook/annex_2/en/.

Box 4.4 Gantt Chart

Step 1: identify the endpoint of a process.

Step 2: decompose the process into individual elements that are prerequisites for each other and for the overall process to succeed.

Step 3: estimate the time necessary for each of the elements.

Step 4: draw a time axis for each of the elements (length equals times), starting with the first elements that need to happen on top and ending with the process outcome.

Step 5: review which elements are not mutually dependent and happen in parallel; redraw the processes with overlapping time elements.

Step 6: review the Gantt chart regarding logical consistency and resource/manpower strains.

Step 6a: for planning purposes add resources/personnel needed and percentage of completion.

Step 6b: for entry point analysis (EPA, see 9.2), assess which process elements would create openings for an intervention due to advantages in resources, knowledge, or network.

Step 6c: for monitoring and forecasting, identify indicators of measurement significant of each element in the process, and monitor these indicators for their occurrence.

4.2.3 SWOT Analysis

The SWOT analysis is a matrix-based analysis tool for organizational management (Table 4.2). It consists of four elements: strengths (S), weaknesses (W), opportunities (O), and threats (T). Sometimes, threats are replaced with constraints (C; SWOC). Strengths and weaknesses are internal forces in an organization, and opportunities and threats are external to it. In contrast to the force field analysis (see section 9.1), which sees decision-making parameters influenced only by two kinds of forces, those that facilitate change (driving forces) and those that resist it, SWOT analysis specifically emphasizes the organization's internal and external elements. Furthermore, given the terminology in the external sphere (opportunities and threats), SWOT puts an emphasis on factors that are yet to lead to certain effects.

Table 4.2 General SWOT Matrix

	Positive	Negative
Internal	Strengths	Weaknesses
External	Opportunities	Threats

At first sight the SWOT analysis looks rather simple; however, the matrix can be expanded to create pairs of internal/external factors that in turn translate into strategies:[15]

- *Strengths and Opportunities (SO Strategy—Maxi/Maxi)*: This is the ideal type strategy in which an organization can maximize the use of its external opportunities through the optimal utilization of its internal strengths.
- *Strengths and Threats (ST Strategy—Maxi/Mini)*: This strategy aims to utilize the organization's internal strengths to overcome external threats.
- *Weaknesses and Opportunities (WO Strategy—Mini/Maxi)*: Conversely, the WO strategy tries to make use of external opportunities to compensate for internal weaknesses.
- *Weaknesses and Threats (WT Strategy—Mini/Mini)*: Worst-case scenario planning is where internal weaknesses meet external threats. The WT strategy aims to minimize internal weaknesses in order to mitigate external threats or to avoid them.

The matrix in Figure 4.5 illustrates the steps that the humanitarian intelligence team takes in the process of creating a SWOT analysis. While

Step 1. Prepare an Organization Profile: (a) Sectors of Activity; (b) Regional Focus; (c) Competitive Situation; (d) Embeddedness in Humanitarian System;				
		Step 4. Prepare a SW Audit in: (a) Management and Organization; (b) Operations; (c) Finance; (d) Outreach and Accountability; (e) Monitoring and Evaluation		
	Internal Factors	Step 5. Develop Alternatives Step 6. Make Strategic Choices; Consider Strategies, Tactics, Action Steps 1 to 6. Test for Consistency. Also Prepare Contingency Plans. (Step 7)		
External Factors			List Internal Strengths (S): (1) (2) (3)	List Internal Weaknesses (W): (1) (2) (3)
Step 2. Identify and Evaluate the Following Factors: (a) Economic (b) Social (c) Political (d) Environmental (e) Health (f) Safety and Security (g) Access and Acceptance (h) Humanitarian Coordination		List External Opportunities (O): (Consider Risks Also) (1) (2) (3)	SO: Maxi-Maxi Strategy	WO: Mini-Maxi Strategy
Step 3. Prepare a Forecast, Make Predictions and Assessment of the Near Future		List External Threats (T): (1) (2) (3)	ST: Maxi-Mini Strategy	WT: Mini-Mini Strategy

Figure 4.5   **Humanitarian SWOT Matrix**

individual analysts can conduct a SWOT analysis, this tool benefits greatly from the cooperation of team members and the team leader in the form of brainstorming processes. Also, since group think and other biases can influence particularly the vision on internal strengths and weaknesses, the SWOT analysis also profits from external input.[16] The following matrix provides a step-by-step plan to conduct a SWOT analysis for a humanitarian organization with field deployments. Steps 1 and 4 concern the organization itself and will require only modifications if regional sections of the humanitarian organization show specificities. Steps 3 and 4 are specific to the external operational environment and need to be adapted to any occurring changes. Steps 5 and 6 are the results of matching the SWOT criteria to develop the four sets of strategies.

4.3   CONTEXT-SPECIFIC ANALYTICAL APPROACHES

4.3.1   Macro-Micro Analysis

Context analytical approaches that aim to compare the change from one situation to another (i.e., after a humanitarian emergency) require an understanding of the causes behind the changing variables and the constant factors before and after major events such as armed conflicts or natural disasters. In order to understand these factors one can employ the macro-micro analysis. This analysis takes macro processes (e.g., A leads to Z) as evidential hypothesis and looks into the micro processes underlying the causal interaction between two or more macro phenomena (e.g., micro processes a, b, c lead to micro outcomes x, y, z; see Figure 4.6). If the analyst observes a change on the surface of a context (A→Z), that is, on the macro level, any intervention would

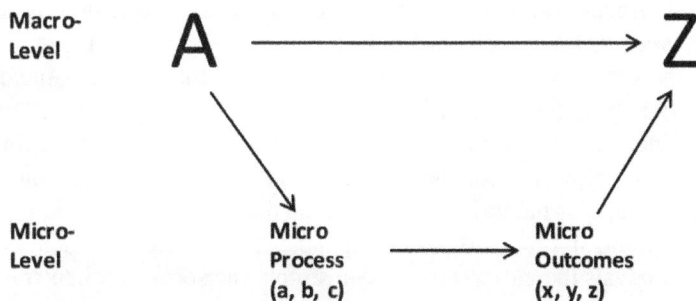

Figure 4.6   Macro-Micro Analysis Scheme

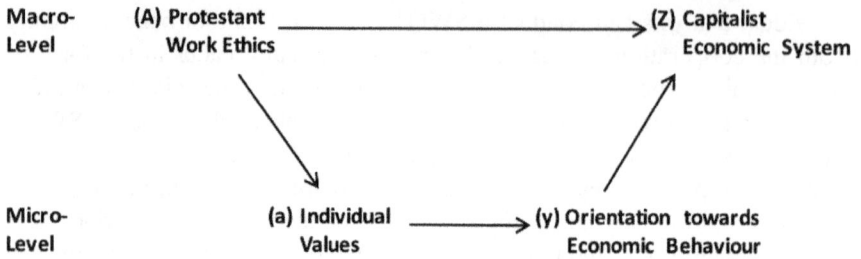

Figure 4.7   Macro-Micro Explanations in Social Science (Coleman 1986: 1322)

also need to take into account the underlying processes. In these cases, the analyst would need to know what the causal mechanisms under the surface are (a, b, c) that lead to the change (x, y, z) with effect on the macro level; thus, the analyst has to look under the surface where actual social interactions take place—the micro level.

We have, therefore, to make a distinction between macro-level problems and micro-level explanations.[17] Macro-level problems (or observations) pertain to the identification of more or less "general" factors that depict a particular empirical problem. Micro-level explanations solve that empirical puzzle. A famous example is based on Max Weber's work on the protestant work ethic. Weber established a relationship between the capitalist economic system and the presence of a protestant work ethic. However, knowing that this relationship exists is not sufficient, since we do not yet know which underlying causal mechanism leads to this relationship. Identifying this causal mechanism is referred to as a micro-level explanation. Weber discovered that a protestant work ethic influences the values of individuals (i.e., try to be a good person during your life) and that this leads to similarities in economic behavior (i.e., work hard, try to be successful; see Figure 4.7).

One additional component that can be part of the macro-micro analysis is the *critical incident technique*.[18] It is of particular value if one wants to analyze the effect that a specific event had, to establish an ex-ante/ex-post (before/after) base line comparison, or to study the processes that led up to a critical incident. The critical incident can be a specific point in time that has particular relevance for the situation, but it can also be the onset of a major man-made or natural humanitarian crisis. It is also possible to simply select two points in time without having a particular critical incident in mind. Then the analysis thereafter will explain simply the social mechanisms in the

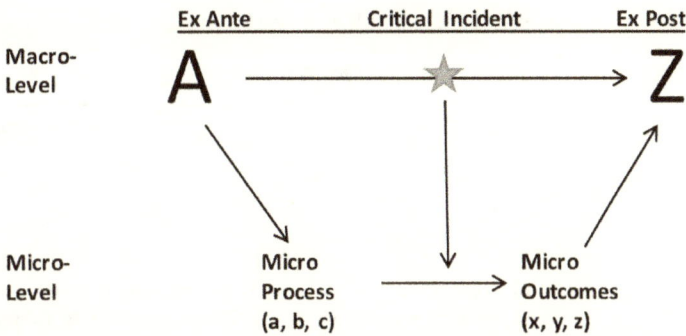

Figure 4.8 **Macro-Micro Scheme with Critical Incident and Ex-Ante/Ex-Post Division**

researched population that kept the situation the same or led to an improvement or decline in the sectors the analyst investigates. Such a snapshot analysis of a pre- and post-incident state informs the researcher about the general sectoral developments and underlying processes over the chosen time frame. This relates to the diagnostic question "What has changed due to an event in the contextual constellation?" Such a diagnostic approach establishes the dependent variable; this means, it tells the researcher about a macro-level phenomenon that requires explanation—"Why did A lead to Z?" (macro-micro analysis) and "What is the role of the critical incident regarding A and Z?" (critical incident technique). In other words, by using the critical incident technique the analyst hypothesizes that the event chosen as critical incident fulfills a certain function in the equation A→Z. For example, the critical incident could have played the role of a catalyst (see Figure 4.8).

In simple terms, with two contextual snapshots, one before and one after a critical incident, the researcher gets to know what has changed due to the critical incident. In order to understand the social mechanisms of how the critical incident actually changed the aspects of the comprehensive context (the explanatory question) one needs to look at the micro level. Since when referring to the micro level we were talking about social mechanisms, it is obvious that this is where actors need to be investigated in more detail. This is where the stakeholder analyses can be tremendously helpful for understanding the social dynamics (see chapter 6).

For example, let us for the sake of clarity look only at economic stability as one core contextual factor. If economic stability was high before a civil war and is low after that critical incident, the question arises how this relates to the change in economic stability. The observation thus takes place on a

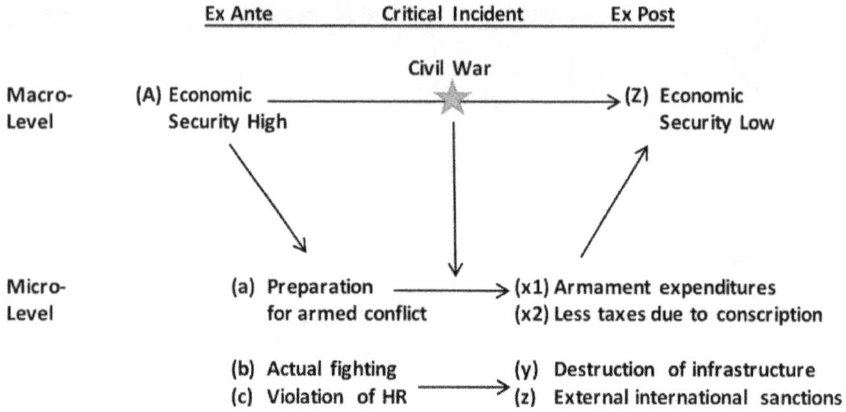

	Ex Ante	Critical Incident	Ex Post

Figure 4.9   Macro-Micro Explanation of Threats of War and Weak Economy

macro level and one assumes a causal connection between the change of economic stability and civil war. While the fact that there should be a causal link seems obvious, the actual investigation into the micro processes might reveal interesting and unexpected connections. In order to find out what these causal connections are, one has to delve deeper with the investigation and trace how the violent conflict affects the actors' ability to engage in economic activities. For example, one of the findings could be that the state had to invest a lot of money and people in the preparation for a possible civil war through military spending and the introduction of conscription; the same might be true for the opposing faction. Furthermore, the state might spend tax money to buy weapons, and people might have to stop working in order to serve in the military or the militia. Insecurity further affects local markets. War expenditures put direct pressure on the economy of the state, and military service reduces the income from taxes. Additionally, the actual fighting might destroy infrastructure necessary for economic transactions (e.g., markets), and possible violations of human rights might trigger international sanctions (see Figure 4.9).

The micro-macro analysis is a useful approach for analyzing cause-effect interdependencies of macro-level phenomena that cannot be readily explained without a closer look at the complex interdependence of variables on the micro level. For an aid agency, this tool is of particular relevance when developing program or project assumptions. It aids in reducing unintended consequences and lends crucial support to the design of targeted and precise interventions.

Box 4.5   Macro-Micro Analysis

Step 1: identify the macro-level phenomenon that requires explanation; select two issues that are apparently connected but for which information as to their exact relationship is missing and which therefore require further explanation.

Step 1a: identify a critical incident in between the macro-level cause and effect or replacing either of the dependent on the subject of investigation:

• Use the critical incident as macro cause (A) if you are interested in which micro relationships have resulted in its apparent effect(s).
• Use the critical incident as macro effect (Z) if you are interested in which micro relationships have contributed to its realization.

Note: for complex macro-cause-and-effect relationships, one needs several macro-cause-and-effect pairs. For that purpose the problem tree analysis (4.3.2) is better suited.

Step 2: brainstorm about possible micro-level relationships (a, b, c . . .) of the macro-level cause (A) by asking questions such as the following:

• How might actors be related to the macro-level cause?
• What is the role of culture with regard to the macro-level cause?
• How does the macro-level cause inform interactions between groups and concerning leadership?

Step 3: investigate these questions and support your findings with empirical information.

Step 4: brainstorm about possible micro-level effects (x, y, z . . .) of micro-level causes (a, b, c . . .).

Step 5: select those micro-level effects (x, y, z . . .) that lead to the macro-level effect (Z) and subject them to empirical investigation.

Step 6: draw a Macro-Micro scheme and fill it with keywords representing the empirical information.

Step 7: check for logical inconsistencies; if found repeat steps 2–5.

4.3.2   Problem Tree Analysis

The micro-macro analysis presented a first step toward the identification of underlying causal mechanisms that pertain to a macro-level observation. The problem tree analysis offers a first step from analyzing the causes leading up to a *focal problem* and the effects caused by it, to developing first objectives (objective tree) and alternatives. Embedding the focal problem (e.g., the outbreak of a disease or the destruction caused by an earthquake) in the causes and effects chain provides a contextual awareness that includes pre- and post-incident factors and can contribute not only to a more coherent project design but even to future DRR and linking relief, rehabilitation, and development (LRRD) efforts. As such, the problem tree analysis is most useful in the program or project management cycle stages of (1) identification, (2) planning (formulation), and (3) appraisal and approval (see chapter 2).

In essence the problem tree analysis can consist of (see Figure 4.10):

1. Problem tree: this mandatory element maps causes and effects pertaining to a focal problem.
2. Objectives tree: this element connects project or program objectives with the causes and effects of the focal problem and helps identify the organization's area of intervention within the larger disaster context.
3. Alternatives analysis: it aims to identify possible alternative options, helps assess their feasibility, and eventually should lead to the decision on a specific project strategy.

Problem Tree: The problem tree consists of three elements: (a) the focal problem, (b) the causes of the focal problem, and (c) the effects of the focal

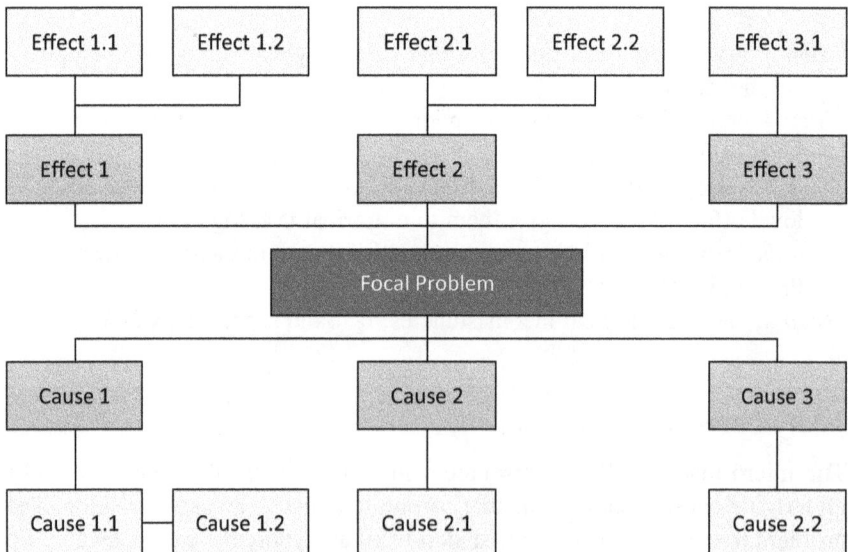

Figure 4.10   Problem Tree Template

problem. Similar to a mind map, the focal problem has to be identified first in order to determine causes and effects. The focal problem might be selected from a list of problems identified earlier. In the process of a focus group discussion mapping out causes and effects, the focal problem might change slightly and may also become more specified. Once the focal problem is clear, one can start developing the problem tree itself (Figure 4.11) by adding information in their cause-effect relation. The steps in Box 4.6 give good guidance for this first phase.[19]

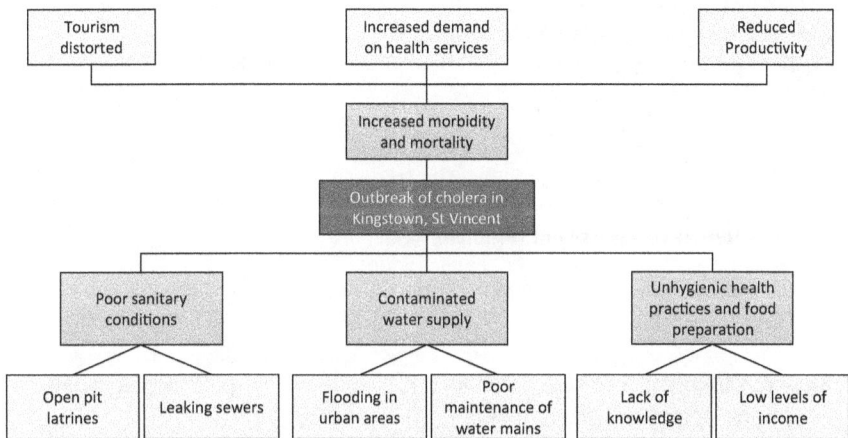

Figure 4.11   Problem Tree Example—Cholera Outbreak. *Note*: Based on Philip Dearden et al., "Tools for Development—A Handbook for Those Engaged in Development Activity" (London: Department for International Development (DFID), March 2003), sec. 3.5, http://webarchive.nationalarchives.gov.uk/20090119062531/http://www.dfid.gov.uk/pubs/files/toolsfordevelopment.pdf.

Box 4.6   Problem Tree Development

Step 1: formulate core problems pertaining to the crisis and the organizational mandate.

Step 2: select one focal problem for further analysis.

Step 3: identify immediate and direct causes of the focal problem.

Step 4: identify immediate and direct effects of the focal problem.

Step 5: construct a problem tree showing the relationships between the problem and its causes and effects.

Step 6: review the problem tree, verify its validity and completeness, and make any necessary adjustments.

Box 4.7   Objectives Tree Development (Problem Tree)

(The Objectives Tree presupposes the development of the problem tree (steps 1–6).)

Step 7: reformulate all the elements in the problem tree into positive desirable conditions.

Step 8: review the resulting means-ends relationships to assure the validity and completeness of the objective tree.

Step 9: if required:
• revise statements;
• delete objectives that appear unrealistic or unnecessary;
• add new objectives where required.

Step 10: draw connecting lines to indicate the means-ends relationships.

Box 4.8   Alternative Assessment (Problem Tree)

(The Alternatives Assessment presupposes the development of the problem tree (steps 1–10).)

Step 11: identify differing "means-ends" ladders, as possible alternative options or activity components.

Step 12: eliminate objectives that are obviously not desirable or achievable.

Step 13: eliminate objectives being pursued by other activities in the area.

Step 14: discuss the implications for affected groups.

Strategy Selection (Problem Tree)
(The Strategy Selection presupposes the development of the problem tree [steps 1–14].)

Step 15: make an assessment of the feasibility of the different alternatives.

Step 16: select one of the alternatives as the activity strategy.

Step 17: develop a Plan B strategy on the basis of possible intervening variables that would affect Plan A but not Plan B.

Step 18: if agreement cannot be reached, then:
• introduce additional criteria;
• alter the most promising option by including or subtracting elements from the objectives tree.

Tourism restored		Reduced demand on health services		Productivity restored

Decreased morbidity and mortality

A B

Outbreak of cholera in Kingstown, St Vincent

A A B

Sanitary conditions improved	Potable water supplied in target areas	Hygienic health practices adopted

A	B A	A	A B B	B
Pit latrines improved	Sewer maintenance improve	Flood control measures implemented	Maintenance of water mains improved	Hygene training in target communities	Income generating activities

Alternative A: Infrastructure	Alternative B: Health Education
Alternative A is focused on infrastructure and could be financed by a donor that has a comparative advantage in supporting this type of activity.	Alternative B is focused on health education and behaviour change and could be supported by donors or NGOs specialising in that kind of activity. Together, the two alternatives offer greater potential for realizing the higher level project objectives.

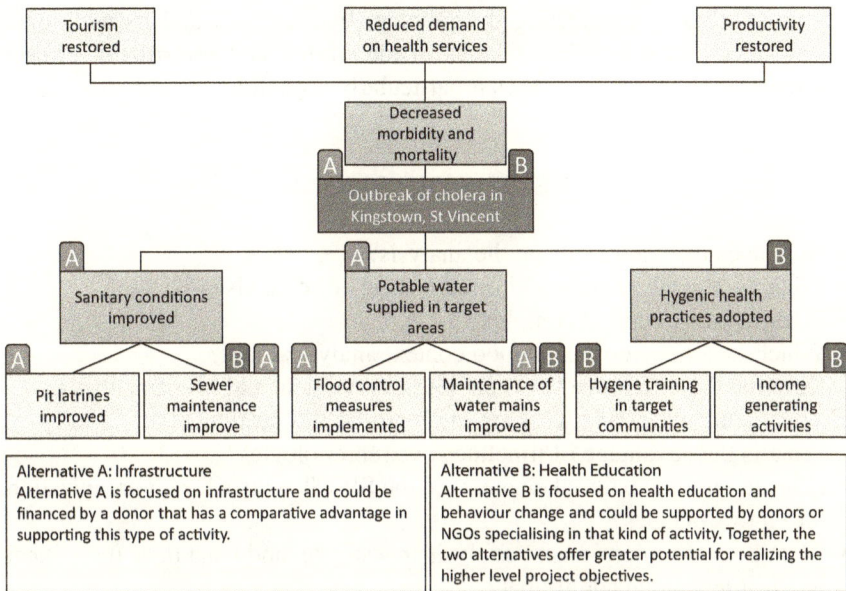

Figure 4.12 Objectives Tree and Alternatives Analysis Example—Cholera Outbreak. *Note*: Based on: Philip Dearden et al., "Tools for Development—A Handbook for Those Engaged in Development Activity" (London: Department for International Development (DFID), March 2003), sec. 3.6, http://webarchive.nationalarchives.gov. uk/20090119062531/http://www.dfid.gov.uk/pubs/files/toolsfordevelopment.pdf.

Objectives Tree: The second phase, the objectives tree, consists of matching causes and effects with project objectives. The transformation of the problem tree into an objectives tree happens by reformulating the causes and effects relationships into a means and ends relationship. Therefore, one should start with reformulating the focal problem into a positive objective (see Figure 4.12). Eventually, the *means-ends* relationship is established by connecting the objectives (i.e., the solutions for causes and effects) with the negative impact that causes and effects have.

Alternatives Analysis: The alternatives analysis represents the third and last phase in the problem tree analysis. Its purpose is the identification of possible strategic pathways and alternative options. The eventual decision which pathway to choose from requires assessment of their feasibility. In addition, alternative strategic pathways provide a plan B in case the original strategy turns out to be nonworkable. The last two steps in the alternatives analysis are the alternatives assessment and the strategy selection.

Problem tree analysis is central to many development and humanitarian project development tools and might even be required by funding agencies.

The possibility of connecting the problem tree analysis and its additional tools directly to a LogFrame helps in identifying and prioritizing project objectives and, therefore, makes it particularly appealing.

REVIEW QUESTIONS

- How does the context shape the analysis?
- What are the advantages and disadvantages of data visualization?
- What makes a context complex?
- Which factors determine a good context analytical tool?
- Describe the difference between needs assessment and needs analysis.
- What is the utility and what are the limits of W-questions?
- What is the advantage of timelines over chronologies?
- How do internal/external elements in the SWOT matrix for an organization turn into strategies?
- What does the micro-macro analysis investigate, and what does the critical incident technique add to that?
- How does problem tree analysis contribute to the development of project objectives?

NOTES

1. C. Tilly and R. E. Goodin, "Chapter 1. It Depends," in *The Oxford Handbook of Contextual Political Analysis* (Oxford: Oxford University Press, 2006), 3–32.

2. Diaswati Mardiasmo and Paul H. Barnes, "Community Response to Disasters in Indonesia: Gotong Royong; a Double Edged-Sword," in *Proceedings of the 9th Annual International Conference of the International Institute for Infrastructure Renewal and Reconstruction*, ed. Paul H. Barnes and Ashantha Goonetilleke (9th Annual International Conference of the International Institute for Infrastructure Renewal and Reconstruction: Risk-informed Disaster Management: Planning for Response, Recovery & Resilience, Brisbane, Australia: Queensland University of Technology, 2015), 301–307, http://digitalcollections.qut.edu.au/2213/.

3. For readers interested in the H-AID framework of analysis, I recommend: Liesbet Heyse, Andrej Zwitter, Rapahel Wittek, and Joost Herman, *Humanitarian Crises, Intervention and Security: A Framework for Evidence-Based Programming* (London: Routledge, 2014).

4. Sarah Collinson, Michael Bhatia, Martin Evans, Richard Fanthorpe, Jonathan Goodhand, and Stephen Jackson, "Politically Informed Humanitarian Programming Using a Political Economy Approach," Network Papers, HPN Resources. London: Humanitarian Practice Network, Overseas Development Institute, December 2002, http://www.odihpn.org/hpn-resources/

network-papers/politically-informed-humanitarian-programming-using-a-political-economy-approach.

5. Wayne Michael Hall and Gary Citrenbaum, *Intelligence Analysis: How to Think in Complex Environments* (ABC-CLIO, 2009).

6. For approaches concerning root causes and permissive conditions in the area of natural disasters and political violence, see, for example, Piers Blaikie et al., *At Risk: Natural Hazards, People's Vulnerability and Disasters* (Routledge, 2004); Edward Newman, "Exploring the 'Root Causes' of Terrorism," *Studies in Conflict & Terrorism* 29, no. 8 (2006): 749, doi:10.1080/10576100600704069; Andrej Zwitter, *Human Security, Law, and the Prevention of Terrorism*, vol. 88 (Taylor & Francis, 2010).

7. For an excellent overview and meta-analysis of the usefulness of these models, I recommend Heyse et al., *Humanitarian Crises, Intervention and Security*, Chapter 2.

8. OCHA, "Ebola Crisis Page—Humanitarian Data Exchange," accessed March 30, 2015, https://data.hdx.rwlabs.org/ebola.

9. "WHO/Factors That Contributed to Undetected Spread of the Ebola Virus and Impeded Rapid Containment," *WHO*, accessed January 17, 2016, http://www.who.int/entity/csr/disease/ebola/one-year-report/factors/en/index.html.

10. Emergency levels:

- *Level 1: Emergency operations within the response capabilities of the relevant Country Office (CO), with routine support from Regional Bureaux (RB);*
- *Level 2: Emergency response operations requiring regional augmentation of country-level response capability;*
- *Level 3: Emergency response operations requiring mobilization of global response capabilities in support of the relevant CO(s) and/or RB—that is, a corporate response.*

Regarding more details on the classification of emergency response operations according to a three-level scale, see: http://documents.wfp.org/stellent/groups/public/documents/resources/wfp264770.pdf.

11. Richards J. Heuer and Randolph H. Pherson, *Structured Analytic Techniques for Intelligence Analysis* (SAGE, 2010), 102.

12. "Measuring Malnutrition (Module 7)," *Unite for Sight*, accessed April 23, 2015, http://www.uniteforsight.org/nutrition/module7.

13. Elaine K. Yakura, "Charting Time: Timelines as Temporal Boundary Objects," *Academy of Management Journal* 45, no. 5 (October 1, 2002): 958, doi:10.2307/3069324.

14. John Hassard, "Aspects of Time in Organization," *Human Relations* 44, no. 2 (February 1, 1991): 116, doi:10.1177/001872679104400201.

15. Heinz Weihrich, "Analyzing the Competitive Advantages and Disadvantages of Germany with the TOWS Matrix—An Alternative to Porter's Model," *European Business Review* 99, no. 1 (1999): 9–22; Heinz Weihrich, "The TOWS Matrix—A Tool for Situational Analysis," *LRP Long Range Planning* 15, no. 2 (1982): 54–66.

16. Val Renault, "Chapter 3. Assessing Community Needs and Resources—Section 14. SWOT Analysis: Strengths, Opportunities, Weaknesses, and Threats,"

in *Community Tool Box*, Work Group for Community Health and Development (University of Kansas, 2015), http://ctb.ku.edu/en/table-of-contents/assessment/assessing-community-needs-and-resources/swot-analysis/main.

17. This distinction was made by the sociologist James Coleman. See, for example, J. Coleman, "Social Theory, Social Research and a Theory of Action," *American Journal of Sociology* 6 (1986): 1309–35.

18. The critical incidents approach is particularly useful if the effect on one particular incident should be analyzed or if one wants to compare the effect of similar critical incidents. See J. C. Flanagan, "The Critical Incident Technique," *Psychological Bulletin* 51, no. 4 (July 1954).

19. Philip Dearden et al., "Tools for Development—A Handbook for Those Engaged in Development Activity" (London: Department for International Development (DFID), March 2003), sec. 3.2–3.3, http://webarchive.nationalarchives.gov.uk/20090119062531/http://www.dfid.gov.uk/pubs/files/toolsfordevelopment.pdf.

Chapter 5

Humanitarian Analysis and Intervention Design Framework

Comprehensive Context Analysis

5.1 INTRODUCTION AND THEORETICAL BACKGROUND

We have seen before that generic context analyses focus on descriptive questions that are applicable in any context. In contrast, context specific tools of analysis focus on causal mechanisms that explain the specificities of a given case. The humanitarian analysis and intervention design (H-AID) framework, as developed in the book *Humanitarian Crises, Intervention and Security: A Framework for Evidence-Based Programming*, combines the two.[1] It was especially developed by a team of researchers from the University of Groningen to aid humanitarian actors in their analysis of humanitarian disasters and the planning of interventions. The framework consists of a variety of tools that can be used both separately as well as in combination for the analysis of actors, contexts, and the assumptions behind intervention designs. This chapter gives an overview of one core tool, the comprehensive context analysis (CCA), as part of the H-AID framework. It does not delve into the H-AID tools of stakeholder analysis, intervention design, and monitoring and evaluation tools, which also make part of the H-AID framework. However, in addition to the CCA tool covered in the book, it does provide an expanded analytical tool kit for the CCA, which is based on the original framework but goes beyond it. An Excel program that performs all calculations and visualizations can be found in the online resources in addition to this book.[2]

The theoretical background of the framework is based on the securitization theory, human security, and the logics of humanitarian action and its principles. This leads to a sectoral approach of context analysis, which divides the overall context into six sectors (called context dimensions) that are mutually interdependent and overlapping. Furthermore, this type of analysis takes into account the different levels on which actors are operating, the so-called

Table 5.1   Matrix of the Comprehensive Context Analysis (CCA)

Level \ Context Dimensions	Political	Economic	Social	Health	Environmental	Food
International						
Regional					State Security	
National		Human Security				
Group & individual						

levels of analysis. Combining both context dimensions and levels of analysis results in the matrix of analysis as depicted in Table 5.1. This approach is also referred to as "CCA."

The matrix itself is useful, first, for the sorting of data; second, for the aggregation of the data into information; and third, for the translation of the information into different security or threat levels. The key questions guiding the analysis are:

1. When, to what degree, and in what way do the following affect context dimensions of a population: (a) disaster events and/or conflicts, and (b) interventions?
2. Which factors within which levels of analysis are responsible for negative and positive effects on the respective context dimensions?

For the translation of the information into different threats levels within specific context dimensions, the Groningen research team has developed a matrix of security (see Table 5.2) that connects the different levels of security with the extent to which indicators for a decline of the situation are present. This means that this scaling departs from the assumption that without any indication of threat to human security and well-being, there is no securitization—that is, the raising of issues as relevant for security through speech acts.

The advantage of an approach that divides the context in preexisting dimensions is that it allows assigning different indicators for each of the context dimensions (i.e., sectors) while retaining the same definitions of threats for all levels of security. A list of key questions and indicators for each of the

Table 5.2 Security Level Matrix

	Level	Threshold in terms of impact on survival
Security	A	Ideal state of security as defined; or state close to ideal with insignificant indication of threats to a security sector
Latent Threat	B1	Average or just below average state of security; some vague indications of threats, which in total are no threat to an aspect of security; no indicators for negative trends
	B2	Below average state of security; some indications of threats, which in total are no threat to an aspect of security in the long-run; accompanied by indicators showing negative trends
Manifest Threat	C1	Single indicators or a combination of indicators, which in total threaten to cause damage to a population in the long run
	C2	Single indicators or a combination of indicators, which in total threaten to cause immediate damage to a population
Acute Threat	D1	Single indicators or a combination of indicators, which already cause damage to a population.
	D2	Single indicators or a combination of indicators, which already cause wide-spread damage to a population or result in a high number of victims.

six context dimensions can be found in the Appendix 5.1. Furthermore, for a politically focused analysis, Appendix 5.2 provides a list of core human rights associated with each context dimension. These lists guide the analysts to ask the right questions for different sectors in humanitarian action.

5.2 APPLICATION OF THE COMPREHENSIVE CONTEXT ANALYSIS

For the actual assessment of the security levels for the different context dimensions (food, health, environment, etc.), the threat levels are visualized in a so-called radar graph. Radar graphs have the advantage that they allow simultaneous representation of all context dimensions, the inclusion of a pre-post comparison (cf. the logic of the Macro-Micro Analysis in section 4.3.1), and the inclusion of *confidence intervals* also in the visualization. Confidence intervals or confidence margins are the expression of uncertainty about the quality of the data or the source, and not about the risk. The higher the uncertainty, the larger the confidence margin, for example, stating that security in one context dimension ranges between B1 and B2 (= confidence margin of 1) expresses a higher confidence than B1 – C1 (= confidence margin of 2).

The CCA in its six dimensions is visualized through a radar graph (see Figure 5.1). Each axis represents a context dimension on which the assessment is projected. This assessment includes both the higher and the lower

Table 5.3   Scale of Security Levels for Translation into a Radar Graph

Security	A	6
Latent threat	B1	5
	B2	4
Manifest threat	C1	3
	C2	2
Acute threat	D1	1
	D2	0

Table 5.4   Comprehensive Context Security Levels after a Hypothetical Disaster Event

Context Dimension	Post-Incident (Lower Limit)	Post-Incident (Upper Limit)
Environment	4	5
Health	1	2
Political	2	4
Economic	3	3
Sociocultural	3	4
Food	1	2

estimate of the confidence margin. In order to compile such a radar graph for the CCA, the estimates of the higher and lower end of the confidence margin for each context dimension need to be mapped into values between 0 and 6 on the following scale of security levels (see Table 5.3), which is a translation of the security level matrix into numbers.

After the aggregation of the information regarding present indicators into threat levels, the outcome has to be translated into a number to be entered into a spreadsheet for each dimension (Table 5.4). This includes the upper and lower limits of the confidence margin. The confidence margin expresses how much confidence the researcher has in his assessment. If the researcher has a high confidence that a situation is a latent threat (B2), she will simply enter the value "4" for both lower and upper limit. If the researcher is less confident about the finding and is indecisive of whether to assign a B2 or a C1, then she would add a "3" for the lower and a "4" for the higher confidence limit. In the radar graph, this is visualized as a gray band—the thicker the band, the more uncertain the state of affairs (e.g., environmental security B2 – B1 = 4 – 5). The spreadsheet can then be used to visualize the radar graph (see Figure 5.1) by means of a spreadsheet program (e.g., Excel).

Figure 5.1 illustrates a CCA mapping of a hypothetical food crisis. It depicts which context dimensions are under pressure (in this case the social, political, and economic dimensions) and in immediate danger (food and health dimensions) and which aspects are in an acceptable zone of security (environmental).

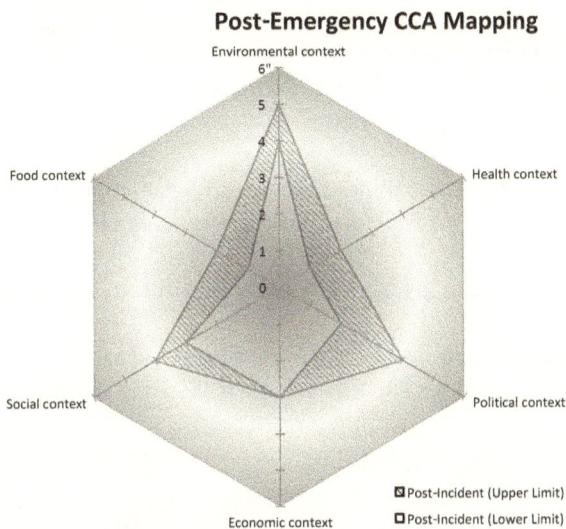

Post-Emergency CCA Mapping

Figure 5.1 **Post-Emergency Mapping of the Six Context Dimensions**

This visualization method allows grasping the basic patterns of a sectoral-ized complex context in one graph. Furthermore, it conveys how confident the analyst is about the findings (e.g., there is considerable uncertainty about the political context dimension, B2 – C2, and much confidence about the economic dimension C1). It is important to realize that neither the order of the different context dimensions, nor the connector lines between them have any specific analytical meaning of causality. They merely represent correlational information, which needs to be further analyzed on the basis of empirical data to provide deeper conclusions. The relational analysis tool (section 5.4) was designed for that purpose.

In this example of a food crisis, the environmental context dimension (B2 – B1) is relatively stable. The health and food dimensions (both C2 – D1) are under much pressure. This might lead, depending on further qualitative information, to the following interpretation. Since both the health and the food context dimensions rank very low, both food and health problems seem to be interrelated—this would require further investigation into their causal relationship. The economic security scores quite well. This suggests that food might generally be available but not accessible to the population in question or that economic resources might be available to mitigate the crisis. In order to establish such a relation, one would need to look deeper into the qualitative data as will be shown below in section 5.4 on "Relational Analysis."

While this CCA gives a quick snapshot about the status quo of a complex context with additional information about interrelations and quality of the data, subsequent analytical steps are necessary in which the following questions become particularly important:

1. What is the current security level in the different context dimensions?
2. What are the major problems and constraints in the different context dimensions?
3. Where are the major capabilities on which future interventions can be built?
4. Which dimensions are influenced by the disaster?
5. Which interconnections exist between the different context dimensions?

Box 5.1   H-AID—Comprehensive Context Analysis

Step 1: determine the level of analysis and the exact period of assessment (pre- or post crisis).

Note: the more precise the level of analysis and the shorter the period of assessment selected, the more informative the CCA becomes. Shorter periods of assessment resemble a snapshot of the context, longer periods of assessment rather an average.

Step 2: use the list of indicators in Appendix 5.1 to sort the data on indicators into the six context dimensions.

Step 3: use the list of key questions in Appendix 5.1 to aggregate data into information and apply it to the security-level matrix (Table 5.2).

Step 4: for each context dimension, evaluate the uncertainty of data (regarding reliability of data and source (see section 3.5)) to determine the confidence margin.

Step 5: draw a radar graph with six axes (one for each context dimension), and mark the axes with 6 steps (from 0 to 6).

Step 6: for each context dimension, plot the higher and the lower confidence interval onto the radar graph.

Step 7: analyze the radar graph, by assessing for each dimensions the reasons behind:
  • the confidence margin
  • the level of security
  • the possible interactions between context dimensions (make a list of hypotheticals)
  • the possible and likely changes and developments in the near future

Different additional analytical tools can be used to answer them, such as the capabilities-constraints analysis or the relational analysis. They will be addressed in turn.[3]

5.3   CAPABILITIES/CONSTRAINTS ANALYSIS

The radar graph maps not only the current security level per dimension, but implicitly it also includes the capabilities (resources, infrastructures, strengths) and constraints (hazards, vulnerability, disaster, risk). The *capabilities/constraints analysis* aims to distill in which context dimension resources are available to use when planning an intervention. In addition, it gives pointers when context dimensions are particularly vulnerable and should not be relied on as a resource for a humanitarian project.

This capabilities/constraints analysis is the simplest way of analysis of the CCA. Essentially, it is based on the assumption that if one context is on the level of security (A) or latent threat (B1 or B2) and no extreme trend indicators point to a rapid deterioration of the situation, then these contexts can be considered assets that can be utilized to ameliorate the weaker dimensions. For the calculation and the visualization this means a threshold point at "3,5" on the radar graph. Before this can be taken for granted, a detailed look at the underlying data to identify the concrete assets and whether they can be used to ameliorate the constraints is necessary.

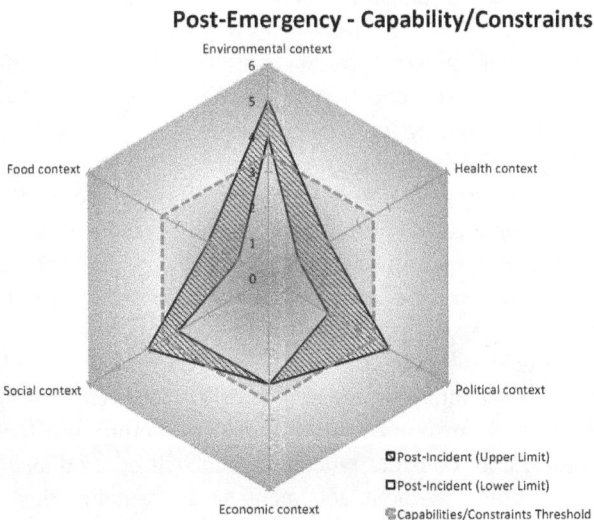

Figure 5.2   Capabilities/Constraints Radar Graph

Taking a look at Figure 5.2, there seems to be a relatively stable environmental context, because both the higher and the lower end of the confidence margin are above the capabilities/constraints threshold (indicated with a dashed line) in the capabilities zone (outside the threshold). The food, health, and economic dimensions are completely below the threshold in the constraints zone (inside the threshold). Building an intervention on remaining local resources in these dimensions runs the risk of further deteriorating them, and may even lead to a cascading effect, where threats in one dimension negatively influence all other dimensions. The higher end of the confidence margin of social-cultural and political dimensions is in the capabilities zone and the lower end is in the constraints zone. This split of the confidence margin above and below the capabilities/constraints threshold indicates that there is an uncertainty whether one can use the resources in the respective dimensions as capabilities, or whether one has to deal with them as constraints. The lower the analyst assesses the confidence in the data (i.e., the broader the confidence margin banner), the higher the uncertainty about how to treat the

Box 5.2   H-AID—Capabilities/Constraints Analysis

(This analysis presupposes the complete CCA analysis of 5.2.)

Step 1: in your radar graph, plot a line at "3,5" on each axis, representing the capabilities/constraints threshold.

Step 2: note for each dimension whether the higher and the lower confidence margin is:
  • below the capabilities/constraints threshold = potential constraints
  • above the capabilities/constraints threshold = potential capabilities
  • split above and below the capabilities/constraints threshold = uncertain, but more likely potential constraints

Step 3: make a list for each context dimensions of all factors that actively constrain the dimension or contribute to being a capability.

Step 4: investigate the reasons why the context dimension is a constraint/capability in the larger context of the situation, that is, what are the underlying processes as presented by the data.

Step 5: investigate which exact resources your project would rely on within a certain context dimension that falls above/below the threshold; if the specific resource is not by itself affecting or affected by the context dimension, consider whether it can still be used as a capability within your project without detriment to the beneficiaries, the larger context dimension, or other context dimensions.

respective dimension. If this uncertainty can be reduced by additional or more specific data regarding the local resources the humanitarian operation would specifically be relying on, then the analyst can make a definitive decision. If a definitive decision is not possible with the available information, then the analyst should consider the context dimension as a constraint.

In this hypothetical case it would be particularly interesting to investigate why the food dimension and the environmental dimension context are not both low and how the deterioration of the health and the food dimensions are related to the economic context. As mentioned already, a sociopolitical relationship between food security and the economic dimension seems to be present here. In cases such as the relationship between the food and the economic context dimension and the apparent lack of a relation with the environmental dimension, cross-cutting issues of contexts deserve special attention. In order to get a solid assessment of the interconnectedness of the factors, one factor needs to depend on factors located in one or more *other* context dimensions. Furthermore, once the stakeholder analysis (chapter 6) is completed, it is recommended to take a close look at those actors that control and facilitate assets in the strong contexts and those that are positively and negatively active in weak dimensions and key dimensions required to improve the security levels.

5.4   RELATIONAL ANALYSIS

The purpose of a relational analysis is to examine the degree to which threats to one context dimension are caused by conditions or processes in the other context dimensions, and to what degree these context dimensions are interdependent in the concrete case. It furthermore indicates which of the context dimensions are the most central to the security threat encountered by the humanitarian organization. The *relational analysis* requires the analyst to take a look at factors (and their indicators) that are of cross-sectoral relevance, so-called cross-cutting themes. For example, indicators concerning nutrition are usually strongly related to health and the food context is often dependent on the economic context. These relations can be present; however, each context is different, and therefore, this analysis is necessary to come from assumptions about interdependence to evidence about interdependence. In other words, this means if a lot of indicators show a high likelihood that they will affect each other, the relation is high. The dimensions that in a concrete case are strongly related to most of the other dimensions occupy a very central role in the problem and are therefore of particular interest. These dimensions might be the most vulnerable or the most resilient depending on their security level and their relation with the other dimensions.

Chapter 5

Table 5.5   Relational Analysis of the Context Dimensions

	Environm. context	Health context	Political context	Economic context	Social context	Food context	Centrality Score
Environm. context		0	1	0	1	0	0,4
Health context			2	1	2	3	1,6
Political context				1	3	2	1,8
Economic context					2	2	1,2
Social context						3	2,2
Food context							2

For the relational analysis the analyst assesses the interrelation based on relational factors on a scale from 0 (for no relation) to 3 (for a strong relation). This is done by ranking the mutual dependency of context dimensions with one and another. Once one has entered all correlations, one can calculate the average centrality score by taking the sum of all interdependencies in one column (e.g., political context: 1, 2, 1, 3, 2 = 9) and by dividing it by the number of combinations possible (9/5 = 1,8). The more one specific area (e.g., the social context) relates to all other contextual areas, the higher it scores on centrality, a measure of how central one context is in a given situation. Context dimensions with a high centrality score are of particular interest as they might point to specific capabilities of actors or structural weaknesses in a given society (see Table 5.5).

For example, in the environmental dimension of our hypothetical case there is no relation with the health, economic, and the food dimension to be found; a weak correlation with the political dimension and the social dimensions are present as we have evidence that some pollution to the environment is caused by culturally accepted negligence, which is also expressed by a lack of governmental oversight. The food dimension, on the other hand, is connected most strongly with the health, social, and economic dimensions. This shows that the food context and the social context are sensible variables in the overall context (centrality score of 2,2). A lack of access to medicines seems also be connected to the social marginalization. The weakening of the economy is only marginally the result of an illness-induced lack of production, but seems to be strongly related to the food crisis (possibly indicated by a lack of purchasing power). Table 5.5 demonstrates the relational analysis of the hypothetical scenario. It is based on the observed interrelationship between the various contexts. With a centrality score of 2,2 for the social context dimension, the relational analysis might, thus, point to a potentially crucial actor that might hamper humanitarian aid, for example, in cases in which the actor would try to divert resources from the beneficiary population. This has to be further checked in a subsequent stakeholder analysis.

As always in these types of analysis, the numbers represent the aggregate analytic effort of the analyst or the analytic team in condensed form and are ready for further analysis or decision-making. The CCA provides an opportunity to visualize potentials and constraints or established relationships between the contexts, which might have been previously unknown or overlooked. The stakeholders, which also influence how the different context dimensions look like, are implicitly present in the data collected. The next chapter will explicate these actors and provide additional tools for visualization and analysis. Hence this first overview conducted through the CCA does not yet lead to a full understanding of the crisis and why relationships exist between various context dimensions. But it gives very good insights into the basic features, the capabilities and constraints, and the correlation between the context dimensions.

Box 5.3 H-AID—Relational Analysis

Step 1: draw a matrix with the six context dimensions dividing both the rows and the columns.

Step 2: distill information (from present data and if necessary from newly collected data) regarding each possible interdependence between context dimensions (e.g., food/health, food/economy).

Step 3: on the basis of information regarding interdependence, rank the interdependence score for each possible combination of context dimensions on a scale from 0 (no relation) to 3 (high relation).

Note: The ranking of interdependence is a relative or dense ranking. In dense ranking, context dimensions receive a number depending on how they compare to all other items. Equal rankings receive equal scores, higher/low rankings receive lower scores.

Step 4: for each context dimension calculate the centrality score by adding all five numbers relating to the dimensions from both rows and columns. Divide the sum by five. The result is the centrality score of the respective context dimension.

Step 5: investigate the reasons for low/high centrality scores. Analyze whether the score indicates that the context dimension has a specific vulnerability or resilience.

Step 6: combine the information regarding resilience/vulnerability with your findings regarding capabilities/constraints.

REVIEW QUESTIONS

- How does the H-AID method disaggregate a context?
- What is the role of the confidence margin?
- How do you determine the level of security in a context dimension?
- What are the possibilities and the limits of visualizing the CCA in a radar graph?
- Which context dimensions can be considered capabilities/constraints, and why? What is the role of confidence intervals in this consideration?
- What does the centrality score in the relational analysis express?

NOTES

1. Liesbet Heyse, Andrej Zwitter, Rapahel Wittek, and Joost Herman, *Humanitarian Crises, Intervention and Security: A Framework for Evidence-Based Programming* (London: Routledge, 2014).

2. http://humanitarianintelligence.net.

3. Please note that the capabilities/constraints analysis as well as the relational analysis are not intrinsic parts of the original H-AID framework but form part of the extended tool pack.

Part III

ACTORS AND INTERACTIONS

Chapter 6

Understanding Actors and Their Impact

6.1 WHAT ARE STAKEHOLDERS?

Stakeholder analysis belongs to the most difficult areas of humanitarian intelligence analysis. There are several problematic areas, which can lead the analyst astray. For example, which individuals, groups, nonstate actors, and states are operating in a given context; which of those actors are relevant for the analysis; what is their power; what is their stake in the situation; what are their intentions; and how will they affect the outcome of the humanitarian intervention? These are just a few of the questions that trouble the analyst in the concrete case. For humanitarian analysis, a stakeholder analysis provides the following two indispensable insights:

1. Identification of key actors, their stakes, action opportunities, and constraints
2. Evaluation of the interactions between actors in terms of dependence, cooperation, and conflict

The stakeholder analysis fulfills two functions, a diagnostic and an explanatory one. The diagnostic function aims to review the social mechanisms behind a given crisis. It asks the following two key questions:

1. Who are the key agents affected by the crisis or affecting the crisis?
2. What are their goals and resources?

The explanatory function of a stakeholder analysis has two purposes. For (1) the *postmortem* analysis it can answer the question of what is the effect of these agents (before, during, and after the crisis). For (2) *forecasting* the stakeholder analysis identifies which agents are likely to support or hinder reconstruction of a secure environment for the beneficiaries.

There is no agreement in the literature regarding "the principle of who or what really counts" when conducting a stakeholder analysis.[1] Broad definitions include all stakeholders present, irrespective of whether they are actually relevant or not. Narrow definitions focus only on stakeholders that have an actual stake in the matter, some sort of risk, or power to decisively inform the outcome.

Stakeholder analysis originality stems from business sciences. Freeman's definition of the stakeholder as "any group or individual that can affect or is affected by the achievement of a corporation's purpose"[2] is frequently cited by academics.[3] Thus, many definitions in the literature describe the stakeholder as an entity with relevance to a specific corporate actor rather than the overall context: "Stakeholders are all those claimants inside and outside the firm who have a vested interest in the problem and its solution" and "[they] are the concrete entities that affect and in turn are affected by a policy."[4] Accordingly, a stakeholder can be external or internal to a corporate actor and depending on the analysis the corporate actor itself can be a stakeholder in the larger context. The stakeholder has a concrete interest in the problem at hand or in its solution. And it is at the same time affected by or is influencing the outcome of a concrete situation. In a broad sense, the term "stakeholder" refers to all individuals, groups, or organizations that are relevant for the analysis and need to be taken into account in some way.[5] Actual or potential stakeholders can include communities, societies, institutions, and even the natural environment.[6] A much bigger point of contestation in the literature than the definition of the stakeholder is the nature of the actual stake and how to define power in a stakeholder field.

Both definitions leave it relatively open to include all groups or individuals without necessarily having to define the notion of the stake. Only those actors with not enough power to affect the corporate actor or the situation, as well as those who have no claim on the relationship with either corporate actor or situation can be excluded from the stakeholder analysis.[7]

According to Freeman, every actor that may prevent reaching objectives of the central actor for which the analysis is conducted needs to be captured by the definition of stakeholders.[8] As such Freeman puts forward the stakeholder relationship itself as a more useful unit of analysis, rather than the issue at stake, for the development of strategies. While issues emerge and disappear through the behavior and interaction of actors, it is the stakeholder that behaves and that remains relatively stable.[9]

In practice, we will see that the analyst will have to include not only actors that she considers legitimate, that is, that interests run in parallel to the central actor and that values are similar, but also very important actors with both the interest and ability to derail a central strategy directly or indirectly. In order to develop a robust strategy, such a strategy needs to be able to compensate for the interference of adversary actors.[10] To contribute to a strategy that is capable of compensating for these forces is the true purpose and capability of a good stakeholder analysis.

Given the varieties of entities that are involved in a certain context, the organization can be faced with a variety of claims and obligations by other stakeholders. A stakeholder analysis becomes particularly useful when it is not possible to treat all claims and obligations equally and thus satisfying all stakeholders. In these cases, a robust analysis allows to determine the minimum level that needs to be achieved to satisfy stakeholders on a basic level or at least to not cause antagonistic reactions.[11] Attention to the stakeholder field is therefore of utmost importance, as it allows for the assessment and enhancement of the political, social, and cultural feasibility of a project. It furthermore allows the identification of key stakeholders that need to be satisfied for an operation to be ultimately successful.

By knowing the stakeholder field, and more specifically the key stakeholders' interests and abilities of interfering with or supporting a plan of action, critical failures in the planning of an operation can be avoided beforehand. Furthermore, understanding the stakeholder behavior allows to some degree to predict emergent needs, adjust ongoing operations, and develop alternate plans of action—the so-called Plan B (for trend analysis, see chapter 8; for scenario planning, see chapter 9).[12]

6.2 ANALYZING STAKEHOLDERS

6.2.1 Stakeholder Matrixes

A very common strategy to analyze stakeholders is a stakeholder matrix. The stakeholder matrix is essentially a mapping exercise in which stakeholders are mapped in relation to each other concerning one or more attributes. The mapping happens in the matrix and requires research about the different stakeholders in advance. The first step is to identify which stakeholders are actually of relevance to this situation. In order to do that it is useful to search for stakeholders using general classification schemes such as PESTLE. As we have already discussed in the previous chapter regarding the H-AID analysis, a classification scheme divides the context into different sectors. PESTLE is a very common scheme in the United Kingdom, and it stands for:

- *Politics*: governments, ministries, political parties, nonstate advocacy actors, developmental NGOs, militias, nonstate armed groups, terrorist organizations, etc.

- *Economics*: banks, financial service providers, donors, charities, organized criminal groups, etc.
- *Social/cultural*: social interest groups, traditional local support communities, churches, religious groups, other organized cultural groups, etc.
- *Technological*: telecom service providers, tech companies, energy sector companies, etc.
- *Legal*: courts, ombudsmen, local or regional quasi-legal structures (e.g., council of elders, Gacaca courts), law firms, etc.
- *Ecological*: wildlife and environmental NGOs, poachers, etc.

Of course, for the purpose of a humanitarian action specific analysis we are adding another set of actors:

- *Humanitarian*: local organizations, international and NGOs; specific expertise—WASH (water, sanitation, and hygiene), shelter, protection, camp management, etc.

The stakeholder matrix divides attributes of stakeholder over one, two, or more dimensions in a diagram. These dimensions vary from one stakeholder analysis to another. Very common attribute pairs are:

- power–interest (Figure 6.1),[13]
- potential for cooperation–potential for posing a threat (Figure 6.2),[14]
- influence of the stakeholder–importance of the stakeholder,[15]
- alignment with a certain issue area of interest–interest in the specific topic.[16]

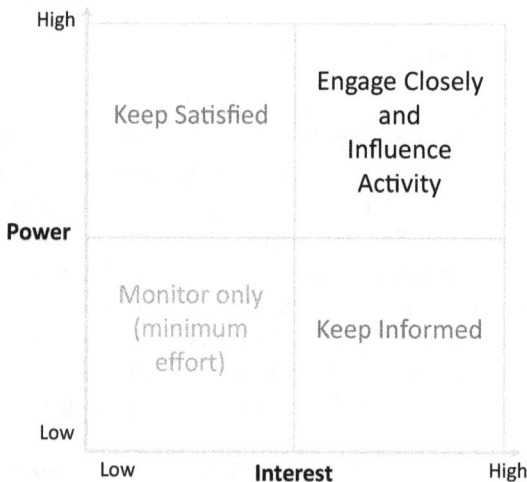

Figure 6.1   Power/Interest Matrix. *Note*: Hovland, *Successful Communication: A Toolkit for Researchers and Civil Society Organisations*, 9.

High

Stakeholder Type 1 **Supportive** *Strategy:* **Involve**	Stakeholder Type 4 **Mixed Blessing** *Strategy:* **Collaborate**
Stakeholder Type 2 **Marginal** *Strategy:* **Monitor**	Stakeholder Type 3 **Non-supportive** *Strategy:* **Defend**

Potential for Cooperation

Low

Low | **Potential Threat** | High

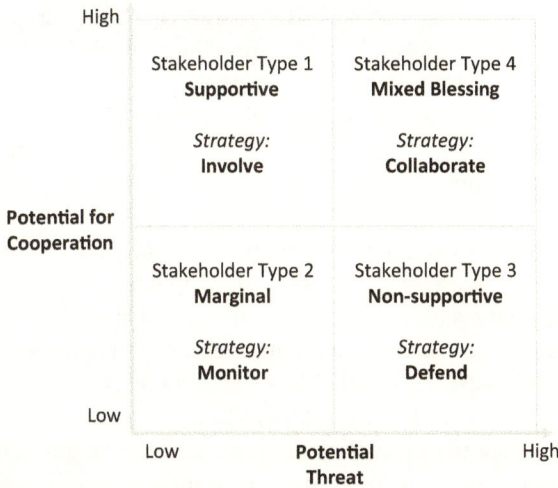

Figure 6.2   Threat/Cooperation Matrix. *Note*: Savage et al., "Strategies for Assessing and Managing Organizational Stakeholders," 65.

When using two attributes, as well as two descriptors for the attributes such as high and low (e.g., high-power/low-power, high interest/low interest), the matrix automatically results in four different fields. These four fields can be considered to describe four kinds of stakeholders relevant to the situation—a diagnostic typology of stakeholders. Figures 6.1 and 6.2 illustrate two very popular stakeholder matrixes. Figure 6.3 illustrates a monodimensional stakeholder continuum based on the justifications scheme from supporter to opponent. As stakeholder positions with respect to these attributes vary, the stakeholders are distributed along the axes of the attribute pairs. Three attribute pairs require a three-dimensional matrix. Given the limits in visualization of a three-dimensional matrix, it is recommended to limit one's visualization to two axes and add another matrix for another attribute pair if necessary.

A stakeholder analysis using such a matrix is most useful for strategy development if the stakeholder typology is at the same time connected with certain strategy of how to approach different stakeholders. In order to be able to attach a specific strategy to a specific stakeholder typology, it is important

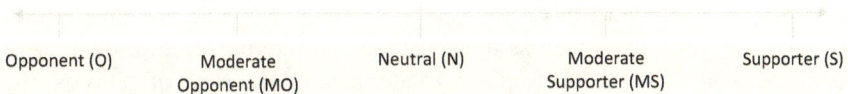

Opponent (O)	Moderate Opponent (MO)	Neutral (N)	Moderate Supporter (MS)	Supporter (S)

Figure 6.3   Mono-Dimensional Stakeholder Continuum. *Note*: http://www.who.int/workforcealliance/knowledge/toolkit/33.pdf.

to keep in mind to conduct a stakeholder analysis always from the perspective of the organization the analyst is performing the analysis for. That means the strategy is of course dependent on the very organization one works for, its mandate, its limitations, and its frames of reference. Figure 6.2, for example, distinguishes four kinds of stakeholders and attaches different strategies of how to approach them:

- Type I: supportive stakeholders [potential high/threat low]— strategy: involve the stakeholder to ensure support
- Type II: marginal stakeholders [potential low/threat low]— strategy: monitor for changes in the nature of the stakeholder
- Type III: mixed blessing stakeholders [potential high/threat high]— strategy: collaborate with stakeholder to bring to your side
- Type IV: nonsupportive stakeholders [potential low/threat high]— strategy: defend against disruptive interventions

Most of the time, a complete list of relevant stakeholders, their interests, and the power are not directly evident from the data collected. This requires investigative efforts, particularly when it comes to interests and hidden agendas. Key informants, secondary political/economic research as well as further academic and journalistic resources can be of help when interpreting the present data, in order to come from data to information. The research side of stakeholder analysis draws its information from the following sources of data to reach its conclusions:

- qualitative information on strengths, opportunities, weaknesses, and threats to the operational humanitarian project;
- human intelligence from key informants familiar with the context, who can help to identify specific stakeholders relevant to the success and failure of the project;
- focus group workshops—when working in groups make sure that the participants come from different disciplines and interest groups in order to limit bias and group think;
- survey work and quantitative analysis of secondary data for purpose of verification and adjustments about the assumptions regarding stakeholder interests and influence.

Since stakeholder analyses rely heavily on the perceptions and preferences of the analytic team as well as the selection and interpretation of qualitative data, the analytic team has to place greater care on the rigor of analysis, the selection of sources, and the triangulation of the data as well as sources (see chapter 3). This kind of analysis aims to depict the status quo and is not meant to predict the developments of stakeholder positions and their interaction over time. For this purpose, other tools such as scenario planning (see chapter 9) and network analysis (see chapter 7) are quite useful (Table 6.1).[17]

Box 6.1 Stakeholder Matrix

Step 1: identify the issue at stake.

Step 2: make a long list of actors and rank them by importance and power.

Step 3: make a short list of actors and start a thorough background research on their interests, the resources, the ability to influence the situation, and their general characteristics (the sample stakeholder analysis table developed by DFID can help you in sorting the data per stakeholder and characteristic; see Table 6.1).

Step 4: select the appropriate classification scheme for your case (e.g., power, interest, potential for cooperation, influence of the stakeholder, etc.) and map all stakeholders onto the matrix. The mapping of stakeholders can be done by intuitively evaluating and discussing the data in the analytic team, or on the basis of a scale of two or more steps (e.g., high, middle, or low power/interest/threat) for each dimension.

Step 5: assign the different appropriate strategies to the respective stakeholders depending on which fields they occupy.

Table 6.1 Sample Stakeholder Analysis Table*

Stakeholder Categories	Relevant Stakeholders	Characteristics (social, geographical, organizational)	Influence (power to facilitate or impede reform)	Importance (degree of priority needs and interests)	Interest (from commitment to status quo to openness to change)
Government policymakers					
Implementing agency staff					
Intended beneficiaries					
Adversely affected persons					
Organized interest groups					
Civil society organizations					
Donors					
Other external stakeholders					

*Jeremy Holland, *Tools for Institutional, Political, and Social Analysis of Policy Reform: A Sourcebook for Development Practitioners*, World Bank (Washington, DC: World Bank, 2007), 128, https://openknowledge.worldbank.org/handle/10986/6652.

6.2.2 AGIRI Stakeholder Analysis

This section will elaborate how to conduct a stakeholder analysis on the basis of AGIRI factors: agents, goals, interactions, resources, and institutions. The AGIRI Stakeholder Analysis (or AGIRI analysis for short) is an extension to and a more precise form of a stakeholder analysis. This kind of analysis is helpful to investigate the *diagnostic problem* more in depth and assists in further thinking through meaningful humanitarian interventions.

The acronym of AGIRI stands for five factors pertaining to stakeholders, which play a role in every social setting where disasters take place. The combination of these five concepts with the general problems of diagnosis results in the formulation of subproblems to be analyzed (see Table 6.2).

By identifying the most relevant agents in a humanitarian crisis situation, their goals and resources, their interactions and the relevant institutions at place, the humanitarian analyst gets more insight into the crisis dynamics. This will be helpful in identifying options and opportunities for as well as limitations and threats to intervention strategies.

As mentioned above, the AGIRI analysis goes beyond the mere stakeholder matrix by adding theoretical depth, better precision of analysis, and further analytical steps that can be undertaken. One basic assumption behind the AGIRI analysis is that agents are rational in nature, meaning that they consciously try to achieve their goals with the means available to them (i.e., resources and interactions). They will strategically interact with other agents to acquire resources or to achieve their goals. In addition, it is assumed that agents are often self-interested, meaning that they do not necessarily always strive for the common good (e.g., in the case of a humanitarian crisis: resolving a particular humanitarian problem) but may have their own particular

Table 6.2 Overview of the AGIRI Factors

AGIRI Factors	Key Questions for Analytic Subproblems
Agents	Who are the individual and corporate agents that are either directly or indirectly affected by a disaster?
Goals	What are the salient goals of the individual and corporate agents affected by a disaster?
Resources	Which of these resources are threatened by the disaster? How important are the resulting losses for the social production functions of individuals and the efficiency of corporate agents?
Institutions	To what degree is the functioning of existing institutions affected by the disaster? Are new institutions emerging, how do they function, and which unintended consequences do they have?
Interactions	Which interactions between agents exist during the assessment period? Which coordination and cooperation problems and opportunities between the involved agents does the disaster event create?

interests (e.g., they might want to earn money due to a crisis situation and hence do not have an interest in resolving the problem). Furthermore, another analytic assumption is that their rationality is limited by the normative framework (e.g., laws, customs, religious practices) to which they feel obligated. Additionally, other factors that influence their decision-making are information available to them, time pressure, and their cognitive abilities—the technical term is "bounded rationality." The assumptions of the AGIRI analysis resonate with publications about the political economy of humanitarian crises, in which the core questions is who has somewhat to lose or gain with a particular humanitarian situation.[18] The well-known "do no harm" approach by Mary Anderson is also based on these basic assumptions.[19] In the following paragraphs, the five factors that constitute this type of analysis and associated theoretical assumptions are elaborated in further detail.

6.2.2.1 Agents

A first necessary precondition for the analysis of the decline, disappearance, and reconstruction of a beneficial environment for a population is to specify the different types of agents that are involved in this process. An initial step toward the analysis of this process has been conducted with the macro-micro analysis (see chapter 4). Also, the stakeholder matrixes provided a classification scheme on the basis of PESTLE+H (H stands for humanitarian actors). On a theoretical level, three types of agents have to be distinguished:

- natural persons and groups of natural persons (e.g., refugees, farmers);
- states as corporate agents;[20]
- other corporate agents such as:
  ◦ intergovernmental organizations (IGOs, e.g., UN)
  ◦ international NGOs (nonprofit INGO, human rights INGOs)
  ◦ multinational corporations (profit INGO, e.g., Shell)
  ◦ local groups and communities (e.g., families, lineages, clans, neighborhood organizations)

The identification of the different kinds of agents is important because each of them can have different goals and resources. Whether or not and how a stabilization of the situation can be achieved will depend on the outcomes of the strategic interactions between these different types of agents. It is obvious that the more types of agents are involved, the more complex such an analysis will be if one assumes that strategic interactions are possible between all pairs of agents.

Disaster events will differ with regard to the different types of agents that are involved in the process of the decline and/or reconstruction of human security. For example, any attempt to analyze the stakeholder interaction in the Balkan region would require the taking into account of the interactions between a large number of different corporate agents (e.g., the United Nations, the UNHCR, NATO, the governments of the Serbia's neighbor states, the Serb military and police forces, different NGOs, political movements in Kosovo), as well as natural persons (e.g., ethnic Albanian refugees, the local population in the areas where the refugee camps have been constructed). In comparison with this highly complex situation, an analysis of the reconstruction of human security after natural disasters (like the hurricanes that hit the United States or the earthquakes in Turkey, Greece, and Taiwan) would certainly require an emphasis on other types of agents, with, for example, the NATO not being important at all, whereas problems of efficiency, functioning, coordination, and control of national, regional, and local state or private agencies will be of major importance.

The relevance of different types of agents also necessitates a careful choice of the right level of analysis. While it is possible to assess the stakeholder field of a certain area in regard to the local population (e.g., within a village), a stakeholder analysis will have to go beyond this setting and include all relevant natural persons and corporate agents that influence the situation from the outside, for example, at national, regional, or international level. (For further details on levels of analysis, please refer to the elaborations with regards to the comprehensive context analysis in chapter 5.)

It should be evident that the identification of relevant agents as well as choosing the initial level of analysis is neither a trivial nor an easy endeavor. The reason for this has to be sought in the often complex internal structure of corporate agents on the one hand, and goal and identity-related processes for natural persons on the other. Thus, while it might be adequate to speak of the strategy of "NATO" in some cases, it will be necessary to differentiate between the policies of the different members of NATO in other circumstances. The same holds true for natural persons. It might be useful to analyze a given situation by referring to "the refugees" in a camp context, for example, if one wants to assess the adequacy of the envisioned material support that is needed locally. However, for other purposes of analysis (e.g., prevention of violence within the camps), it might be necessary to further differentiate this group (e.g., to distinguish between the ethno-religious background of refugees or gender and age) and thereby closing in to assess the situation on a smaller scale.

In some cases, it might be easy to identify the type of agents involved, whereas in others this task will be more difficult because some agents have an interest in hiding their involvement in an ongoing conflict (e.g., the weapon industry or high-tech firms delivering products into embargo regions). In such cases, the availability and reliability of information concerning the role of these agents will be low, though their potential impact on the decline and reconstruction of the humanitarian project context can be high.

A good approach that has proven useful in practice when deciding whether or not to disaggregate corporate agents into several stakeholders is to take a look at whether to separate stakeholders who share the same goals and resources. If this is indeed the case, there is no good reason to complicate the analysis by creating more stakeholders than necessary. For example, when analyzing the involvement of the United Nations there might be little reason to separate between UNDP and UNOCHA if on the local level both are represented and act through the senior UNDP staff member functioning as humanitarian/resident coordinator (HC/RC). If, however, they act independently, with slightly different goals (humanitarian versus development aid), and with the availability of different resources, then it makes sense to separate them for the purpose of a more refined analysis.

6.2.2.2 Goals

The second element is closely related to the previous one, but extends it in some important aspects. After having identified the relevant agents in a particular humanitarian situation, it is necessary to analyze their goals. In order to do so, various approaches can be taken, depending on the assumptions one has about the nature of agents and their goals. Based on academic insights about human behavior, the basic assumption behind an AGIRI analysis is that all involved agents are "resourceful and maximizing agents" rather than passive objects. They derive their goals from their own knowledge and the behavior of other agents. It is therefore important to identify the goals of agents in relation to their interests. The notion of "resourcefulness" refers to the fact that humans are inventive, can learn, and are able to substitute between different means to reach their goals. The notion of "maximizing" refers to the idea that agents will try to achieve their goals by choosing the most efficient alternative that bears the least costs.

There is much evidence in the literature that goals are crucial determinants of the behavior of natural persons and corporate agents alike. In fact, the notion of "human security" itself refers to a higher-level goal. It is based on the assumption that at least some people in a given setting prefer to live under conditions that reflect security in different aspects (such as food, health, economy, environment). Consequently, an analysis of the production and decline of human security requires the existence of measurable indicators of goals and their achievement that are valid across particular situations in time and space or across cultural settings. This will require the appropriate selection of indicators for the respective context (see Appendix 5.1).

6.2.2.3 Resources

The third step in the analysis consists in the identification of the resources and constraints of the involved agents. Resources can be seen as a means for the rehabilitation of the project context from the effects of a crisis, but also for the achievement of goals opposed to that. Constraints, in turn, refer to the absence of particular resources that would be necessary for the realization of goals. Therefore, in order to realize their goals, agents will be forced to obtain control over those resources that are necessary to realize physical and social well-being as well as other goals dictated by their interests and normative institutions. One can think of resources in terms of money, information, authority, services, contacts, etc.

However, it is important to stress that the nature of resources differs in their accessibility and divisibility.[21] A common characteristic of disaster situations is that one or more particular resources that are necessary for the realization/restoration of human security of beneficiaries are either lacking/disappearing, or that (some) people are likely to lose the right to control particular resources (in the sense of a lack of entitlement). It is obvious that the sheer reduction of the availability of some resources for (some) agents can create resource imbalances, which might in turn influence the power structures within a population, possibly affecting intergroup relationships and the relative importance attached to the constituent elements that support the protection or realization of assets within a certain context dimension.[22] Thus, a detailed analysis of which agent has control over which resources and events before, during, and after the disaster will be of crucial importance for specifying the threats, obstacles imposed, and interferences by actors within the project context.

The analytical problem emerging here specifically for the development of a humanitarian project consists in an assessment of the types of resources that are needed to facilitate the realization of physical and social well-being of the beneficiaries in a given situation, and to what degree there are possibilities for substitution among resources that are difficult to provide. In addition, it is important to assess the degree of access to and control over resources (entitlements) of the agents involved, and the structure of social relationships that produces entitlements over resources. Furthermore, it has to be taken into account that any provision of resources has the potential to alter existing power structures or to create new ones, thereby changing the bargaining position of the agents in the system.

6.2.2.4   Institutions and Structures

The fourth element of an AGIRI analysis consists in the identification of the institutional structures in which actors are embedded. "Institutions" can be defined as "systems of ideas such as norms, symbols, rules, conventions, and so on." Institutional structures are rules that define agents' modes of operations. Having said before that agents behave according to their goals one has to add that the way in which they define and reach their goals is informed by the institutional structures they follow. For example, religion (as an institutional structure) might demand from a farmer (the agent) that before getting the crops from the field to serve as food (goal) he must do a small sacrifice to his gods (element of the institutional structure religion); the UN Security Council (agent) in order to make binding decisions for an embargo to stop a state from committing crimes (goal) needs a consensus of the permanent members as demanded by the UN-Charter (institutional structure)—the Security Council's potential in achieving its goal depends on the one hand on the UN members states to fulfill the resolution's mandate (resources). As such institutions provide the structural foundation for the different means for the realization of a humanitarian goal.

In the analysis it is important to realize that every agent is bound by institutional structures. These structures often overlap between agents, but at the same time some agents can also be bound by very specific institutional structural elements, not applicable to all. For example, all citizens might be bound by the same state laws, but only some are bound by specific religious institutional norms. These institutional structures can be an entry point for planning interventions, but they could also mean an obstacle. Faith-based NGOs might, for example, have considerable advantages for entry into and operation in areas of the same religious background and severe problems in areas of other religious backgrounds.

The nature of this part of the institutional context, in which people are embedded, plays a major role for bringing about social and physical well-being. For example, the local, regional, and international market can be considered as an institutional structure with money as its symbol (i.e., it is a symbol of values, because the material worth of paper money is much lower that the value that the market assigns to it). Institutional market structures affect the relative prices for resources either directly (e.g., states setting price limits of particular goods, like bread) or indirectly (e.g., through reducing or increasing the transaction costs associated with the acquisition or exchange of particular resources, such as by tax laws).

On a more informal level, institutions provide "rules of the game." For example, there can be particular norms regarding food sharing in communities. Humanitarian organizations often divide food according to need (the most vulnerable and needy will get priority with regards to food provision), whereas in some cultures food distribution is determined according to status in the group. This means that those with the highest status (community leaders, head of the household) will receive the most food and are often also obliged to divide the rest of the food in accordance with what they think is right. Knowing these kinds of rules, norms, or values is thus of importance to think through, for example, why some groups are more vulnerable than others in times of insecurity. It can also be considered an advantage when these normative structures are used to facilitate aid delivery.

An important, though frequently neglected aspect of the role of institutional structures in the context of disasters is their flexibility. That is, where one institutional structure fails in providing the needed resources, other structures might be able to do so. For example, where enduring food shortages lead to a breakdown of market mechanisms as the principal source for the provision of food, other institutional arrangements, which have their roots in local primordial social structures, like patterns of delayed reciprocal exchange or distributive justice mechanisms (e.g., traditional forms of social security, charity, or *zakat*) might take over this role.[23] Not only will primordial institutional structures take over when market institutions fail, but they will to a large extent determine the effectiveness and actual functioning of other institutional structures. The goals of local people in a specific environmental context often involve coping with certain insecurities in order to maximize their profit in making a livelihood (pastoralist systems present a good example of this). Knowing the risks and dealing with insecurities are the reasons for the existence of certain institutional structures. Thus, apart from the often immediate and self-evident short-term consequences like shortage of food, housing, or medical services, disasters are likely to affect the broader institutional structure in which the involved agents are embedded. This may result in structural disruption or transformation of existing institutional structures and thereby affect other context dimensions than those in which it originated (e.g., food shortage and inadequate distribution or entitlement might lead to conflicts in the social dimension).

Identifying the institutional structure and the way in which it is affected by a disaster already constitutes a very complex task in analyzing the opportunities and constraints of a project. At least as challenging as the diagnosis of institutional structures will be the solution of the intervention problems related to these processes, and especially the task of designing or rebuilding those institutions that might contribute to an efficient realization of human security for beneficiaries and the wider population. Apart from dealing with the issues of legitimacy and justice in distribution and efficiency, such efforts will also have to solve the problem of how to enforce the rules of these institutions. For example, in areas where the reliable enforcement of legal rules declined due to a disaster, the opportunity for carrying out secure market transactions frequently also disappears. One consequence of this development might be processes of segmentation of a population into sharing groups, which allow reducing the risks in interactions with outsiders in the absence of enforceable legal structures. In the long run, this can lead to the intensification of solidarity toward in-group members and increasingly opportunistic behavior against out-groups. This will make mutually beneficial exchanges between groups of agents increasingly difficult and impose considerable obstacles for the construction of boundary spanning institutional structures.[24] In short, conflict between groups might increase as a result.

A related analysis problem consists in assessing the potential unintended consequences that support for or changes to institutional structures might have introduced. An example for such unintended consequences can be found in the withdrawal of refugee aid to Somalia in 1990. This decision facilitated the breakdown of the fragile market-independent sharing arrangements that had developed between the local population and the refugees in the camp, thereby constituting an important prelude to the civil war, which would result in the fall of Said Barre.[25] Another issue to be considered is that both humanitarian interventions and development projects last only for a limited time span. With respect to the institution of refugee camps the situation is the reverse. People expect the situation to be temporary, whereas it may continue for generations to come.

6.2.2.5 Interactions

If agents are interested in the resources controlled by other agents, then their goal will be to obtain the right to control these resources. This (inter)dependence requires some sort of exchange or transfer of resources taking place between the agents if it should not come to a violent outcome. On the one hand, these exchanges are likely to be guided by strategic reasoning of the involved parties, and are extremely subject to opportunistic behavior. On the other hand, these exchanges are constrained by norms of reciprocity, fairness, etc. Especially when important social relations are concerned, people do not merely act opportunistically but also consider their social capital.

The resulting exchange might lead to suboptimal outcomes, as has been so well underscored by game theory. For example, corporate agents like national governments or supranational organizations have to cope with the risk of potential policy deviations by their implementation agencies. Contrarily, the sheer need to get immediate access to resources for natural agents might very well augment their vulnerability vis-à-vis corporate agents in the long run. An assessment of the impact of disasters on comprehensive security therefore requires identifying the specific interdependencies linking the involved agents and the problems that this creates for the exchanges between them. In some local contexts, for example, it demands our attention to the nature of the social relationships through which property regimes can be accessed.[26]

The emerging analysis problem is to assess which additional interaction problems will be created by the hazard itself. Intervention strategies can then facilitate or deteriorate the chances for mutually beneficial exchanges between conflicting parties, for example, through mediators that help to rebuild trust between conflicting parties or through brokers that operate between aid organizations and local people.

6.2.2.6   *Conducting a Stakeholder (AGIRI) Analysis*

In the previous sections, the five factors in the AGIRI analysis have been discussed on a more abstract level. The question that derives from this discussion is how to conduct an AGIRI analysis in the practical sense. Later, the AGIRI approach will be introduced step by step.[27] One way to visualize these interactions is to draw a network graph of the agents involved, in which the size of the dots/circles represent the effective power of the agents and the distance between and strength of the relationship between the agents are illustrated by the length and thickness of lines. This approach will be explained in more detail in chapter 7.

Each of the AGIRI elements fulfills a specific function in the analysis of the stakeholder field. Every agent has a set of goals, which it is willing to pursue in accordance with the institutions (norms that guide its behavior), and to the extent made possible by the resources that the agent possesses. Furthermore, interactions also determine the extent to which and the manner in which agents realize their goals. Interactions also inform about which groups of actors collaborate and which groups are adversaries.

Not every goal is equally important to an actor. One can express the differences in importance of goals for an actor with the term "salience." A salience of a value 1 expresses 100 percent willingness to invest one's resources into achieving the goal. A salience of 0 expresses that the goal is not present or a mere lip service. Resources can, among other ways, also be estimated in relation to the context dimension (for the six context dimensions representing societal sectors, see chapter 5) that they're placed in. If the resources are able to change the context dimensions from one level of security to the next (say B2 to B1), one can attribute a value of 1, if they are able to change the security level two steps a value of 2, and so on. This leads to a theoretical scale of capabilities from 0 to 6. The level of analysis plays an important role here. The more local the level of analysis of the context, the more powerful actors are in relation to it. The direct connection between salience and capabilities allows us to calculate "effective power," which is defined by the degree to which an actor is willing and able to pursue its goal given the resources present. Furthermore, the goal informs how the power is used and whether it has a negative or a positive effect of the humanitarian project or the beneficiaries. We can attribute a value of −1 to negative goals. While all this sounds relatively complicated, the formula is quite simple:

Goals[−1, 0, 1]×Salience [0 to 1]×Capabilities [0 to 6] = Effective Power

Table 6.3 provides an overview of how to structure the analysis of actors in a table and how to calculate the effective power. Furthermore, it distinguishes between the six context dimensions that we have introduced in chapter 5. By splitting the analysis of each actor and their relevance and effect in each context dimension, the analyst can achieve deeper insights into the degree to which actors position themselves with regards to different issue areas pertaining to the six context dimensions. Table 6.3 then illustrates that Agent 1 has a medium salience with regard to all context dimensions except the political context and the environmental context. Additionally, this agent has goals that are positively affecting the environment, food, and economic context, but goals that have a negative impact on the social and health context. This information can then be mapped on a graph (see, e.g., Figure 6.4) for each context dimension resulting in six actor maps ready for analysis.

Table 6.3   AGIRI Calculation Table

Agent	Goals	Interaction	Context Dimension	Goal as It Affects Context Dimension	Salience	Capabilities (Resources)	Effective Power
Agent 1	Goal 1	Agent 2	Environmental context	1	0,2	5	1
	Goal 2	Agent 3					
	Goal 3	Agent 4	Health context	−1	0,5	4	−2
	Goal 4		Political context	0	0	0	0
			Economic context	1	0,5	1	0,5
			Social context	−1	0,5	3	−1,5
			Food context	1	0,5	2	1

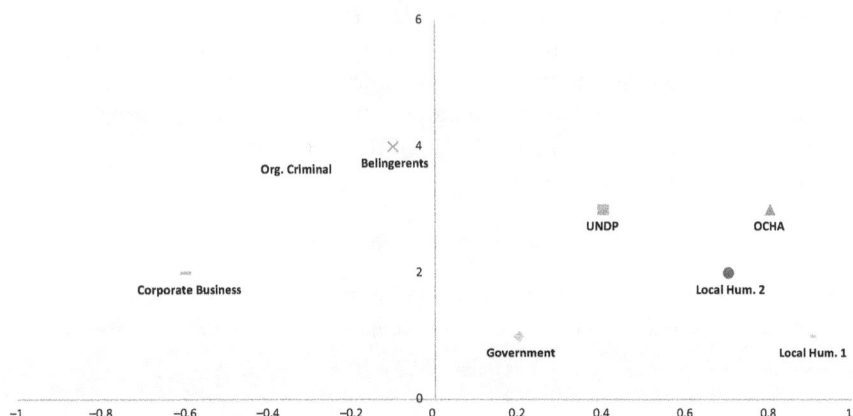

Figure 6.4   AGIRI Mapping of Stakeholders in a Specific Context Dimension

Box 6.2   AGIRI Stakeholder Analysis*

Step 1: identification of agents.
- Based on the information collected, who are the most relevant corporate agents and natural persons?
- Do corporate agents need to be taken as one actor, or do they need to be disaggregated? For that purpose look specifically at unity in goals and resources (e.g., does it suffice to analyze "the state" as a unitary actor, or is it necessary to further subdivide this agent into, say, departments and ministries).
- Create a long list of agents.

Step 2: rank the actors by importance and shorten the list to no more than 10–15 actors, unless you would miss out on very important actors. Consider that for each of the selected actors all AGIRI factors have to be analyzed.
[Steps 3–5 can be done for all six context dimensions: food, health, economic, social-cultural, environmental, political]

Step 3: analysis of goals and interests.
- Natural agents: Assuming that natural agents strive for physical and social well-being, what essential elements of their well-being is lacking or threatened that they will strive for?
- Corporate agents: What formal goals can be distilled from policy statements, public speeches, press releases, etc.?
- Can hidden agendas be identified? Look, for example, at inconsistencies between actions and formal goals, partisanship, ideologies, lobbying on behalf or behest, etc.
- All agents: Which agents have something to gain with the humanitarian situation (i.e., can be assumed to want to maintain the situation) and which agents have something to lose with the humanitarian situation (i.e., can be assumed to be in favor of improving/changing the situation)?
- Salience: How salient are these attitudes toward the humanitarian situation? This encompasses an analysis of the importance of these attitudes per actor. Select a number between:

0 (unimportant) / 1 (very important).

- Goals: Assign a value to the goals of actors as it is positioned vis-à-vis the goals of your organization or the beneficiaries that you are preparing the project for:

0 = neutral goals / −1 = opposing goals / 1 = assisting goals

Step 4: analysis of resources (or capabilities).

For all agents identified: What resources do each of the agents possess to achieve their salient goals? Think about formal and informal resources (e.g., laws and veto powers, or information and network contacts), as well as material and immaterial resources.

Try to quantify these capabilities by assigning a value between 0 and 6:

$$0 = \text{no capabilities} / 6 = \text{high capabilities}$$

Note: the capabilities are ranked in a way to be compatible with the H-AID CCA and Trend Analysis. Therefore, the maximum score to be awarded to capabilities is 6 (for six levels of security).

Step 5: analysis of effective power.

Multiply the salience scores with the capabilities (resources) scores in order to get an insight into the effective power of agents. Knowing the effective power of agents gives an indication of whether agents actually can pursue their goals or lack the power to do so. This information is valuable for humanitarian analysts to find out whether agents are sufficiently interested and powerful to pursue their goals and to sustain the current status quo or want to alter the situation, and if so, in which direction. Regarding the direction (positive or negative effect on the project goals), use the value for the goals to multiply it with the effective power (salience × capabilities). This will result in a value between –6 and 6. Negative numbers represent effective power directed against the goals of your project/organization. The formula is:

Goals [–1, 0, 1]×Salience [0 to 1]×Capabilities [0 to 6] = Effective Power

Draw a matrix (see Figure 6.4) with two axes: horizontal = Position (Salience) / vertical = Effective Power [for each context dimension if applicable].

Step 6: analysis of interdependencies and interactions.

Analyze the matrix in terms of: groups of potential allies, groups of potential adversaries, interactions among and between potential allies/adversaries (e.g., communication networks, resource flows), interdependencies among and between potential allies/adversaries (e.g., contractual obligations).

(continued)

Box 6.2   AGIRI Stakeholder Analysis* (*continued*)

Step 7: analysis of institutional structures.

Analyze how institutions inform possible lines of action regarding the achievement of the goals that actors have.

Analyze further the positive and negative interactions that respective institutional structures (beliefs, areas of worship) suggest.

Step 8: strategy development.

Given the information about goals, resources, salience, and interactions, decide which agents your project/organization should cooperate with, communicate with, shield against, rely on for information, rely on for resources, etc.

What do institutions tell you about acceptance of your organization in the field; what do they tell you about whom to associate with to increase acceptance (humanitarian space)?

*The AGIRI Stakeholder Analysis and additional visualizations are supported by the Excel programme available at: http://humanitarianintelligence.net.

REVIEW QUESTIONS

- What is the purpose of a stakeholder analysis with regards to its diagnostic and explanatory functions?
- What is a stakeholder?
- How can a robust stakeholder analysis contribute to strategy development?
- Which classifications of actors are useful for the stakeholder matrix in a humanitarian intelligence analysis?
- How are stakeholder matrixes utilized for strategy development?
- Which assumptions about decision-making of actors does AGIRI analysis assume?
- How does one decide whether to disaggregate corporate actors into subactors?
- How do goals determine the position of actors?
- What is the role of institutions regarding the goals of actors?
- What is effective power, and how is it calculated?

NOTES

1. R. Edward Freeman, *Strategic Management: A Stakeholder Approach* (Cambridge University Press, 2010).

2. Ibid., 46.

3. Grant T. Savage, Timothy W. Nix, Carlton J. Whitehead, and John D. Blair, "Strategies for Assessing and Managing Organizational Stakeholders," *The Executive* 5, no. 2 (February 1, 1991): 61–75.

4. R. Mason and I. Mitroff, *Challenging Strategic Planning Assumptions: Theory, Cases, and Techniques* (New York: John Wiley & Sons, 1981).

5. J. M. Bryson, "What to Do When Stakeholders Matter," *Public Management Review* 6, no. 1 (2004): 21–53.

6. Ronald K. Mitchell, Bradley R. Agle, and Donna J. Wood, "Toward a Theory of Stakeholder Identification and Salience: Defining the Principle of Who and What Really Counts," *The Academy of Management Review* 22, no. 4 (October 1, 1997): 853–86, doi:10.2307/259247.

7. Ibid.

8. Freeman, *Strategic Management.*

9. R. Edward Freeman, "The Stakeholder Approach Revisited," *Zeitschrift Für Wirtschafts-Und Unternehmensethik* 5, no. 3 (2004): 228–41.

10. Freeman, *Strategic Management.*

11. Bryson, "What to Do When Stakeholders Matter."

12. Savage et al., "Strategies for Assessing and Managing Organizational Stakeholders."

13. Ingie Hovland, *Successful Communication: A Toolkit for Researchers and Civil Society Organisations*, Rapid Research and Policy in Development (London: Overseas Development Institute (ODI), 2005), 9, http://www.odi.org/publications/155-successful-communication-toolkit-researchers-civil-society-organisations.

14. Savage et al., "Strategies for Assessing and Managing Organizational Stakeholders."

15. http://www.dse.vic.gov.au/effective-engagement/toolkit/tool-stakeholder-analysis-stakeholder-matrix.

16. http://policyimpacttoolkit.squarespace.com/library/the-alignment-interest-and-influence-matrix-aiim.html.

17. Jeremy Holland, *Tools for Institutional, Political, and Social Analysis of Policy Reform: A Sourcebook for Development Practitioners*, World Bank (Washington, DC: World Bank, 2007), 126, https://openknowledge.worldbank.org/handle/10986/6652.

18. See, for example, Sarah Collinson, et al., Politically Informed Humanitarian Programming: Using a Political Economy Approach, HPN network paper 41, 2002.

19. M. Anderson, *Do No Harm, How Aid Can Support Peace—or War* (Boulder: Lynne Rienner, 1999).

20. The choice for the state as separate corporate actor has been deliberate. Placed in between the supranational and subnational level, this intricate position stresses the increasing number of restraints states experience in the international arena due to the process of political and socioeconomic globalization. On the other hand, at the national level, states are confronted with a growing demand of their citizens to act on their behalf in solving political and socioeconomic problems. See among others W. F. Hanrieder, "Dissolving International Politics: Reflections on the Nation-State," in *Perspectives on World Politics*, second edition, ed. R. Little and M. Smith (London: Routledge, 1996), 143.

21. J. Coleman, *Foundations of Social Theory* (Cambridge: Belknap, 1990), 34.

22. E. Vonken, *Threat to the Power Relation and Negative Intergroup Behaviour* (Tilburg: Tilburg University Press, 1997).

23. M. Bollig, "Bridewealth and Stockfriendship. The Accumulation of Security through Reciprocal Exchange," *Angewandte Sozialforschung* 20, no. 1–2 (1997): 57–72.

24. Ch. Laughlin, "Deprivation and Reciprocity," *Man* 9 (1974): 380–96.

25. Th. Zitelman, "Refugee Aid, Moral Communities and Resource Sharing. A Prelude to Civil War in Somalia." *Sociologus* 41, no. 2 (1991): 118–38.

26. Franz von Benda-Beckmann, Keebet von Benda Beckmann, and Melanie Wiber (eds), *Changing Properties of Property* (New York/Oxford: Berghahn Books, 2006).

27. This approach is inspired by the work of Frans Stokman on EU negotiations. See F. N. Stokman, A. L. M. Van Assen, J. Van der Knoop, and R. C. H. van Oosten, "Strategic Decision Making," *Advances in Group Processes* 17 (2000): 131–53; and T. Allas and N. Georgiades, "New Tools for Negotiators," *McKinsey Quarterly*, 2001.

Chapter 7

Social Network Analysis and Interpretation

7.1 FROM STAKEHOLDERS TO NETWORKS

A thorough stakeholder analysis is a prerequisite of any resilient plan of operation. While it is crucial to understand the influence of stakeholders within the stakeholder field, stakeholder theory focuses mainly on the stakeholders themselves and less on the interaction between stakeholders.[1] This limits the stakeholder analysis to some degree. Analyzing the stakeholder field can be seen as taking a snapshot of the current situation, but it provides the analyst with only a limited amount of data to conduct further investigations in trends that result from stakeholder interaction. To add another layer that focuses on stakeholder interactions might therefore be useful, if not even necessary, to predict the effects that the humanitarian operation would have on the present stakeholder field. In other words, social network analysis (SNA) allows to some degree to predict what would happen if one inserts oneself as a new actor into the present situation. Furthermore, it gives clues about possible responses of other stakeholders, possible alliances, important gatekeepers, and entry points that might be crucial for the planning stage of a humanitarian operation. Compared to stakeholder matrices, in which stakeholders seem to operate in relative independence from each other, network theory considers the stakeholder field as a network of relationships between different stakeholders and their mutual interdependence. Consequently, network analysis entails "a series of multilateral contracts among stakeholders."[2]

This sort of analysis does not only shed light on how stakeholders might influence the objectives of other stakeholders and ultimately inform the objective of one's own organization, but also allows to predict to a certain degree the effects of introducing oneself as a new stakeholder and/or the effects of changing power relationships that a humanitarian operation might result in. In effect, analyses based on network theory produce explanations and insights of an organization's response to multiple stakeholders within the complex environment of interactions.[3]

Rowley argues that "employing social network concepts will generate an explicit theory of stakeholder influences based on the structural characteristics of an organization's network of relationships."[4] That means, by using the concepts and tools associated with network theory (i.e., SNA), one is able to examine the characteristics of both individual stakeholders and the overall stakeholder field, whether the stakeholder network is resilient or fragile, and which new connections are worth establishing. This establishes a definitive added value in addition to stakeholder analyses based on the relatively rigid classification schemes.

Law enforcement and state intelligence rely already since the 1980s on SNA.[5] Also for a humanitarian analyst SNA can be of invaluable use. One particular advantage is that with the right software updating the stakeholder field can be done by the click of a button. This provides immediate insights into how the addition of new actors or the disappearance of others as well as the establishing of new connections and the loss of old ones affects the overall network.

7.2   INTRODUCTION TO SOCIAL NETWORK ANALYSIS (SNA)

As a method, SNA has become a key technique in contemporary social sciences, having found significant application in the fields of anthropology, biology, communication studies, economics, information science, social psychology, etc. The concept of a "social network" has been loosely used for over a century to describe complex sets of relationships within a social system.

Traditionally, SNA makes the distinction between whole/complete networks and personal/egocentric networks. This distinction largely depends on how an analyst is able to gather the data. For settings in which the analyst has access to the complete information (i.e., within the humanitarian organization, the members of a humanitarian cluster, or people in an Internally Displaced Persons [IDP] or refugee camp) one would speak of a complete network. In such complete networks every actor is potentially an *ego* and an *alter*. In egocentric networks the analysts would start with one or more actors as a point of departure (*egos*) and investigate using tools such as surveys and snowballing techniques who these actors are associated with; the analyst would then conduct the analysis of new ties on the basis of newly identified connections.

In contrast to stakeholder analysis, both network approaches (complete and egocentric networks) have in common that they do not treat stakeholders as discrete units of analysis but focus on the relationship among actors, rather than individual stakeholders and their attributes. The overall structure of the social network helps to determine the utility for each of its individual members (nodes). For example, tight networks, in which individual members have a lot of ties to other members, are considered to be more resilient as they tend to have more redundancies; at the same time, they tend to be more closed and might inhibit the introduction of new actors and new ideas. Open networks with many weak ties (i.e., actors with many connections outside the main network) have a tendency to allow for new connections to be made and ideas to be introduced, while simultaneously they might be less resilient. For example, a humanitarian organization, whose staff has a lot of connections to different sections within a beneficiary group, the government, other humanitarian NGOs, and the donor community, is more likely to hear about new developments, identify emergent threats, and utilize new opportunities than organizations operating in relative isolation. Organizations that have ties to many stakeholders, which other organizations don't have, are in a relatively strong position to exercise influence or act as brokers within the social networks by bridging two networks that are not directly linked—this is called "to fill structural holes."

These examples show already that network theory adopts a different definition of "power" than traditional stakeholder analysis. Whereas in stakeholder analysis power is an attribute of an actor (e.g., funding, equipment, political support), in network theory power is an expression of how well an actor is connected to other actors. This general description sounds quite intuitive. However, it is very useful to make these network connections of one's organization explicit and to compare it to other organizations as well as identifying one's position in the overall network to determine both overall organizational strategy as well as developing concrete humanitarian action plans. In short, SNA delivers an alternative approach to stakeholders, their interactions, and their power. In its approach, based on network theory, it puts less emphasis on the attributes of actors than on relationships and ties within the whole social network.

A well-conducted SNA provides additional insights over traditional stakeholder analysis matrices such as:

• *Patterns of Interaction*: SNA helps to identify which common patterns of interaction, and the lack thereof, are present in the given stakeholder field; understanding these patterns of interaction helps the humanitarian organization to adopt the right strategy to ensure synergies, avoid conflicts, engage with existent (e.g., traditional) modes of behavior, etc.

- *Identification of Structural Holes*: the visualization of social networks allows to intuitively identify structural holes (i.e., the lack of connections between actors and networks); sometimes, the bridging of structural holes increases the resilience of a social network by creating redundancies; in other cases these structural holes help identify certain power relationships that one was unaware of.
- *Diffusion of Information*: information management is a crucial component in every humanitarian operation, whether it pertains to needs assessments or safety and security; SNA helps to deliberatively distribute or contain the spread of vital information by identifying important members of the social network that can act as broadcasters; furthermore, SNA allows to identify the structural holes that need to be closed to overcome settings in which crucial information does not reach one's organization.
- *Identification of Groups and Group Properties*: specific tools allow analysts to identify, on the basis of interactions, which actors cluster around each other (cluster analysis) and also how these clusters interact with other actors in the network.
- *Identification of Cooperation and Conflict*: not every form of interaction is necessarily a positive one; in cases of negative interactions, it is useful to know which kinds of conflicts the humanitarian organization needs to avoid or to steer free of by disassociating oneself with actors or by associating oneself with others.
- *Prediction of Network Effects* (and power shifts): the introduction of new actors or new humanitarian interventions invariably changes the dynamics of the social network; context and stakeholder analysis alone do not provide tools to predict the effects of such interventions; here the tools of SNA can simulate the addition of the new actor and envision new connections and how this affects the overall network; this ability to predict effects is also useful for identifying entry points and for designing sustainable and resilient humanitarian operations.

7.3   TERMINOLOGY

Before we go on to discuss the theory that underpins SNA, it is important to clarify a few terms that are crucial in SNA and used in a specific manner. First of all, any network consists of nodes and ties.

Nodes are the individual actors, and *ties* are their links to other actors. The nodes are also referred to with the terms "ego" and "alter." Any network

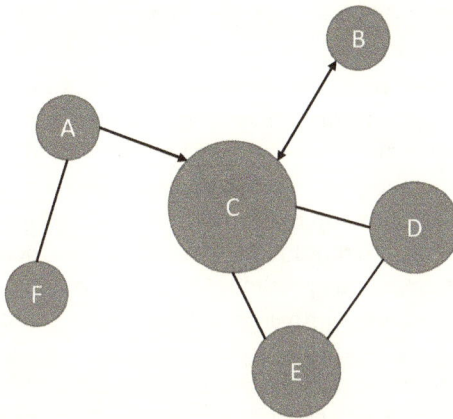

Figure 7.1 Example of a Simple Network with 6 Nodes and 6 Links

consists of as many egos as there are nodes—ego is one individual node, which one takes as a focal point of departure for the analysis; all other nodes are alters.

The *neighbourhood* is the collection of all nodes that connect to a focal node, that is, all alters an ego has connections to. In Figure 7.1, if one takes A as an ego, only F and C belong to its immediate neighborhood—C and F are the only alters. However, if one takes C as an ego, its neighborhood consists of the alters A, B, D, and E. Sometimes the analysis can include further steps beyond the immediate connection; we are then speaking of an "N-step neighborhood," with N standing for how many additional ties are included in addition to the first step.

Dyads are the smallest social structure in which an actor can be embedded. They are pairs of actors that form a binary relationship. This relationship can either be present (i.e., there is a link between the two nodes—e.g., C–B) or absent (E–F). The investigation into dyadic structures of social networks is one of the key features of SNA. Dyadic relationships can be *directional* or *nondirectional*. Directional relationships are depicted with an arrow for the link (A–C), and nondirectional ones (e.g., C–D, D–E) with a simple line. In cases of directional relationships, which are reciprocated, the arrow goes both ways (C–B). Reciprocated ties indicate that some sort of cohesion or trust is present. For analytical purposes it is worthwhile to decide beforehand whether or not to use directional or nondirectional annotation. Mixing annotations might result in confusion when trying to analyze the stakeholder network. Another important structure in SNA is the so-called triads. These structures consist of any three actors that together form a small society (C–D–E). In triadic structures one can note the emergence of hierarchies particularly when using directed graphs.

7.4   THE SOCIAL NETWORK PERSPECTIVE

Taking the perspective of a social network means going beyond the level of dyadic relationships, which is more typical when operating with stakeholder matrices, given the complexities that understanding more than one relationship at a time and judging its consequences entail. A social network captures the influence of multiple independent relationships and their interactions. J. Clyde Mitchell's definition of social networks focuses on actors and their impact on outcomes: "a specific set of linkages among a defined set of persons, with the additional property that the characteristics of these linkages as a whole may be used to interpret the social behaviour of the persons involved."[6] Barry Wellman summarizes his approach to SNA as "describing underlying patterns of social structure, explaining the impact of such patterns on behaviour and attitudes."[7] One can summarize the analytic layers of SNA as encompassing three elements:

- The effect of individual nodes,
- The effects of interconnections between actors,
- The effect of the overall structure on actors.[8]

Wellman developed principles that provide the theoretical cornerstones for analyzing social networks:

- behavior should be interpreted as a result of constraints imposed by the structure of the network, rather than a result of the node's capabilities;
- the analysis should focus on the relations between units rather than their individual attributes;
- a central consideration to the analysis is how patterns of relationships among actors in total affect the individual behavior of an actor;
- the overall structure of all related networks (a network of networks) is treated as a whole and not a priori analytically sub-structured into groups of tightly bonded units.[9]

In essence, instead of "analysing individual behaviours, attitudes and beliefs, social network analysis focuses its attention on how these interactions constitute a framework or structure that can be studied and analysed in its own right."[10]

In addition, structural ties and obstacles are socially constructed by relations among actors, and the behavior of social actors must be understood within the relational system they are embedded in.[11] Given the influence that social interactions have on actors themselves, these interactions within social networks affect beliefs, actions, and perceptions. Interactions between actors shape their social behavior not only through constraints and opportunities, but also through their perception of their environment.[12] The interpretation of the environment is informed through direct or indirect contacts. Actors might gain better information, are more susceptible to be influenced or capable to influence others, are exposed to new ideas, and may gain access to new information and useful resources. Furthermore, tight and cohesive groups may indicate solidarity within the group but also prejudice and conflict with other groups.

Finally, structural relations are dynamic and continue to change the interactions among the actors of the network. When individual actors apply knowledge about the network and exert influence (e.g., by connecting to new actors, by assuming some sort of brokering function) this not only transforms their own immediate environment but has a transformative effect on the overall network structure as well. For the purpose of analysis and forecasting, the humanitarian analysts should in particular consider the effects of (1) systemic transformations, (2) combined network preferences, and (3) intended activities of individual actors.

7.5   LEVELS OF ANALYSIS

Any analysis that involves actors implicitly or explicitly should take into consideration which levels of analysis it concludes. For example, it is of limited use to conduct an SNA that includes individual beneficiaries on the one hand, and international organizations (IOs) such as the United Nations or states on the other. Such a mix of analytical levels would result in a misrepresentation of reality. Hanneman and Riddle elaborate that "actors are embedded in networks that are embedded in networks that are embedded in networks."[13] However, as already explained in the previous chapter, it makes sense to restrict one's analysis to one of the four distinct levels of analysis: the local level, the national level, the regional level, or the international level. Individual actors might form bonds within neighborhoods, communities, or other social entities that in themselves are again embedded in other networks. How these individual actors are tied to each other in one network and how different networks are tied together are interesting angles of analysis for the humanitarian analysts. (Regarding the level of analysis, refer to section 6.2.2.1 on the aggregation and disaggregation of corporate actors.)

7.6   INTERPRETATION[14]

The interpretation of social networks is as much a science as it is an art. Looking at Figure 7.1 one becomes immediately aware that in this social structure not all nodes have an equal amount of ties. On either side of the social network there is a cluster of nodes. And in between them two notes seem to assume particular importance with many ties to other actors. Intuitively, we can also predict that these two players will probably assume quite dominant roles.

In the bottom center, we can see an isolated actor. Furthermore, nodes have different shades and different sizes. However, SNA goes far beyond these obvious, intuitive characteristics. For example, the structure of Figure 7.2 is not random, but apparently it is the result of how different nodes relate to each other and others do not. That means that already the representation suggests one form of relational analysis. Before we go deeper into these more complicated analytical tools, let us look at relatively simple measures.

7.6.1 Basic Features of a Network

Societies with a lot of "isolates" (i.e., nodes without ties) would probably exhibit entirely different social dynamics than societies in which all actors are very closely connected. The simplest measures of social networks are, thus, the size and the density of the network. The size of the network is determined by the number of actors. The larger the network grows, the more the potential connections that are possible, and the greater is its potential power over other networks. Another measure is density; this is the ratio between the sum of all ties divided by the number of possible ties. On the one hand, very dense networks have the advantage of being quite resilient because of a sufficient amount of redundancies. Furthermore, information spreads relatively quickly to every single actor. On the other hand, these dense networks are also quite resistant to change, to the introduction of new actors, or to new ideas.

Structural holes are of particular interest in predicting the behavior of actors. They are characterized by a gap between two or more networks, connected only by the few weak ties or even none at all. The social capital that is buried in structural holes can be generated by brokering between the networks. Thereby, new ideas can be transferred from one group to another, new and nonredundant resources connected, and new synergies created. The idea of structural holes is based on the assumption that dense networks have a lot of overlapping contacts and that it is unlikely that there is a lot of unknown and novel information distributed within this dense group.

> Structural holes separate non-redundant sources of information, sources that are more additive than overlapping. There are two indicators of redundancy: cohesion and equivalence. Cohesive contacts (i.e. contacts strongly connected to each other) are likely to have similar information and therefore provide redundant information benefits. Structurally equivalent contacts (i.e. contacts who link a manager to the same third parties) have the same sources of information and therefore provide redundant information benefits.[15]

Thus, connecting groups previously not well connected might allow for the exchange of new information and the access to new resources. This, of course, puts the broker, who bridges the gap between two groups, in a very powerful position. In Figure 7.9, the structural hole between the left and the right group is bridged by two central actors. As the network grows larger, the density decreases and structural holes are likely, because any single actor can only support a limited amount of connections. These structural holes are of key importance also for identifying possible entry points for the humanitarian organization into the overall social network. Being able to identify these structural holes in social networks enables the humanitarian organization not only to fill gaps where cohesion is necessary, but also to insert itself into the social fabric as powerful actor.

The network observed will most probably be incomplete. It would require extensive research to record all actors and all connections between the observed actors, which goes beyond the capabilities and the time frame within which humanitarian analysts operate. However, as observed in law enforcement intelligence, the incompleteness is not per se a problem of sampling, but the systematic effect representing the covert features of a network and the biases of investigative methods and contextual assumptions.[16] Furthermore, it will be difficult to distinguish between relevant and less relevant actors (e.g., representatives or a group and their family members). Also this issue of fuzzy boundaries should not be considered a big problem. It disappears quite readily when applying network measurements of power, which eliminate weak actors from the analysis, as we will see in this chapter.

7.6.2 Roles Actors Play

Actors can play different roles depending on their position in the network. As will be expanded upon in more detail, power in a social network is a structural element rather than being an intrinsic feature of an actor. The concept of *brokerage* is of particular interest when analyzing who the powerful actors are. Gould and Fernandez shed light on the different positions an ego can assume in relation to its neighborhoods concerning the exchange and flow of resources and information.[17] As such "brokerage" is a process in which the lack of access or trust between two parties is bridged by a third party. In a more systematic way, Gould and Fernandez distinguish between five distinct kinds of brokerages:

- *Coordinator*: all three actors (A, B, C) may belong to the same group. The intermediary actor (C) functions as a coordinator within that group. An example is UNOCHA within the cluster approach. All NGOs and IOs, including UNOCHA, belong to the cluster system, but UNOCHA is coordinating their actions (Figure 7.3).

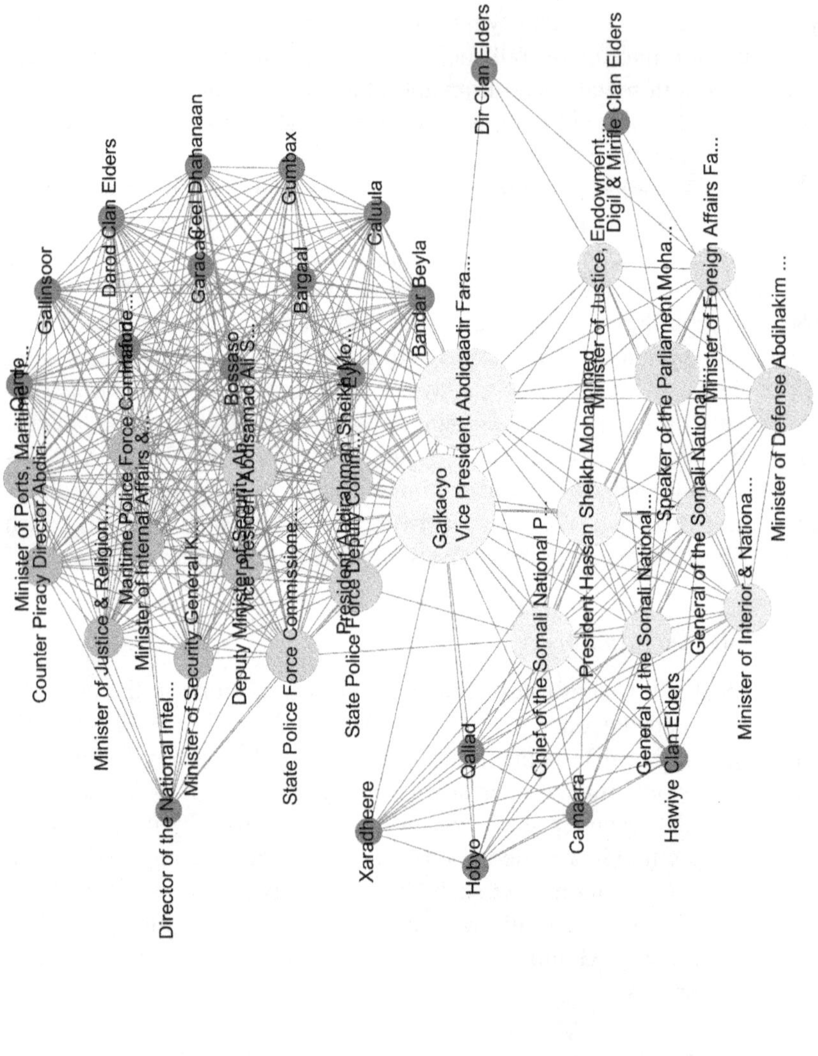

Figure 7.2   Network Analysis of Actors Relevant with Regard to Piracy in Somalia

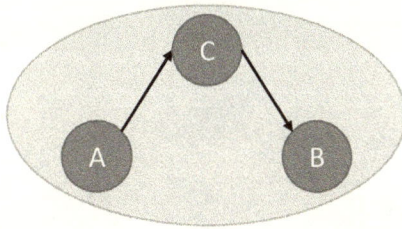

Figure 7.3 Coordinator

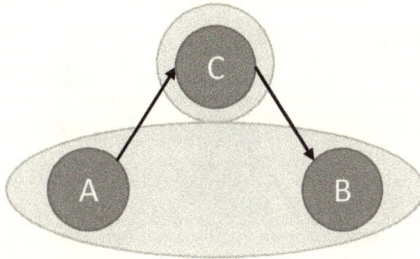

Figure 7.4 Consultant

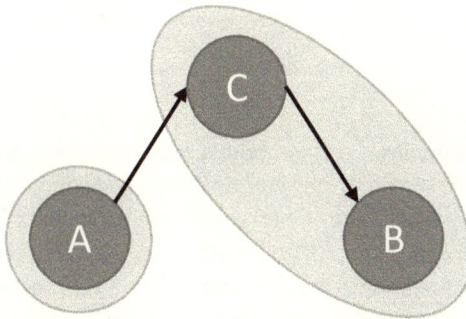

Figure 7.5 Gatekeeper

- *Itinerant (Consultant)*: the two principal actors belong to the same subgroup (A, B) while the intermediary (C) belongs to a different group. In these cases, the intermediary (C) acts as a consultant to the same group and mediates from outside between the actors of the core group (Figure 7.4). These cases are common when humanitarian organizations hire external consultants for issues such as conducting monitoring or evaluation functions within projects.
- *Gatekeeper*: in cases in which A belongs to another group than B and C, who belong to the same group, the intermediary (C) functions as a gatekeeper if it is in A's interest to establish contact with B (Figure 7.5).

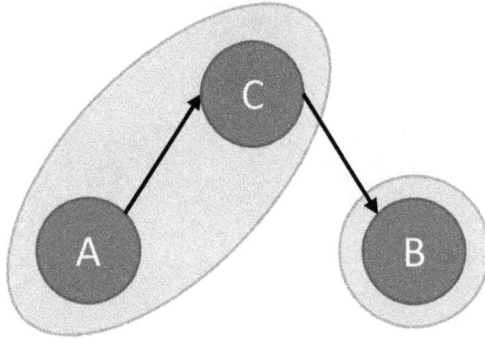

Figure 7.6   Representative

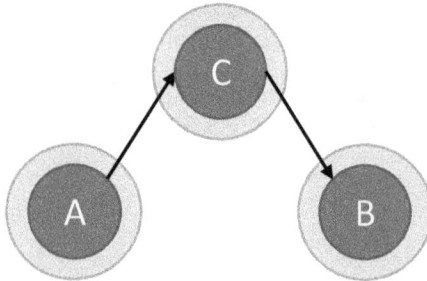

Figure 7.7   Liaison

- *Representative*: conversely, if A and C are in the same group, and A wants to establish contact with B but can only do so through C, C takes on the function of a representative. Gatekeeper and representative functions are often encountered in organizations where the access to the organization and its outside appearance are managed by a single actor or a dedicated group; these could be elders in a beneficiary community, or the secretary of the head of an organization who controls the information flow to him[18] (Figure 7.6).
- *Liaison*: if both principal actors (A, B) as well as the intermediary (C) belong to distinct groups, then C's power stems from the fact that he has contacts to A and B and either of them wants to have contact with the other but cannot do so without the liaising of C (Figure 7.7).

The graphic representation of these five types of brokerage relation symbolizes solid circles as actors; ellipses correspond to subgroup boundaries, and the top point in each triad represents the intermediary or broker—the arrows (in this case we work with a directed graph) represent the interest in connecting with another actor.

7.6.3 Power Distributions within the Network (Centrality)

Ultimately, the analysis of social networks for humanitarian operational planning should result in the knowledge of who are the most powerful actors, why they are so powerful, and with whom they are connected. Having such knowledge enables the humanitarian analyst to estimate the risks of entering a certain social network and identifying the power brokers. Ultimately this reduces the risks for humanitarian personnel and maximizes the benefits for the project and ultimately for the beneficiaries by knowing who to collaborate with and who to stay away from.

The key operational factor in all these questions is the element of power. We have already discussed above how network theory is distinct from other social theories about actors and their behavior. Power, according to network theory, is a structural element that is the result of the actor's position in the social structure. The position in the structure determines to what extent an actor may extract a good bargaining position, exert influence on other actors, receive information and resources as well as forge alliances and collaborate with partners of its choice. Since power is a consequence of the patterns in the structure of relations, a social network varies in overall power depending on whether its nodes are loosely coupled (low density—little power can be exerted) or highly connected (high density—much power can be exerted). We have already discussed this form of the power of a network (power as macro property) above with the concept of density (subchapter 7.6.2). At the same time there is also a relational power between actors (power as a micro property). The more central an actor is to the whole structure, the more opportunities to exert power it has—we refer to this sort of power in network theory as centrality. While the macro power (density) in two social networks might be the same, they might differ immensely in the way power is distributed among actors (centrality) and, thus, also in how decisions are made, how efficient processes in the network can be realized, in short, how these networks work. In terrorism studies, for example, analysts have witnessed the transition from hierarchical to cell structures—this change meant that counterterrorist efforts had to change to adapt to the nature of a new social network with increased resilience due to redundancies in informational capacity as well as isolated pockets in terms of capabilities helping these cells sustain themselves independently.

Centrality is the operational measure of power in SNA. There are several forms of centrality with different reasoning for their importance, some of which we will discuss in turn on the basis of the star, line, and circle network (see Figure 7.8 for the different forms of centrality).

- *Degree Centrality*: In undirected graphs, degree centrality is the number of nodes an ego is connected to or in other words "the sum of edges attached

Star-network   Line-network   Circle-network

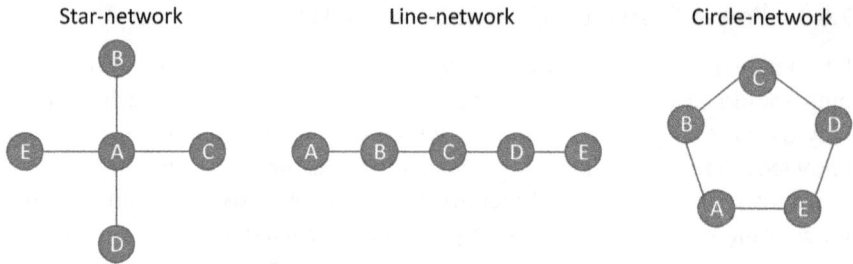

Figure 7.8   Different Forms of Power in Social Networks

to a node u." The more ties an ego has, the more powerful it is vis-à-vis the alters and their ties. The underlying theory is that the more ties an actor has, the more readily it can connect to other actors and the more it is able to assume a brokering position. The power equation is: the higher the number of ties, the higher the number of choices and opportunities and the less the dependence on single other actors. The degree centrality in the different networks of Figure 7.8 varies. In the star network A has the most ties; in the line network B, C, and D have the most, and in the circle network every actor has equally many ties. Degree centrality might be criticized for only taking into account the immediate neighborhood of a node.

- star network   [A: 4; B, C, D, E: 1]
- line network   [A, E: 1, B, C, D: 2]
- circle network   [A, B, C, D, E: 1]

- *Closeness Centrality*: This measure of power assumes that actors are the more powerful, the closer they are to all other actors. It is defined as "the inverted sum of geodesic[19] distances from each node u to all other nodes." Actors that have a shorter path to all other actors are in an advantage to those that have longer path lengths to travel. In our cases of Figure 7.8, A has the shortest distance to all other actors in the star network; all other actors are equal. In the line network, C has the closest path to all other actors, the second-best structural position is taken by B and D, and A and E on the periphery are in a structural disadvantage. In the circle network all nodes are equal.

- star network   [A: 0.25; B, C, D, E: 0.143]
- line network   [C: 0.167; B, D: 0.143; A, E: 0.1]
- circle network   [A, B, C, D, E: 0.167]

- *Betweenness Centrality*: This is a measure of the number of shortest paths that pass through a node. This form of power can be considered in the sense of transaction costs. "Removing a node of high 'betweenness' will, by definition, lengthen the paths connecting several other nodes, rendering communication or transactions between them less efficient."[20] In our star network every actor has to pass A to get to any other actor; A does not have to pass through any other actor. In the line network A and E have no brokering power as they do not divide between any pairs. C is the most central in the line network and has most programming power vis-à-vis all other actors.

- star network   [A: 6; B, C, D, E: 0]
- line network   [C: 4; B, D: 3; A, E: 0]
- circle network   [A, B, C, D, E: 1]

Assume, for example, that a humanitarian organization (A) needs to coordinate with a specific department of the Ministry of Interior (E) to negotiate for access to beneficiaries. The more the steps that this organization needs to take in order to reach the department that decides over access to a certain territory, the more the intermediary actors can control the final outcome. The line network might be the closest resemblance to such a hierarchical structure. In order to increase the speed of decision-making, it might be worthwhile if the humanitarian organization could directly connect with this specialized department, that is, closing the structural hole between A and E. Another scenario to humanitarian organization (A) might be coordinating different implementing partners (B, C, D, E)—let us take the star network as an example of this. In this scenario the humanitarian organization is very strong as it is the only actor connecting all of the actors; however, the network itself is not very resilient, since if A disappears all remaining actors are disconnected and cannot continue their work in coordinated fashion. In practice, betweenness centrality has shown to be a quite useful measure, whereas closeness centrality becomes more arbitrary when the sampling of the network is incomplete.[21] Because the three approaches mentioned above focus on the structural location of individual actors in terms of how close they are to the center of action, it has become more common in SNA to describe actors' capabilities as a measure of centrality rather than power.

7.7   ADVANCED VISUALIZATION AND ANALYSIS

With regards to visualizations of network graphs, decisions over layouts are an important element preceding the analysis. Visualizations can be made by hand. But more complex layouts are best generated by applying an algorithm. The manual approach is only feasible with limited amount of nodes (approximately 10–15). When the humanitarian context presents a large number of actors, the analyst will have to resort to layout algorithms, such as Force Atlas or Fruchterman-Reingold, that determine how the network graph is visualized. These algorithms apply parameters of attraction and repulsion to visualize the nodes in relation to each other based on their links and the relative importance. Which of the many layout algorithms to use in order to visualize one's dataset is largely subjective and depends on the data present and on the analytical needs. Applying the right algorithm will allow to disentangle complex social networks and identify core groups and structural holes.

There are many more visualization techniques that usually combine analytical elements. For example, it might bring analytic advantages to visualize actors with a high degree centrality as larger nodes than actors with a lower degree centrality. Furthermore, it is possible to associate the size or the color of the nodes with other attributes, such as resources, allegiance, or salience.

Of particular utility is the so-called clustering coefficient. This measure defines the degree to which nodes in the graph tend to cluster together. It is based on the real-world experience and evidence in SNA that distinct groups, which share a tightly knit network, are characterized by a high density of ties. The clustering coefficient can be used to identify groups within the network that were previously unknown to belong together. It can, for example, be visualized by applying the same color to actors that have the same clustering coefficient.

The network graph in Figure 7.9 represents the case of the social network concerning piracy and antipiracy efforts in Somalia.[22] The size of the nodes corresponds to the betweenness centrality of each node. The shading is based on the index of the clustering coefficient. As one can see, the groups are not necessarily distinctly separated in all cases and tend to transition from one color to another, with the exception of a few distinct groups. It is also interesting to note that the two actors with the highest degree centrality are the Galkacyo community and Vice President Abdiqaadir Farah Shirdoon Saif, with a total number of 37 and 33 direct relations respectively. The density score of the whole network is 0.456 (from a range of 0, indicating no connections, to 1, indicating that all actors are connected among themselves). This indicates that the overall network is moderately cohesive, which means that diffusion can occur at reasonable speeds and information must on average transfer across three actors in the network to reach everyone. With regard to structural holes the density score indicates that while the network is actually quite large, there should be many structural holes to be exploited to gain entrance into the social network.

Furthermore, with regard to brokerage "several federal government officials are only connected to Puntland communities via indirect relations. Those actors that benefit from serving as intermediaries between other actors who are not directly connected themselves are, most obviously, Galkacyo and Vice President Saif. They serve as a bridge (brokers) between the two components that make up the network. This advantageous position gives these two actors the potential to broker the information flow or synthesize ideas forming strategies that can work its way to the different parts of the network."[23]

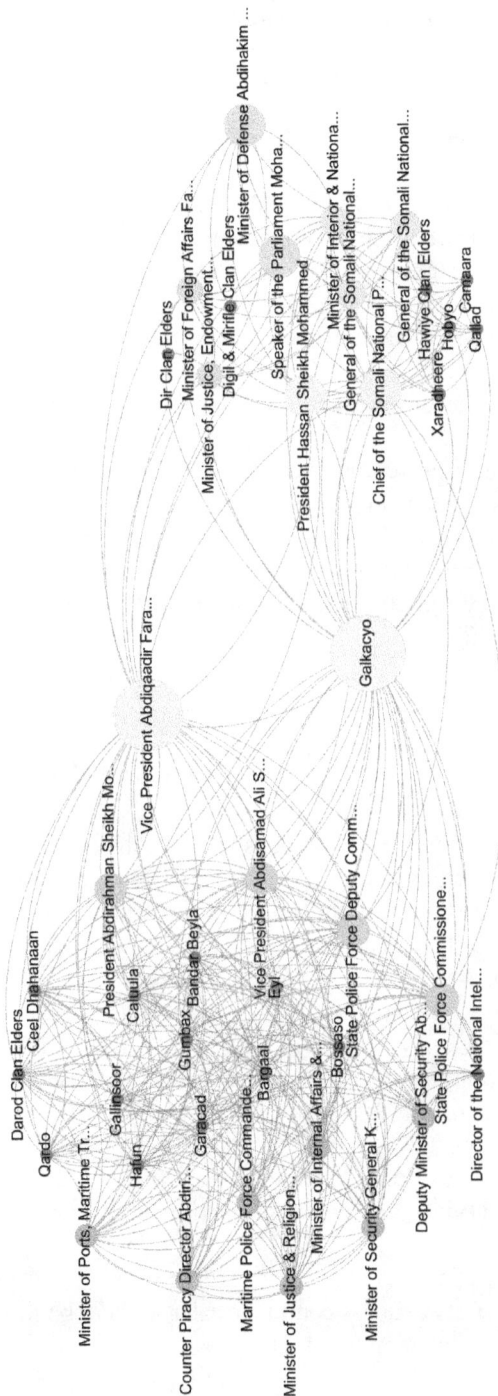

Figure 7.9 Network Analysis of Actors Relevant with Regard to Piracy in Somalia. *Note:* The clustering coefficient is depicted with corresponding shades of gray for corresponding groups; the size of the nodes represents degree centrality.

Box 7.1 Social Network Analysis and Interpretation

Step 1: decide upon your level of analysis, that is, which actors to include and to what extent to disaggregate corporate actors (like the UN or states). This decision should be based on your operational and intelligence needs.

Step 2: collect data about different stakeholders. Use different sampling techniques like snowballing or convenience sampling or distill your data from surveys, focus groups, informants, etc.

Data necessary: actors, interactions between actors.

Note: Based on the available data, decide whether to use directed or undirected graphs.

Step 3: create a node for each actor and label them or assign a color or symbol.

Step 4: create edges representing the interactions identified for each actor.

Note: When using pen and paper, make sure to leave enough space between the nodes to be able to distinguish the different edges. If necessary, redraw the graph. When using an SNA software, this is the time to try out different layout algorithms (e.g., Force Atlas, Fruchterman-Reingold).

Step 5: calculate and analyze the density of the network:

$$\text{Density} = \frac{\text{Actual connections}}{\text{Potential connections}}; \ Potential\ connections = \frac{n*(n-1)}{2}$$

The lower the percentage of density (i.e., the result is a number between 0 and 1 representing 0 percent and 100 percent, respectively), the more likely are structural holes. Look for structural holes and mark them clearly. Look for isolates and briefly assess whether they are worth further research.

Note: For all further calculations, resort to one of the software solutions.

Step 6: calculate and analyze the centrality score of actors in the network. Assign the centrality score to the size of the nodes in order to visualize more powerful actors are larger nodes.

Which actors are the strongest? What is their role in the network? Which brokering positions do they occupy vis-à-vis different interest groups and vis-à-vis your own organization if inserted in a specific structural hole.

Note: Brokerage positions change depending on who you look at (i.e., who the ego is). Betweenness centrality has shown to be most useful as a measure of incomplete networks.

Step 7: calculate the clustering coefficient and assign the result to the color of the nodes, in order to identify different groups in your network. Investigate how the nodes in these groups are connected and which interaction (positive/negative, resources, information, etc.) connects them.

Step 8: in order to identify possible entry points for your humanitarian organization/operation, create a node representing your organization. Try which connections with previously unconnected actors put your organization in stronger positions with regard to:

- *Key Stakeholders*: which actors do you need to cooperate with or avoid to succeed with your project/operation.
- *Structural Holes*: which structural holes connect you to actors that were previously not linked? Which brokering positions do you assume through that?
- *Betweenness Centrality*: calculate your own centrality score and compare it with similar organizations.
- *Clustering Coefficient*: with which groups will you most likely be associated with; what does this mean for your humanitarian space?

It will exceed the purpose of this book to go deeper into the Somali case. However, the above description presents a rough ad hoc analysis and demonstrates how SNA can be readily conducted once core information about actors has been collected.

7.8   SOFTWARE SUPPORT

A lot of software for SNA is available online as open source or freeware. Most of it is quite easily accessible. Particularly recommendable are Gephi[24] and Social Network Visualizer (SocNetV).[25] Both programs can be downloaded free and provide good support and clear tutorials. Furthermore, they are both available across different platforms. For a quick analysis without the additional analytical capabilities, Lynks, a project of the Peace Informatics Lab (Leiden University), is also recommended.[26] In addition to network visualization, Lynks allows sharing the network graphs and cooperating collaboratively in teams online.

7.9   LINKING IT TO AGIRI

It is also possible to link SNA to the AGIRI Stakeholder Analysis (see section 6.2.2). Using the information collected in the AGIRI analysis is quite simple,

Table 7.1 Linking AGIRI to SNA

Agents	Nodes—create as many nodes as there are actors to be distinguished based on Goals/Resources/Identity
Interactions	Links—connect nodes that interact (undirected/directed), label them (thickness of the link can symbolize strength of the interaction), color of the link can represent positive or negative interaction
Resources	Nodes—size of the nodes usually symbolizes either power or resources
Institutions	Institutions help to explain centrality, density, brokerage, and structural holes—can be indicated by the color of the links
Goals	Goals determine the interpretation of centrality, density, brokerage, and structural holes—can be symbolized by the color of the nodes

as most of the elements relate also to information necessary to draw social networks (see Table 7.1). For this purpose, it is necessary to change some assumptions about power. Whereas in the AGIRI analysis resources in combination with salience were assumed to be associated with effective power (salience × capabilities = effective power), in SNA the factor of resources can be used to either inform the size of the node depicted in the network or be kept as quantitative data in the analyst's research notes to inform the interpretation.

REVIEW QUESTIONS

- What is the difference of focus between stakeholder and network analysis?
- What are the analytic advantages of SNA?
- What are the advantages and disadvantages of loose/tight networks?
- What are structural holes, and how can they help to define a strategy?
- How do nodes form neighborhoods?
- Which analytic layers and cornerstones of analysis are relevant for SNA?
- What is the role of perceptions and knowledge in social networks?
- What is the relationship between density of a network and structural holes?
- Define brokerage and explain its utility in analyzing social networks.
- Why is power a structural element in network theory?
- How do you measure micro power? Explain the three different forms of power.
- How do you identify groups within a network?

NOTES

1. Grant T. Savage, Timothy W. Nix, Carlton J. Whitehead, and John D. Blair, "Strategies for Assessing and Managing Organizational Stakeholders," *The Executive* 5, no. 2 (February 1, 1991): 65.

2. R. Edward Freeman and William M. Evan, "Corporate Governance: A Stakeholder Interpretation," *Journal of Behavioral Economics* 19, no. 4 (1990): 354, doi:10.1016/0090-5720(90)90022-Y.

3. Timothy J. Rowley, "Moving beyond Dyadic Ties: A Network Theory of Stakeholder Influences," *Academy of Management Review* 22, no. 4 (1997): 887–910.

4. Ibid., 887.

5. Malcolm K. Sparrow, "The Application of Network Analysis to Criminal Intelligence: An Assessment of the Prospects," *Social Networks* 13, no. 3 (September 1, 1991): 253, doi:10.1016/0378-8733(91)90008-H.

6. James Clyde Mitchell, *Social Networks in Urban Situations: Analyses of Personal Relationships in Central African Towns* (Manchester University Press, 1969), 2.

7. Barry Wellman, "Structural Analysis: From Method and Metaphor to Theory and Substance," in *Social Structures: A Network Approach*, ed. Barry Wellman and Stephen D. Berkowitz (Cambridge University Press, 1988), 19–61.

8. Rowley, "Moving beyond Dyadic Ties."

9. Wellman, "Structural Analysis," 20.

10. Stanley Wasserman and Katherine Faust, *Social Network Analysis: Methods and Applications* (Cambridge University Press, 1994), 7.

11. Mark Granovetter, "Economic Action and Social Structure: The Problem of Embeddedness," *American Journal of Sociology* (1985): 481–510.

12. Wasserman and Faust, *Social Network Analysis*.

13. Robert A. Hanneman and Mark Riddle, *Introduction to Social Network Methods* (Riverside, CA: University of California, 2005), Chapter 1, http://faculty.ucr.edu/~hanneman/nettext/C10_Centrality.html.

14. This subchapter is based on Hanneman and Riddle's excellent open access introductory textbook on social network analysis (ibid.).

15. Ronald S. Burt, "Structural Holes versus Network Closure and Social Capital," in *Social Capital: Theory and Research*, ed. Nan Lin, Karen S. Cook, and Ronald S. Burt (New Brunswick, London: Transaction Publishers, 2001), 35.

16. Sparrow, "The Application of Network Analysis to Criminal Intelligence," 262.

17. Roger V. Gould and M. Roberto Fernandez, "Structures of Mediation: A Formal Approach to Brokerage in Transaction Networks," *Sociological Methodology* 19 (1989): 91–94.

18. Reinhard Selten and Rolf Stoecker, "End Behavior in Sequences of Finite Prisoner's Dilemma Supergames—A Learning Theory Approach," *Journal of Economic Behavior & Organization* 7, no. 1 (March 1986): 50, doi:10.1016/0167-2681(86)90021-1.

19. Geodesic distance means the shortest distance between two nodes in terms of the number of edges connecting them.

20. Sparrow, "The Application of Network Analysis to Criminal Intelligence," 264.

21. Ibid., 265–66.

22. The data and graphs have been reproduced with permission of the author: Tamara van der Heijden, "Countering Piracy in Somalia—A Social Network Approach to Stakeholder Analysis" (Master Thesis, University of Groningen, 2013).

23. Ibid., 51.
24. https://gephi.org.
25. http://socnetv.sourceforge.net.
26. https://lynksoft.com.

Part IV

FROM TRENDS TO OPERATIONAL PLANNING

Chapter 8

Humanitarian Analysis and Intervention Design Framework

Trend Factor Analysis

8.1 FROM CONTEXT AND ACTORS TO TREND FACTORS

At this stage of analysis, we presuppose that the humanitarian analyst has conducted a thorough context and stakeholder analysis. This chapter is an extension of the humanitarian analysis and intervention design (H-AID) framework that combines the comprehensive context analysis (CCA) with intelligence about stakeholder interaction and other trend factors, such as natural hazards and technological disasters. It is an extension of the H-AID framework discussed in chapter 5 and, in addition, of the book *Humanitarian Crises, Intervention and Security: A Framework for Evidence-Based Programming.*[1] It further draws on the AGIRI stakeholder analysis, which can be used as a stand-alone tool as well as in conjunction with the CCA.

Given the knowledge about the project context and its stakeholders, the next analytical step would be to apply this knowledge to identify trends that are presently observable. In general, one can state that the best predictor of future behavior is past behavior. On the basis of this assumption, one can identify trends in the given context that are presently observable in different context dimensions. However, due to the complexity of stakeholder fields these trends are relatively hard to assess without the aid of additional analytical steps. This chapter provides such an analytical tool that helps to synthesize the effects of actors and other trend factors into discernible trends. Also this tool is available to the reader as a software solution.[2]

In section 4.3.1 the Macro-Micro Analysis, with its distinction between macro-level problem and micro-level explanation, has been introduced, and in chapter 5 the diagnostic problem on the basis of the H-AID method has been extensively addressed. The CCA was proposed as a tool to study the diagnostic problem, whereas the AGIRI analysis in section 6.2.2 related to the explanatory question. The context analysis in combination with the stake-holder analysis can be pushed still one step further concerning the *explanatory problem*.

The general factors pertaining to the macro-level phenomenon are at this stage already known to the researcher. The CCA analysis of the pre- and post-incident situations and the AGIRI stakeholder analysis give plenty of information about the structural settings of environmental and social dynamics. The basic assumption until here was that most of these factors come about due to social interaction between actors, with goals and resources, in a particular institutional context. Which concrete interactions lead to which insecurities still remains unknown. To take a closer look at how the interaction of actors influences one or more context dimensions is part of the trend analysis. To repeat utilizing Coleman's distinction between macro- and micro-level factors: (1) the CCA analysis represents the macro-level phenomenon. (2) The critical incident connects two elements based on the hypothesis that the incident had a certain effect on the context dimensions. (3) The AGIRI analysis causally connects the critical incident with the change in context dimensions through social mechanisms.

For example, how can one explain the high death toll of the earthquake in Haiti (January 2010)? In terms of the above typology, we might find out that vulnerabilities in the physical environment resulted in the high death toll. The low quality of buildings was raised as one of defining problems in the disaster.[3] The macro-micro level question to be answered then is this: How can the low quality of buildings be explained?

In order to come to such a macro-micro explanation, one needs to investigate the AGIRI factors, which are a set of factors of potential importance in understanding humanitarian problems: the actors (agents) involved, their goals and interests, their resources, the interactions among these actors, and the institutional setting in which they operate. Questions deriving from an AGIRI analysis in relation to Haiti could be, for example:

- Which agents were involved in or responsible for buildings in Haiti?
- Which agents had an interest in, for example, formulating and upholding building regulations, and which agents did not do so?
- What resources did the agents have to address the low quality of buildings?
- How did agents cooperate to achieve better quality buildings?

The role of the government is probably of highest interest here. If our investigation would lead to the conclusion that the government had done nothing to improve the quality of construction, then the question would be: why not? What other interests and goals might have interfered with intervention in this domain, and what resources were lacking to do so; or what resources did stakeholders gain by not doing so? If some intelligence points to the fact that the government and other agents knew the quality of the buildings was low, then information was not the resource lacking in this respect. What could then be an alternative explanation? An AGIRI analysis can thus be of help in explaining this lack of collective action in this particular case.

8.2   THE LOGIC OF TRENDS

There are two CCA graphs necessary in order to know the impact of a disaster (the critical incident) on the context dimensions; one CCA before, describing the status quo ante as a baseline and one after the hazard took place (i.e., critical incident approach). It requires the mapping of the different context dimensions at two periods in time. Comparing the two sheds light on how the context dimensions change before and after the disaster. At this stage the underlying social dynamics, which were present before and which unfolded during and after the critical incident, are only implicitly present in the data. This is not enough to understand the trend factors and assess further developments.

Since the CCA is only a contextual snapshot, it does not indicate whether and/or where the incident could still cause problems and which role the actors play with regard to the individual context dimensions. Therefore, the Trend Factor Analysis, which bases on the previous steps (the CCA and the AGIRI analysis), assesses the trends within the context dimensions. It uses the status quo CCA as a baseline and projects onto the status quo the current actor dynamics and other extraneous (environmental and technological) factors. This projection of trend factors then forms the trend. In other words, applying trend factors (AGIRI and hazards) to a status quo CCA of the different context dimensions projects the current effects of actors and hazards into the near future. We will see in chapter 9 that for the purpose of scenario planning, the Trend Factor Analysis can form the basis of reflection—the so-called baseline scenario.

The interplay of the AGIRI factors gives a strong indication of present trends (the actor-based trend factors) within the different contextual dimensions of the project environment, as already pointed out with each of the AGIRI factors. These actor-based trend factors should be analyzed with reference to each of the specific context dimensions they are impacting on.

Let us take a hypothetical example of a complex emergency—a flooding in a region that also deals with a civil war. If there is a strong presence of rebels in the assessed area and therefore a rigid counterinsurgency is conducted by state authorities, which impacts negatively on the political context dimension of the population, this trend has to be taken into calculation (depending on the concrete situation also in terms of the societal context dimension). At the same time the hazard, the flooding, persists for a certain time leading to a lack of food and to water-borne diseases. One can see in this example that social mechanisms alone cannot explain the postincident state of the context but persistent or intervening effects of hazards have to be taken into account as well (the environmental/technological trend factors—hazards). One has therefore to ask the following *predictive question*: What is the effect of hazards and stakeholders on the context dimensions of the research object (beneficiaries)?

The trend analysis can be summarized with the following simplified formula:

$$\left\{ \begin{array}{l} \text{Impact of Actors on Context Dimensions} \\ +\text{Impact of Hazards on Context Dimensions} \end{array} \right\} = \text{CS-Trend Analysis.}$$

8.3   APPLYING TRENDS TO THE STATUS QUO

Applying the impact of hazards and actors to the postincident state (Z), provided that nothing has changed, answers the predictive question of how the trend seems to continue after the last evaluation (see Figure 8.1). Although it is a predictive question the aim is not to forecast the future, but to find valuable entry points for an intervention, resources and allies one can draw on, and restraints to action, access, and security one has to take into consideration.

The trend analysis draws on the data collected for the CCA of the situation after the critical incident (state Z), which represents the present situation (status quo) into which the humanitarian project should be implemented.

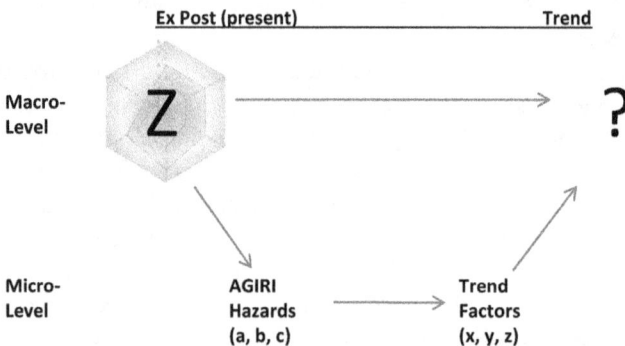

Figure 8.1   Applying Trend Factors to the Status Quo

It further presupposes that based on the AGIRI method the stakeholder analysis has been conducted and the effective power of all stakeholders in different context dimensions has been calculated (see section 6.2.2.6). In addition to this information, it is now necessary to extract data on the effect of present hazards or nonactor-related occurrences (such as floods, disrupted infrastructure, technological impacts and droughts) still or newly affecting the context. In order to disentangle the actors' influence from the CCA we have previously conducted the AGIRI stakeholder analysis. What still needs to be done is filtering out the actor-independent factors (hazards) that persist or emerge after the outbreak of the crisis (or the critical incident). Examples of these hazards and their continuous effect could be:

- forest fires, which could lead to increased erosion and therefore to more landslides;
- floods, which could lead to more water-borne diseases and therefore to a higher mortality rate;
- earthquakes, which could result in destruction of cultural facilities necessary for social support networks;
- disruption of storage facilities for waste consisting of poisonous products could lead to water and land degradation;
- damaged nuclear facilities could lead to radioactive contamination of the surrounding.

The evaluation of hazards and their persistent effects happens in the same way as the assessment of effective power. With hazards we refer to ongoing or emerging natural and technological occurrences that have negative effect on the research object—for example, the population of beneficiaries, the state, or region. The following hazards are of particular interest because their occurrence is independent of the researched population, but also because their possible effect on the population strongly depends on its vulnerability to such a hazard (in the sense of the formula "Disaster Risk = Hazard × Vulnerability" (see chapter 4)): geophysical, atmospheric, or hydrological event (e.g., earthquake, landslide, tsunami, windstorm, wave or surge, flood or drought; see Table 8.1).

For example, let us assume that a drought continues to persist and further reduces the food production. As this is a negative effect on the food context dimension (which is currently at a level of [3 = C1 Manifest threat]) and only partially affects the beneficiaries in the region, as there are disaster risk reduction (DRR) measures in place, we select a value of –0,5 for the impact on the food dimension. This will result in a value that deducts this from the number CCA—a negative impact. Furthermore, one has to estimate the potential of the hazard in decreasing the security level (as we did for the assessment of

Table 8.1   Overview of the Processing of Hazards for the Trend Analysis

	Positive or Negative Impact on Context Dimension	Force of the Hazard	Hazard Effect on Context Dimension
Description	Does the hazard have a positive or a negative effect on the context dimension?	How much force does the hazard exert relative to the context dimension?	Effective power of the hazard
Processing	Between [–1 and 1]	Between [0 and 6]	Impact × Force

resources in effective power) if it continues to affect the context. In our case it might be eventually resulting in bringing the general context dimension to an acute threat (D1). There are two steps between C1 (3) and D1 (1) that signify the potential force of the hazard (3 – 1 = 2). Multiplying force with impact (2 × –0.5) results in the effective power of the hazard (–1). This evaluative step can be repeated for each relevant hazard.

In order to calculate the effective power of the stakeholders, multiply the salience scores with the capabilities (resources) scores (see section 6.2.2.6 (Step 5)). Once the evaluation of the persisting effect of actors and hazards is done, the next analytical task in the trend analysis is to combine this information on the specific effect of hazards and actors on the security aspects with the CCA analysis. That means the data of the CCA serves as a starting point onto which the latest information on continuous hazards and on the stakeholder field is applied. Knowing this allows assessing capabilities and restraints of a region, which is the fundament of any intervention design.

Adding the effects of hazards and actors to the result of the postincident CCA analysis for the respective context dimension results in the trend for this aspect from the point of the status quo CCA to the future (see Figure 8.2). In this figure α and β are stakeholders, whereas δ stands for the hazard. Stakeholder α has a negative effective power on the status quo of the context dimension, and stakeholder β has a larger positive effective power. The persistent hazard δ also has a negative effect on the context dimension. One calculates, therefore, in our case:

$$Z \text{ (status quo)} + \beta - \alpha - \delta = \text{Trend.}$$

In this graphical representation (Figure 8.2), the positive effect of stakeholder β outweighs the negative effect of stakeholder α and hazard δ. The trend vector points toward an improvement of the situation.

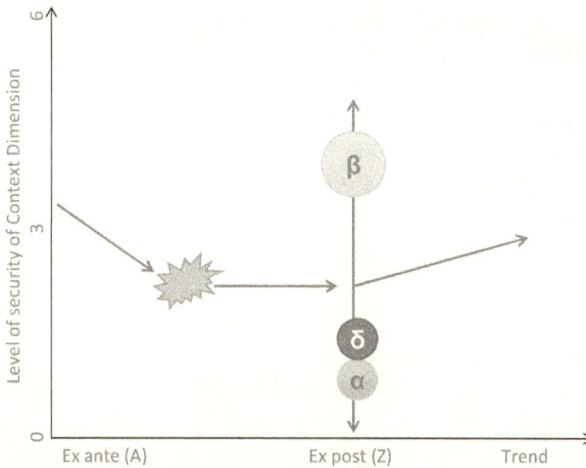

Figure 8.2 Graphical Representation of the Trend of One Context Dimension

When this is done for all the aspects it is possible to map the trend as vectors onto the graph by adding positive effects and subtracting negative effects from the ex post state of the context dimension. This point is then plotted onto the graph one step further in the timeline; it marks the direction of the trend vector. It is important to note that the trend line should indeed be considered a vector indicating the direction and does not point at an end result. This has to do with the fact that Trend Factor Analysis is the analysis of trends in the present situation and not the prediction of developments at a certain point in the future (in contrast to that, see scenario planning in chapter 9). The rule of thumb for assessing the strength of the trend is: the steeper the vector, the stronger the trend and the faster its progress. In other words, the angle of the vector (the steepness of the arrow) gives information about of the acuteness of the trend.

8.4   TREND FACTOR ANALYSIS IN PRACTICE

In the stakeholder analysis, information has been collected on the AGIRI elements that, when related to the context dimensions, give considerable information on how actors will impact on the different context dimension. From the data necessary for the CCA we can also distill information regarding hazards and their impact.

As already explained in the previous section on the AGIRI analysis (6.2), the salience is measured on a scale from 0 to 1. In order to integrate the analysis of effective power (salience × capabilities) into the CCA analysis it is now important to ask whether the goal of the actor would result in an improvement of the security aspect or in a deterioration of it. Depending on whether the goals of the agent affect the context dimension of the research object positively or negatively the salience is multiplied with −1 (for negative effect of goals) or with 1 (for positive effect of goals). Note that actors can have different impacts on different context dimensions. Therefore, assess the effective power of an actor regarding each context dimension separately. Table 8.2 summarizes the necessary steps.

Conduct the same assessment for the effect of hazards in each context dimension based on the steps outlined in Table 8.2.

Calculate the sum of all effects caused by hazards and the sum of all effective powers of stakeholders within one dimension. Next, add the sum of hazard effects and effective powers of actors to the security level (see section 5.2 for the table on security levels), which results in the trend vector.[4]

Trend Vector = Security Level+ Effective Powers (Stakeholders) + Hazards Effects

One further element provides an additional level of analysis. In section 5.2, we have introduced the lower and the upper limits of the confidence margin— that is, confidence the researcher has in the assessment of the security level of the context dimension. The trend vectors can then be projected from the lower and the upper levels of the context dimension resulting in a worst case trend and a best case trend (see Figure 8.3).

Table 8.2   Overview of the Processing of AGIRI Factors for the Trend Analysis

	Agent	Goals	(Inter)action	Salience	Capabilities	Effect on Context Dimension
Description	Actor of relevance for context dimension	Goals of relevance for context dimension	(Inter) action of the actors with relevance for context dimension	How much is the action or interaction directed toward the context dimension	How much force or capability of action or interaction with relevance for context dimension	Effect on context dimension
Processing	Name the agent	1 or −1	Reference to AGIRI analysis	0–1	0–6	Context dimension + (Goals × Salience × Capabilities)

Combined Dimensions - Best Case Trend

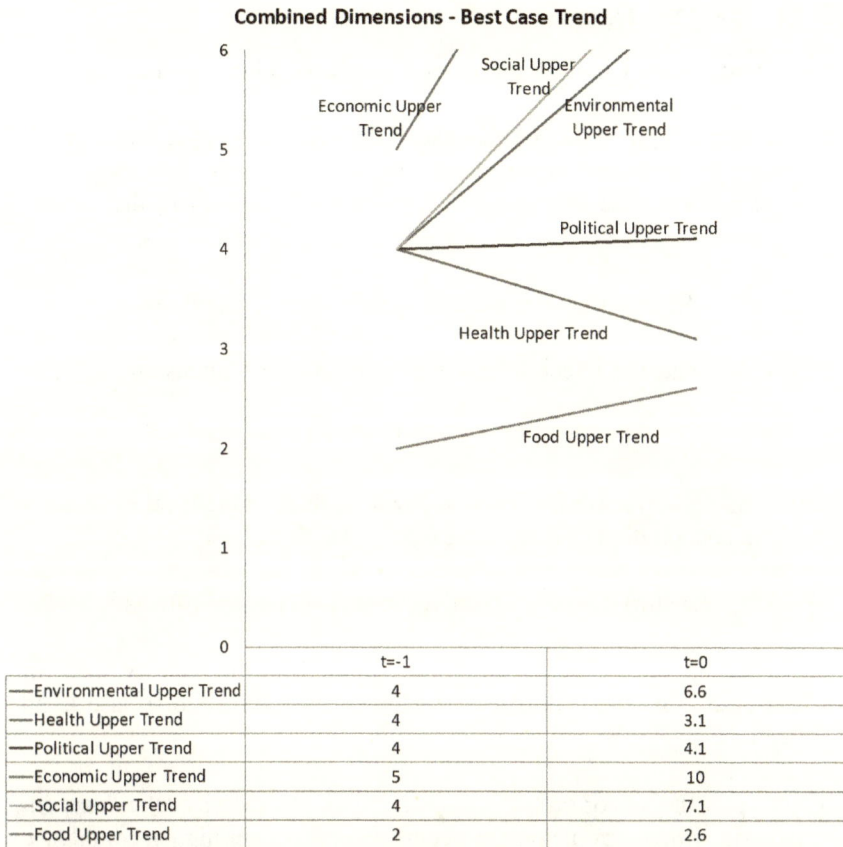

	t=-1	t=0
——Environmental Upper Trend	4	6.6
——Health Upper Trend	4	3.1
——Political Upper Trend	4	4.1
——Economic Upper Trend	5	10
——Social Upper Trend	4	7.1
——Food Upper Trend	2	2.6

Figure 8.3   Example of a Best Case Trend Project of the Combined Context Dimensions

If the trend analysis shows that the respective context dimension is negatively impacted by the resulting trend (see e.g., the health trend in Figure 8.3), then the carrying capacity for this aspect will be only limited or maybe not present at all. The contextual restraints reflect the areas in a given situation where interventions have to take place.

The trend analysis in summary follows these analytical steps:

- AGIRI factors impacting on the respective context dimensions of the project environment;
- actor-independent environmental variables (hazards) impacting on the respective context dimensions of the research object;
- applying Trend Factors (AGIRI factors + Hazard factors) on the postincident CCA leads to a trend assessment for each context dimension.

Box 8.1   H-AID Trend Analysis

Step 1: conduct a CCA for the ex-post situation following the steps outlined in chapter 5.
Step 2: conduct an AGIRI of all stakeholders for the ex-post situation following the steps outlined in chapter 6.
Step 3: calculate the effective power of all stakeholders in the context
dimension.

$$\text{Effective Power} = \text{Goals} \times \text{Salience} \times \text{Capabilities.}$$

Step 4: calculate the effect of hazards for the context dimension.

$$\text{Hazard Effects} = \text{Impact} \times \text{Force.}$$

Step 5: add all effective powers and hazard effects to the level of security
of the context dimension of the ex-post situation.

$$\text{Security Level} + \text{Effective Powers} + \text{Hazards Effects.}$$

Use the upper level of the confidence margin for the security level for
a best case trend projection; use the lower level for a worst case trend
projection.

Step 6: plot the vector on a graph (vertical axis = security level/horizon-
tal axis = time) by using the security level (lower/higher confidence
level respectively) as a starting point and add the effective powers and
the hazard effects to the security level to draw the next point in time.
Connect the two points on the graph to create the trend vector.
Step 7: repeat steps 3–6 for the other context dimensions of the ex-post
situation.

8.5   USING TREND FACTORS TO CHECK ASSUMPTIONS

Trend factors are not only useful to identify ongoing development, they can
also be used to check whether the assumptions about the effective power
of stakeholders and the effects of hazards have been correctly estimated in
previous analytical steps. This can be done by applying the trend analysis to
the CCA of an ex-ante state (A) before the critical incident, which should
lead to the CCA of the post-incident state (Z)—the present (see Figure 8.4).
In other words, if one applies a CCA to the situation in the past and adds the

trend factors to this equation, the result should show that trends have been realized in the CCA of the present, provided that the CCAs are not too far apart or close together. For example, if the results of the trend analysis do not match up with the previously assessed postincident level of security (the trend should have been positive but the security level of the ex-post CCA is lower than before), this informs the researcher that the effective power of one or more stakeholders and/or the effect of hazards have been misevaluated in the previous steps (CCA and AGIRI).

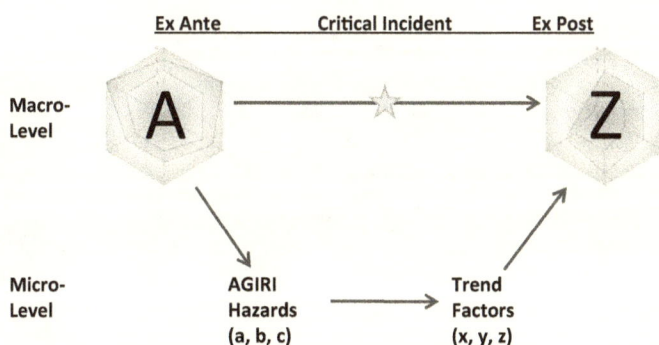

Figure 8.4   Applying Trend Factors for Assumptions Check

Box 8.2   H-AID Trend Factors Assumptions Check

Step 1: conduct a CCA for the ex-ante and the ex-post situation following the steps outlined in chapter 5.

Step 2: conduct an AGIRI of all stakeholders of the ex-ante situation following the steps outlined in chapter 6.

Step 3: calculate the effective power of all stakeholders for the context dimension of the ex-ante situation.

Step 4: calculate the effect of potential hazards for the context dimension of the ex-ante situation.

Step 5: add all effective powers and hazard effects to the level of security of the context dimension of the ex-ante CCA.

Step 6: repeat steps 3–5 for the other context dimensions.

Step 7: compare whether the trends projected onto the ex-ante CCA point into the same direction as the developments analyzed in the ex-post CCA. If this is not the case, go back to your assessment of effective power of the stakeholders and the effects of the hazards.

This formal check should not be considered as precise measure. As explained before, the trends are vectors pointing into a direction and not at an end point. Since the effects of trend factors take time to unfold, trends might not yet be detectable if ex-post/ex-ante CCAs are too close together. It provides, however, a structured approach to check one's assumptions regarding the context and the stakeholders. Keep in mind, for the purpose of assumptions checking, it is important that one can use the trend factor information (i.e., information about AGIRI and hazards) from the ex-ante period only and not from the ex-post period. Otherwise, one would project the present capacities of actors and hazards onto the CCA of the past, which would not yield the desired results.

REVIEW QUESTIONS

- Which analytical steps form the baseline for the H-AID Trend Factor Analysis?
- Which trend factors inform the trends?
- How do you assess the impact of a hazard?
- How can trend factors help to check assumptions about ex-ante/ex-post relationships?
- What are the limits of the assumptions check using trend factors?

NOTES

1. Liesbet Heyse, Andrej Zwitter, Rapahel Wittek, and Joost Herman, *Humanitarian Crises, Intervention and Security: A Framework for Evidence-Based Programming* (London: Routledge, 2014).

2. The software can be downloaded at: http://humanitarianintelligence.net.

3. J. E. Daniell, B. Khazai, and F. Wenzel, "Uncovering the 2010 Haiti Earthquake Death Toll," *Natural Hazards and Earth System Sciences Discussions* 1, no. 3 (2013): 1913–42.

4. In Appendix 8.1, for those interested in what the mathematics behind this looks like, a more detailed formula for the calculation of the trend for the individual aspects can found. Please also note that the software combines the multiplication of Goals and Salience into one step only. This means Salience is then a range from −1 to 1 depending on whether it affects the context dimension negatively or positively.

Chapter 9

Operational Planning and Forecasting

Operational planning tools complement the analytical tools discussed in the previous chapters. These tools are meant to incorporate the intelligence generated in the analysis stage into project hypothesis underlying the humanitarian operation. Operational planning tools presuppose that the humanitarian analyst has already conducted his or her research, as well as collected and analyzed the data to generate information. The analyst has now reached a point at which intelligence (i.e., actionable information) has to be distilled from information. The purpose of these tools is to assist in the creation of actionable information necessary in the planning stage by looking into core elements of a humanitarian operation, namely:

1. Entry stage: (9.1) Force Field Analysis and (9.2) Entry Point Identification
2. Operations stage: (9.3) Worst Case Anticipation and (9.4) Scenario Planning
3. Concluding stage: (9.5) Exit Strategy Assessment

These three stages assume that the humanitarian analyst has already conducted thorough context and stakeholder analyses to prepare the groundwork for the operational planning.

9.1 FORCE FIELD ANALYSIS

Force field analysis is a simple yet powerful decision-making tool that maps the forces for and against change with regards to the specific policy or project planned. Thereby, one becomes more aware of the driving and constraining factors that will eventually inform operational planning and strategic

Driving forces	Strength	Agency control	Total Force		Total Force	Agency control	Strength	Restraining forces
Dropping prices of food products	2	2	4	Food Production and Sustainable Agriculture	4	2	2	Decreasing agency budget
Better agricultural techniques and processing	2	4	6		6	1	5	Irregular annual precipitation
Improved operational planning	4	5	9		8	4	4	Poor procedures for hiring and paying field workers
Increasing public support	2	2	4		8	3	5	Losses to fires and grazing

Figure 9.1 Force Field Analysis Example Adapted from Food and Agriculture Organization (FAO) Regarding Food Production and Sustainable Agriculture Programs. *Note*: Ben Ramalingam, *Tools for Knowledge and Learning: A Guide for Development and Humanitarian Organisations, Rapid – Research and Policy in Development* (London: Overseas Development Institute (ODI), 2006), 33, http://www.odi.org/publications/153-tools-knowledge-learning-guide-development-humanitarian-organisations.

decision-making. The theory of force fields was initially developed by Kurt Lewin in 1951. The analytical tool that has been developed on this basis is widely used for the planning and implementation of change in the management of programs.[1]

For the purpose of a proper force field analysis, the analysts must exhaustively list the forces that surround the decision-making area or policy. As it is the case with many brainstorming techniques, this kind of analysis is best conducted in a small group of five to eight people. A further step in the analysis is the weighing of the forces among each other by either assigning a value (5 for strong, 1 for weak) or using dense ranking for a more nuanced approach. In dense ranking, items receive a number depending on how they compare to other items. For the purpose of force field analysis, start numbering the weakest force with 1 and work your way up. For example, if force A ranks stronger than forces B and C (which are equal in force), both stronger than force D, then the ranking looks as follows: D = 1; B,C = 2; A = 3. In addition to the forces for and against a certain issue area, the analytical team can also decide to add a third column detailing the agencies' control over the force (see Figure 9.1).

Once the analyst has got a good overview about the positive and negative forces that surround a certain issue area by listing and weighing all relevant forces, the force field analysis can contribute to decision-making and planning of humanitarian operations by informing the analyst which forces can be used to further the project, program, or policy and which forces need to be overcome. Ideally positive forces can be used to overcome negative forces.

The steps in Box 9.1 describe the process of force field analysis.[2]

Box 9.1   Force Field Analysis

Step 1: define the problem, goal, or change clearly and concisely.

Step 2: use a form of brainstorming to identify the main factors that will influence the issue.

Step 3: make one list showing the strongest forces for and against the problem, goal, or change.

Step 4: array the positive forces in one column of the table and parallel to it the negative forces in another column.

Step 5: assign a value to each factor indicating its strength vis-à-vis the other factors by assigning a value between 1 and 5 or by dense ranking.

Step 6: calculate the total score for each list to determine whether the forces for or against a problem, goal, or change are dominant.

Step 7: examine the two lists to determine if any of the forces neutralize each other and can therefore be neglected.

Step 8: analyze the lists to determine how changes in forces might affect the overall outcome.

9.2   ENTRY POINT IDENTIFICATION

Everybody is implicitly aware that a bad start can reflect on the success of an overall project. Thus, one of the first problems one encounters when planning an intervention is the question of where to start it. This question is more critical than one initially assumes, because it rests on implicit assumptions that need to be made explicit. Entry point identification (EPI) tries to answer key questions to make the start to any project a success. In order to be of any aid to a good project start, EPI needs to answer at least questions that concern the base of operations, logistical routes, cooperation and implementation partners, and possible threat factors. In general, the humanitarian analyst needs to be able to answer questions regarding strategic planning and tactical planning. The strategic-level entry point questions are of a more general nature, whereas the tactical-level entry point questions translate strategic objectives into practice. The operational-level elements concern the day-to-day practice and require an operational awareness (called "battlefield awareness" in military circles), that is, up-to-date local intelligence.

9.2.1   Strategic-Level Entry Points

As mentioned above, in this stage the humanitarian analyst should be able to answer the strategic-level questions associated with EPI on the basis of already present information. In essence, as with other planning tools, EPI is not a tool of analysis but of decision-making. Hence, the following questions aim to give concrete answers for strategic-level decisions:

- Basic questions:
  - What are the humanitarian needs? (Context analysis—chapters 4 and 5)
  - How and where are the vulnerable populations? (Stakeholder analysis—chapters 6 and 7)
  - What are the parameters and the mandates of the humanitarian operation? (LogFrame—chapter 2)

- Location questions:
  - Where do we locate the humanitarian operation?
  - What infrastructure is necessary to conduct the humanitarian operation to ensure the sustainable flow of resources necessary to conduct the project?

- Actor questions:
  - Who are partners to cooperate with, and who are actors to stay away from? (See specifically step 8 of Box 7.1 in chapter 7)
  - Which cross-cultural elements would facilitate or hamper the initial access and eventual success of a humanitarian operation? (See specifically section 6.2.2.4)

- Identity questions:
  - How do we ensure humanitarian principles and humanitarian space? (Chapters 6 and 7)
  - What kind of profile with regard to the humanitarian agency's identity (low/high profile) would be most beneficial from the very onset of the humanitarian operation with regard to minimizing risks and maximizing benefits?

9.2.2   Tactical-Level Questions

With regard to the tactical level, the European Interagency Security Forum has developed a comprehensive guide around the questions surrounding the opening of offices in the field.[3] Figure 9.2 summarizes the most important elements that need to be taken care of. It differentiates the entry stage into three phases: (1) planning phase; (2) acquisition phase; (3) preoperations phase. The manual prepared by the European Interagency Security Forum (EISF) contains a lot of important guidance and is highly recommended. For the purpose of EPI I will refer only to elements of the first phase.

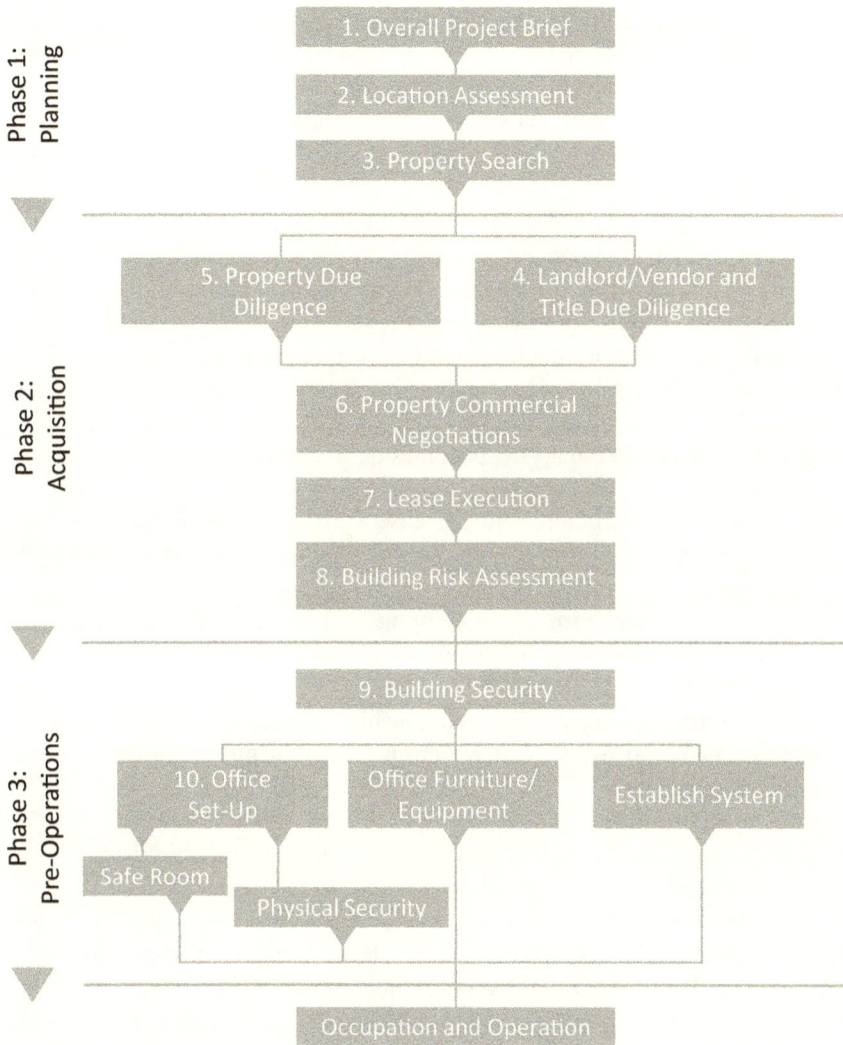

Figure 9.2   Office Opening Process and Key Factors. *Note: Source* 8, "Office Opening: A Guide for Non-Governmental Organisations," EISF publication (European Interagency Security Forum, March 12, 2015), 4; https://www.eisf.eu/library/officeopening/.

In the planning phase, the humanitarian analysis and planning team should develop an overall project brief, which contains key information relevant for the choice of the location based on the project parameters. Crucially, this starts with a brainstorming session to identify the sine qua non requirements, that is, conditions without which the project cannot start. Typically, such conditions include elements that are always present, such as electricity, infrastructure, and telecommunication facilities, and elements that are project specific, such as proximity to local authorities and proximity for public health infrastructure. This then leads to developing an idea of what kind of premises are needed.

In this regard, it is indispensable to understand the local context (see chapters 4 and 5)—the context will also define the kind of facilities that are necessary—for example, if it becomes cold at night, heating might be necessary; if gender-based violence is an issue, the toilets might not be located outside the premises or should at least be somehow protected and well lit; certain neighborhoods might be avoided due to crime. At the national and regional level the following checklist, against which to check the information acquired in the context analysis, becomes quite useful:[4]

- the national infrastructure and the ease with which personnel, supplies, and equipment travel into country as well as ease of movement within the country itself;
- health facilities and current or emerging health risks, telecommunications and Internet networks and providers, power generation, utilities, and power supply reliability;
- security infrastructure and the relationships between security institutions such as police, army, special police, presidential guards, tribal factions, warlords and militia;
- political environment;
- natural elements such as hurricanes, rainy season, or seismic risk;
- religious issues;
- rule of law programs;
- potential strategic upheavals such as elections or successions that may change the landscape while the program is running;
- economic factors such as currency fluctuation and inflation, as they may affect the stability (current and future) of a country;
- national payment regulations such as withholding taxes or the inability to remove money out of country, or restrictions on receiving payments from external countries;
- taxation—what regulations/restrictions exist that can benefit or hinder the agency, especially the process of setting up and registering a legal entity? (also bear in mind local nuances or customary dealings that will affect timeliness);
- corruption—endemic in some contexts, this will invariably have an impact on conducting negotiations, transactions, or even operations and threaten the organization's reputation;

- the level of education—ascertain the ease with which it is possible to source and train local staff/volunteers;
- national employment law should be investigated as it might affect HR management.

At the local level, the general considerations the humanitarian analyst should address are:

1. *Security*: Crime and political violence are events to be reckoned with. Given the fact that humanitarian operations entail expensive equipment and valuables, the site selection matters to reduce the likelihood of crime for profit. The neighborhood is also of relevance with regard to political violence, particularly if in the vicinity embassies of unpopular governments or UN buildings are located, and there is a history of protests or attacks on such buildings. Furthermore, perception management is also a matter to be considered. Having one's headquarters in the vicinity of organizations that are unpopular might taint the humanitarian organization's fame and make collaboration with the local population difficult.
2. *Real Estate*: "You should ask the question: Which neighborhood offers the quality of property best suited to the agency's needs and reputation?"[5]
3. *Utilities*: Water, food, power (alternatively reliable generators), and uninterrupted communications and connectivity are key prerequisites of a successful project execution.
4. *Environment*: Natural hazards (earthquakes, floods, etc.) might be an issue. In these cases, the building should provide adequate protection.
5. *Local Ethnic Affiliations*: Intergroup, intertribal, or clan relationships might result in tensions when a third external actor with little local help is added to the equilibrium. Knowledge of these relationships as well as customs and protocols between them might be crucial to avoid allegations of favoritism. For example, a humanitarian organization operating in Somaliland rented an office from one group and ensured to rent the warehouse from another ethnic group in order to avoid negative allegations.

Appendix 9.1 provides a form developed by the EISF to support the thinking process about an organization's needs regarding premises.

EPI, as already mentioned, is not an analytical tool, but a decision-making tool on the strategic and tactical level by the use of guiding questions. It is important that the analyst remains aware of this difference. Being a decision-making tool means that the analyst has to have already conducted a thorough context and stakeholder analysis. If the analyst would skip the analysis and simply search for the information to answer the guiding questions, the findings might be biased or skewed, since, differently from context and stakeholder analytical tools, decision-making tools are not built on an extensive sociological fundament necessary to deduce unbiased and objective original findings.

9.3   WORST CASE ANTICIPATION

The three tools summarized in this section are related to scenario building and do not develop the full narrative of a scenario based on contextual forces, but rather depart from the project itself as a starting point. The best way to generate ideas for worst case anticipation is the brainstorming method in a group with mixed expertise (technical, contextual, logistical, etc.). Worst case anticipation utilizes brainstorming methods based on conflictual antici- pation and critique of project assumptions similarly to a dialectic approach (thesis/antithesis)—a form of constructive conflict. Research has shown that these approaches lead to quicker and better decisions than, for example, free discussions and consensus building. In free discussions and consensus building the probability to come to faulty decisions is higher than in conflic- tual approaches, because consensus-seeking groups prefer group harmony over critical evaluation. While consensus building, a quite frequently used approach in managerial decision-making, supports free expression in groups, it does not provide formal procedures for testing and evaluating the state- ments formulated through consensus. There are, of course, downsides to the conflictual approach; for example, individuals might feel defeated and demeaned. Furthermore, distance, distrust, and suspicion between team mem- bers might inhibit future teamwork. A structural approach to conflict-based methods helps to mitigate some of these effects in comparison to free floating conflictual discussions, and it reduces the emotional identification with ideas.

The following three tools provide a structural approach to conflict-based worst case anticipation: critical failures checklist, point of no return analysis, and devil's advocacy. The critical failures checklist is the most structural of these tools and provides the most guidance for the brainstorming process.

9.3.1   Critical Failures Checklist

Differently than devil's advocacy, the critical failures checklist is an approach that can be done with the whole team and does not necessitate two adversary groups. It is most useful once the general parameters of the projects are clear, the entry point is assessed, and logistical cornerstones are set—in other words, it is of particular use during the planning process before the project parameters are set in stone. Its basic aim is to test all project components for their susceptibility to critical failures. Critical failures are project internal or

Table 9.1 Critical Failures Checklist

Project Component		Critical Failure	Likelihood		Counter measure	Feasibility	Explanation
A. Transportation							
	a.1	road block	low	a.1/1	pay-off	high	
	a.2	road flooded	high	a.2/1	alternate route	low	no direct routes
				a.2/2	air transport	medium	costly
B. Security							
	b.1	theft	medium	b.1/1	install security measures	high	
	b.2	armed robbery	low	b.2/1	provide security to staff	high	decreases acceptance and access
C. ...							
	c.1	...	...	...	...	...	

external problems that endanger the whole mission success and/or the safety and security of the staff.

Since every project has several components, which are susceptible to critical failures in a different way and to a different degree, it is worthwhile to isolate these components in a project first. Furthermore, not every component is equally susceptible to critical failures. Sometimes, it might turn out that a project component contains many possible critical failures. Particularly, if a few of the critical failures are very likely regarding a specific project component and/or countermeasures to the critical failures are unfeasible, then one might want to consider exchanging the project component for another alternate component that is less susceptible to critical failures. Table 9.1 helps to assess the critical failures and develop countermeasures.

9.3.2   Point of No Return

A point of no return is a point in time or a condition of a project after which the commitment costs have reached a point where stopping the project is costlier than finishing it. Establishing a point of no return for a project is crucial, as this determines also the point before which "return" is feasible and advisable if the costs of proceeding are prohibitively high. Being aware of this point of no return is important to avoid an escalation of commitment; this is the pattern of behavior in which actors continuously rationalize actions

Box 9.2   Point of No Return Assessment

Step 1: develop the project implementation time Gantt chart (see section 4.2.2).

Step 2: calculate the costs involved over time and per Gantt chart item.

Step 3: identify the point in time when the costs of continuous commitment are becoming higher than the expected result.

Step 4: during the project execution monitor ongoing vis-à-vis projected total project costs, and if necessary readjust the estimations of remaining costs in view of the point of no return.

and decisions while incurring increasingly negative results. In other words, an escalation of commitment occurs when actors prefer persistence over withdrawal as well as over other changes in the course of action. This form of commitment bias is sometimes facilitated by the faulty arguments, among many possible others,[6] that the already invested costs justify or even require a persistence in course so that the time invested is not wasted, or because of personal identification with the project or compassion with the people. It is often perpetuated by an expectation that no further obstacles will be coming up. Commitment bias might also be facilitated by the familiarity with the decision-making context, particularly if a new course of action would intro- duce a new decision-making context.

Particularly in humanitarian operations, the point of no return analysis might be criticized for seemingly putting a value on the life of beneficiaries when considering the consequences of commitments beyond the point of no return. However, one should always consider that the ethical obligations of a humanitarian organization concern both beneficiaries and staff members. Furthermore, reputational damage of an organization can also prevent future projects and even undo the results of good projects if the beneficiaries (in the sense of stakeholders in the project) cannot rely on the professional execution of projects through this humanitarian organization anymore.

When conducting step 3, also take into consideration reputational dam- age, as well as risk to safety and security of staff vis-à-vis the negative effect that altering the course of a project or its discontinuation would have for the beneficiaries. In order to assess the costs of an alternate course for the project implementation, resort to scenario planning (see section 9.4).

9.3.3   Devil's Advocacy

Devil's advocacy is a conflict-based approach in which an adversary team crit- icizes the analytic judgments and the project assumptions of a humanitarian

Box 9.3   Devil's Advocacy[8]

Step 1: identify a problem needing group analysis and decision-making.

Step 2: divide the group or team into two equally sized subgroups. Assign one subgroup to play devil's advocate (DA subgroup) and the other to develop an affirmative recommendation (AR group).

Step 3: after separating into subgroups, instruct the AR group to develop a set of recommendations and build an argument for them, supported by all key assumptions, facts, and data that underlie them. That group writes out the recommendations, assumptions, facts, and data on a white board or on large piece of paper. Meanwhile, instruct the DA subgroup to prepare for their critique by discussing the case and identifying critical assumptions, data, and facts the other group might miss.

Step 4: then, join both subgroups together. Instruct the AR subgroup to present its recommendations and assumptions to the DA subgroup, which critiques the recommendations, attempting to uncover all that is wrong with the recommendations, assumptions, facts, and data and explaining why the recommendations should not be adopted.

Step 5: then, separate the subgroups again so that the AR group revises its recommendations to answer the critiques, while the DA group works to find more critiques that would strengthen the recommendation.

Step 6: repeat steps 4 and 5 until both subgroups can accept the recommendations, assumptions, and data.

Step 7: once both subgroups agree on a recommended solution, move forward and enact the recommendations.

project or a decision to be taken. It is a tool that is preferably used before a final decision has been taken. Devil's advocacy helps to identify factors that can go wrong by building the strongest arguments against the proposed course of action and its prospect of achieving the final result. This often happens by examining critical assumptions and sources of risk and uncertainty and by trying to anticipate surprise. It is usually recommended to start with the strategic goals of the project and the underlying assumptions by identifying gaps, mistakes in the project logic, or too rigid cause-and-effect chains (i.e., where causes and effects are too naturally assumed without allowing for alternate narratives).[7] The devil's advocacy tool promotes diversity and mitigates tendencies toward conformity.

For the purpose of a more structural approach to devil's advocacy, Hartwig has developed step-by-step instructions as shown in Box 9.3.

In contrast to the relatively modest approach to avoid homogeneity through the devil's advocacy, a related but more sophisticated approach, the system of multiple advocacy, additionally addresses the problem of pathological conflict among the advisors. This approach requires a moderating third party in addition to the subgroups to objectively evaluate the pros and cons of different argumentative lines. "In addition to balancing actor resources and maintaining the rules for effective multiple advocacy, the executive must consider how to define his or her own role. When making use of multiple advocacy, the executive should adopt the stands of the magistrates—one who listens to the arguments made, evaluates them, poses issues and asks questions, and finally judges which action to take either from among those articulated by advocates or as formulated independently by himself or herself after hearing them."[9] Furthermore, it is recommended to have more than two subgroups trying to develop alternative views regarding propositions, hypotheses, and project assumptions. For the rest follow the steps described for devil's advocacy.

9.4   SCENARIO PLANNING

During the implementation phase of projects, humanitarian analysts and decision-makers need to remain aware of the changes in their environment. How to identify changes and what to do next (the famous plan B) form the core of another set of tools described with the label "scenario planning." The main purpose of scenario planning is to prepare the humanitarian organization for the expected by reducing the unexpected through developing multiple plausible futures. There are more than two dozen techniques of scenario planning available; however, one dominates the field, namely, the matrix approach developed by Royal Dutch Shell/Global Business Network (GBN) (see section 9.4.2).

For the purpose of the present chapter, let us define a "scenario" as *a possible alternative future relevant for the humanitarian organization with specific focus on the humanitarian project embedded in its context and stakeholder field.* The reason why scenario planning is important particularly for humanitarian organizations is that these operate in complex contexts, which by their very nature produce a lot of uncertainties. Scenario planning helps to reduce these uncertainties by scoping possible scenarios and helping to prepare for them. In general, despite the variety of tools, there are generic elements and steps that are always relevant when conducting some sort of foresight project. This starts with the framing of the project and collecting information about the context. It proceeds with forecasting alternative futures and envisioning preferred futures for the basis of a plan of action to achieve the preferred future. Bishop, Hines, and Collins summarize these reoccurring generic elements in Table 9.2.

Table 9.2   A Generic Approach to a Comprehensive Foresight Project by Bishop, Hines, and Collins*

Step	Description	Product
Framing	Scoping the project: attitude, audience, work environment, rationale, purpose, objectives, and teams	Project plan
Scanning	Collecting information: the system, history, and context of the issue and how to scan for information regarding the future of the issue	Information
Forecasting	Describing baseline and alternate futures: drivers and uncertainties, implications, and outcomes	Baseline and alternate futures (scenarios)
Visioning	Choosing a preferred future: envisioning the best outcomes, goal-setting, performance measures	Preferred future (goals)
Planning	Organizing the resources: strategy, options, and plans	Strategic plan (strategies)
Acting	Implementing the plan: communicating the results, developing action agendas, and institutionalizing strategic thinking and intelligence systems	Action plan (initiatives)

*Peter Bishop, Andy Hines, and Terry Collins, "The Current State of Scenario Development: An Overview of Techniques," *Foresight* 9, no. 1 (2007): 7.

The different tools of scenario planning range from intuitive narratives (based on unaided judgments) to structural qualitative approaches to quantitative and formal modeling.

One form of unaided group judgment is a role-playing exercise. In this form of scenario development, a group of people is putting themselves into the shoes of those whose future they want to predict as well as their stakeholders. The participants have to assume the role and its context to accurately portray the behavior of the simulated actor. Most commonly role-playing is used in emergency preparedness and in dangerous technical missions. It is less useful for forecasting long-term contextual developments that contain a lot of actors, chiefly because every player also brings to the table their own vision and emotions. This leads to a low reliability and validity as such complex long-term scenarios are hardly reproducible through this method.

Wildcards are one of the most persistent problems in complex contexts. Nonlinearity and complex adaptive systems are evidence pointing at these wildcards. They may be described as surprising factors that have the power to completely change the scenario, such as discontinuous events like natural disasters or coup d'états, discontinuities with significant unintended consequences, like the Arab Spring destabilizing the Middle East and North Africa, or factors functioning as catalysts and accelerant of present developments. Wildcards are inherently difficult to predict, if predictable at all; however, using a set of wildcards based on the present context helps in generating

ideas of what needs to change in the project development in order to accom-
modate a certain range of game changers. Markley's new classification of
wildcard types helps thinking of possible intervening events (type V added
by the author):

1. Type I: low probability, high impact, high credibility
2. Type II: high probability, high impact, low credibility
3. Type III: high probability, high impact, disputed credibility
4. Type IV: high probability, high impact, high credibility
5. Type V: low probability, high impact, low credibility

Disputed or low credibility (type I and II) might be the result of: active or
passive disbelief, denial, disinformation, taboo, censorship, disrepute.[10]

9.4.1   Baseline, Best Case, Worst Case, and Indicators

The simplest technique that also provides the basis for other techniques is the
development of baseline, best case and worst case scenarios with the help of
drivers from the known PESTLE-H or the STEEP categories (social, technological, ecological, economic, political). Equally valid and quite overlapping
are the context dimensions of the H-AID methodology: environment, health,
political, economic, social-cultural, and food dimension. The advantage of
using the H-AID methodology dimensions is the possibility to use the indicator lists for each dimension and the provided set of human rights norms in
Appendices 5.1 and 5.2. Working through these indicators and key questions
will help the analyst define the key drivers of stability and of change.

Constructing best/worst case and baseline scenarios (as well as alternative
scenarios) requires analyzing the key driving forces and uncertainties through
interviews with scenario teams and key decision-makers. In order to distinguish key driving forces from uncertainties, the following two questions are
very useful:

> *Which key forces seem inevitable or pre-determined?* These are trends already
> in the pipeline that are unlikely to vary significantly in any of the scenarios. [...]
> *Which forces are most likely to define or significantly change the nature
> or direction of the scenarios?* This assessment should be measured by two
> criteria—how uncertain are you of its outcome and how important is it to your
> organization?[11]

Once the analyst has determined these factors, it is necessary to assess their
impact on the project relevant scenario—are they drivers of change or drivers
of stability for the baseline future?

Table 9.3   Baseline, Best/Worst-Case Scenario Template

Project Context	Worst Case	Baseline	Best Case	Alternative 1	Alternative 2
Economic	−	=	+	=	+
Social-Cultural	+	+	+	+	=
Health	−	=	=	−	=
Food	−	−	=	=	−
Environment	−	=	=	−	=
Political	=	+	+	=	+

In general, it makes sense to start by constructing a *baseline future* (most likely future) and exploring derivations of it. Also called "official future," the baseline scenario usually connotes "a plausible and relatively non-threatening scenario, featuring no surprising changes to the current environment and continued stable growth."[12] The baseline scenario forms the starting point for several techniques. One alternative way of developing a baseline scenario is using the Trend Factor Analysis (chapter 8).

In order to construct the different scenarios, one constructs a table by listing the key drivers in a column and by evaluating them: [+] for strong/improving; [−] for weak/worsening; [=] for stable/unchanged. Table 9.3 provides the template for such an analysis. It is worthwhile to keep the baseline in the middle and to the right and the left, respectively, add the columns for the worst case and the best case scenarios. It is important to note that the alternatives one develops do not need to fall to either side of the baseline future, that is, that they represent a natural stage of progression between baseline and best/worst case. They can be alternative futures in their own right.

Indicators are very helpful when monitoring the change in these scenarios toward another scenario. Appendix 5.1 provides indicators for each of the context dimensions. However, it is important to select the right indicators for the purpose of monitoring. Heuer and Pherson, two of the key figures in intelligence analysis, propose that besides *reliability* and *validity* (see chapter 3), indicators should be:

Observable and Collectable: Indicators to which the analyst has no access due to the lack of data are redundant. However, some indicators can be substituted by proxy indicators, that is, secondary indicators that are causally connected to the primary indicator and are bound to change similarly, for

Box 9.4   Baseline/Best Case/Worst Case Scenarios

Step 1: define the focal area and the project context including its parameters.

Step 2: assess the key forces of stability and change by looking at your context data (with a view at the indicators and key questions in Appendix 5.1) based on the following two questions:

- Which key forces seem inevitable or predetermined?
- Which forces are most likely to define or significantly change the nature or direction of the scenarios?

Step 3: organize the key forces into four to eight groups or into the context dimensions (i.e., the rows in Table 9.3).

Step 4: write a brief description of the key forces and assign indicators.

Step 5: compile the scenario matrix, including at least baseline, best case, and worst case, as well as one alternate scenario in the header line and the dimensions or key drivers in the first column.

Step 6a: generate the scenarios by assigning the values +, =, and – to each column.

   Note: When using key drivers (rather than dimensions), not every scenario will relate to these key drivers. In these cases leave the value cell empty.

Step 6b: if necessary reconsider key drivers descriptive of a specific scenario.

Step 7a: assign indicators for each key driver or dimension with a view to observability, collectability, stability, and uniqueness.

Step 7b: if necessary reconsider indicators descriptive of a specific scenario.

Step 8: write a short scenario narrative (300–500 words) describing the characteristics of the scenario and the progression toward it.

Step 9: assess the implications of each scenario for the project success and highlight necessary adjustments in project parameters.

example, a common proxy indicator for quality of life is per-capita Gross Domestic Product (GDP).

Stable: An indicator must remain a valid and reliable measure of the specific phenomenon over time. If it ceases to be representative of a scenario or phenomenon or becomes valid only in its final stages, then its usefulness to anticipating surprise is limited.

Unique: An indicator should be specific for the scenario it predicts. If it predicts several scenarios, its diagnosticity is limited. In that case, it might be necessary to use other indicators within the context dimension or indicators in other dimensions to determine toward which scenario the situation is developing.[13]

9.4.2 GBN Matrix

The GBN matrix or "double uncertainty" method is one of the most commonly used tools for scenario planning. Developed by Peter Schwartz in his book *The Art of the Long View* for Global Business Network,[14] the popularity of this method in part stems from its relatively simple approach (at least from its outset) and the limitation to four scenarios.

In the center of the GPN matrix stand two axes that represent the most important uncertainties concerning the context in which the project is placed. These axes should represent the most important drivers of uncertainty, which are not dependent on each other. A SWOT analysis (chapter 4) or the analysis of the context through H-AID framework by using the indicator list should help to identify these key drivers of uncertainty. Combining the two factors in their extreme expressions on the axis results in four possible scenario kernels in the four squares of the matrix, on the basis of which the analyst then has to develop narratives (see Figure 9.3). One might think that reducing a complex context to two variables would do harm to the analysis by oversimplification. However, the complexity comes back in when one starts fleshing out the four scenarios in more detail for the narrative.

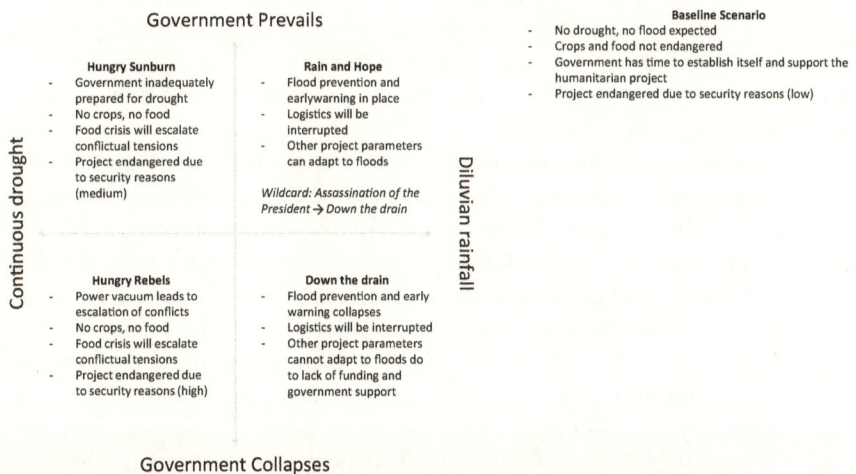

Baseline Scenario
- No drought, no flood expected
- Crops and food not endangered
- Government has time to establish itself and support the humanitarian project
- Project endangered due to security reasons (low)

Government Prevails

Hungry Sunburn
- Government inadequately prepared for drought
- No crops, no food
- Food crisis will escalate conflictual tensions
- Project endangered due to security reasons (medium)

Rain and Hope
- Flood prevention and earlywarning in place
- Logistics will be interrupted
- Other project parameters can adapt to floods

Wildcard: Assassination of the President → Down the drain

Hungry Rebels
- Power vacuum leads to escalation of conflicts
- No crops, no food
- Food crisis will escalate conflictual tensions
- Project endangered due to security reasons (high)

Down the drain
- Flood prevention and early warning collapses
- Logistics will be interrupted
- Other project parameters cannot adapt to floods do to lack of funding and government support

Continuous drought / *Diluvian rainfall*

Government Collapses

Figure 9.3 GBN Matrix for Hypothetical Humanitarian Project, including Baseline Scenario and Wildcard

Box 9.5   GBN Matrix for Scenario Building

Step 1: conduct a context analysis for the specific project context.

Step 2: from the context analysis deduce the key forces of stability through this question: Which key forces seem inevitable or predetermined?

Step 3: construct the baseline future narrative on the basis of these key forces.

Step 4: from the context analysis deduce the key forces of change through this question: Which forces are most likely to define or significantly change the nature or direction of the scenarios?

Step 5: select the two most important forces of change/instability and draw a matrix, in which these forces stand in the center of a continuum between two extreme outcomes for each uncertainty.

Step 6: develop scenario narratives on the basis of other relevant factors and variables around the resulting four squares in the matrix and give them catchy titles.

Step 7: identify possible wildcards and try to see how they fit or do not fit into either of the four squares of the matrix.

Step 8: analyze how the scenarios will influence your project framework and plot courses of action (including exit strategies if relevant; see 9.5).

9.4.3   Manoa Technique

The Manoa approach was developed by Wendy Schutz at the University of Hawai in 1991 for long-term policy planning.[15] Rather than focusing on drivers of change, the Manoa approach aims to reveal opportunity spaces that uncertainties create by emphasizing a "maximising difference" through a focus on emerging issues. As a method, this focus on opportunity spaces separates it from other methods.[16]

In order to achieve this, the process starts with the triangulation of at least three different emergent issues, currently detectable in the STEEP, PESTLE-H, or the H-AID categories, respectively. The further these emergent issues are distinct from each other, the better the resulting analysis will be triangulated. Highly orthogonal starting points reduce the likelihood of weak triangulation caused by interdependent variables and increase the creative space between the emergent issues. The next step is to explore their impact cascade over primary impacts, which in turn result in secondary impacts, these in tertiary, and so on. For example, the emergent issues of "drought" and "food shortage" are mutually interdependent; as one forms the basis of the other, one is the primary or secondary impact of the other, thereby reducing the creative space between the two. An example of relatively independent

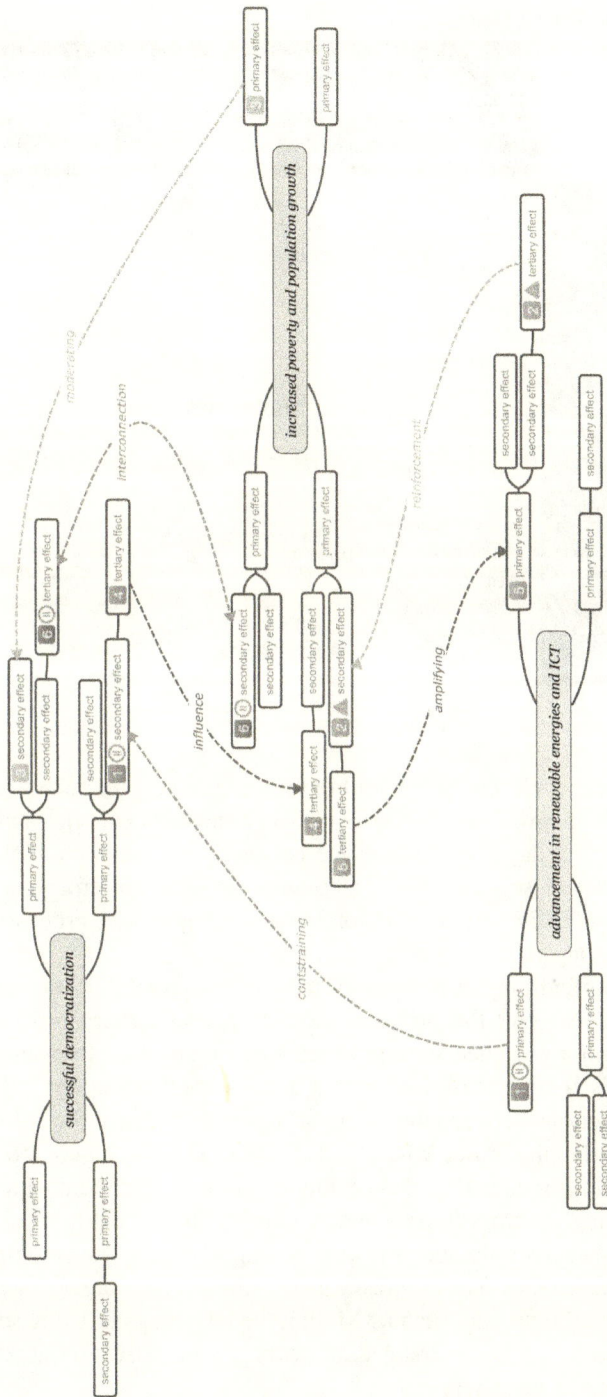

Figure 9.4 Futures Wheel Sample Diagram with Indications of Interactions and Interconnections

Table 9.4   Cross Impact Matrix

	successful democratization	increased poverty and population growth	advancement in renewable energies and ICT
successful democratization	Effects of the futures wheel	Political violence by disenfranchised workers	International energy trade with Western nations / stricter internet regulation
increased poverty and population growth	Polarization of political parties / nationalization of domestic and intern. policy	Effects of the futures wheel	???
advancement in renewable energies and ICT	Moving from development aid recipient to donor – extending extra territorial soft power	General access to internet and electricity but internal digital divide	Effects of the futures wheel

emergent issues would be "successful democratization," "increased poverty and population growth," and "advancement in renewable energies and ICT"; these three form a larger creation space between each other to allow for a more diverse set of scenarios. It is recommendable to use emergent issues from different STEEP, PESTLE-H, or H-AID categories in order to maximize this creation space.

Similar to a mind map or a problem tree (see chapter 4.3.2), the mapping of emergent issues and the primary, secondary, and tertiary order effects is being done in a so-called futures wheel (see Figure 9.4). In essence, this *futures wheel* is composed of overlapping mind maps that map the influences and interconnections between the emergent issues and their effects. Between them is an overlapping space where various order effects can collide. These collisions amplify or constrain change and help identify different patterns for scenario building. A cross-impact matrix (similar to the relational analysis, see chapter 5.4) assists the identification of amplifying or constraining collisions (see Table 9.4). The futures wheel can easily be created with any software for mind mapping, such as Xmind; the advantage of using software is that the effects can be rearranged as necessary to cluster influences and interconnections as necessary.

Box 9.6   Manoa Technique

Step 1: use the STEEP, PESTLE-H, or H-AID categories to identify three or more emerging issues of change; state them as mature conditions for the end of your time horizon.

Step 2: create the *futures wheel* by drawing up the three or more emerging issues and their primary-, secondary-, and tertiary-order effects (or even more if necessary):
- *Step 2a*: brainstorm at least five primary-order effects, by pushing them to their extreme logical conclusions.
- *Step 2b*: brainstorm at least three secondary-order effects using the same logic.
- *Step 2c*: brainstorm one or two tertiary-order effects using the same logic.

Step 3: identify the influences and interconnections between effects of different emerging issues; if necessary redraw/restructure the effects in the *futures wheel* to cluster logically the influences that connect different effects.

Step 3a: create a cross-impact matrix in order to assist the thought process of interactions and synergies between different emerging issues of change; if necessary, develop new primary and secondary effects connecting the findings of the cross-impact matrix with the emerging issue.

Step 3b: refine your analysis by asking the following questions:
- What changes might amplify or accelerate other changes?
- What changes might balance or constrain other changes?
- What causal loops emerge as a result?

Step 4: use effects, influences, and interconnections to develop scenario kernels by imagining catchy titles to describe different scenarios.

Step 5: develop narratives for each of the titles on the basis of the scenario kernels; try to describe "a day in the life" of your project/program within each of these scenarios; try to reflect how these scenarios impact on your project/program implementation.

Step 6: double check whether you have stretched the projection of scenarios far enough by challenging your current project assumptions, by combining changes and impacts to distort familiar processes in the presence, or by modifying constraints/threats as well as strengths/opportunities you currently take for granted.

Step 7: ask what these scenarios mean for the project implementation and the project assumptions in practice; which indicators can identify the emergence of either of these scenarios; which measures have to be taken if either of these scenarios occurs (the plan B).

9.5   EXIT STRATEGY ASSESSMENT

9.5.1   Humanitarian Criteria for Exit Strategies

When it comes to office closure, a well-developed exit strategy is of prime importance, particularly since in this last phase the humanitarian organization faces the highest risk in terms of theft, sabotage, pressure from suppliers (also local ones), interference by government and tax officials, demands for "favours" by corrupt officers, etc. To have enough time to respond to unexpected events and to have an exit strategy that mitigates these risks is therefore indispensable.[17]

In order to determine an appropriate exit strategy, the World Food Programme operates with different triggers that initiate corresponding strategies (Table 9.5).

Exiting too early from a complex emergency can be just as damaging to the population as an exit that happens too late. When exiting too early the conflict might resurge, peace negotiations might fail, and the lack of aid might play in favor of any party trying to draw advantages from a deprived community. Too late exits might actually result in aid dependency of the beneficiary population and in hope of continuous support, which donors might be willing or able to fulfill. For the purpose of developing exit strategies and deciding upon the right moment in such complex emergencies, the Interagency Standing Committee (Office for the Coordination of Humanitarian Action [OCHA]) has developed criteria that indicate conditions that might make a situation ripe for the deployment of an exit strategy:[18]

a. the reduction of a significant number of civilians affected by the emergency;
b. a successfully negotiated peace settlement bringing about the cessation of hostilities;

Table 9.5   World Food Programme Triggers for Exit Strategies*

Type of Trigger	Triggers
Programmatic	Progress toward objectives
Contextual	Improvement in the overall humanitarian situation
	Refugee return (<5,000 remaining)
	Security constraints making effective aid provision impossible
Systemic	Government capacity to meet needs and for emergency response
External	Diminished donor contributions
	Commitment by other donor

*"Exiting Emergencies: Programme Options for Transition from Emergency Response," Executive Board Decision (World Food Programme, 30 December, 2004), para. 14, https://www.wfp.org/sites/default/files/Exiting%20Emergencies%20-%20(2005).pdf.

c. the resumption of normal social, political, and economic activities;
d. the government's capacity to resume its obligation toward the population, in particular the victims of the conflict.

A resource mobilization strategy should be in place that covers the strategic framework for postconflict activities.

There is a difference between office closures at the end of the project and forced office closures. Forced office closure may, for example, be:[19]

a. permanent closure of programs and office;
b. closing a program while maintaining an office in that locality;
c. closing an office but continuing the program through remote management/ partners;
d. a temporary rapid closure, which may last from a few hours to a number of days (suspension).

Planned office closures and exits usually happen when the project reaches a time limit, when the project impacts have been achieved, or when benchmarks have been reached. In planned exits one can speak of three different approaches:[20]

a. *Phasing down* describes a progressive reduction of program activities due to reduced resources, or as a preliminary stage before phasing out or phasing over. It might involve local partners to sustain program benefits with little or no renewed resources.
b. *Phasing out* means the discontinuation of a project without its transferal to other actors. This should ideally happen when permanent or self-sustaining changes have successfully been realized, and no further resources are necessary to ensure the durability of the project goals.
c. *Phasing over* describes the transition of program activities to other specialized international actors or to local institutions or communities. In the latter case, it is important to consider whether local communities sense ownership and commitment to continue program activities, whether they have the necessary knowledge and skills to do so, and whether they have sufficient, financial, institutional, and human resource capacity to ensure a successful continuation.

Particularly in planned office closures, humanitarian actors are implicitly or explicitly obliged by principles such as linking relief, rehabilitation, and development (LRRD) or sustainability, meaning that they have to ensure that projects are transferred into local ownership or transitioned into development aid. Frequently mentioned principles that should inform humanitarian exit strategies of planned office closures are:[21]

- planning the exit from the outset;
- thinking about sustainability of the project;
- regularly consulting with partners and stakeholders;
- communicating your status internally and externally.

Forced office closures due to contextual issues such as security constraints, which make effective aid provision impossible, are less a matter of strategic decision-making than tactical decision-making. Whereas the term "exit strategy" might in practice still be used, the tactical and operational-level decision elements will prevail over strategic objectives formulated in the project or program proposal. While assets recovery and theft prevention will occupy some thought, the utmost priority will concern staff security.

9.5.2   Staff Security in the Exit Phase

As mentioned above, staff safety and security should remain a key concern particularly during the exit period irrespective of whether it is a planned or a forced one. The following recommendations by the EISF should serve as a general guide regarding security consideration:[22]

a. When staff becomes isolated and therefore more vulnerable due to reduced numbers, consider moving them into alternative accommodations (e.g., hotels, other residences by nongovernmental organizations (NGOs), or UN compounds).
b. Staff should maintain means of communication through mobiles, satellite phones, or radios until the exit is completed.
c. Ensure that you continue using security communication check procedures throughout the exiting period.
d. Maintain up-to-date staff movement lists in order to coordinate a possible evacuation with embassies and UN offices.
e. Keep detailed information about exiting procedures, such as exact date and time of final departure, externally on a need-to-know basis.
f. Ensure that staff who are thought to be carrying significant assets are under increased security measures to reduce potential risks.
g. Particularly when information cannot be contained, plan goodbyes with relevant stakeholders after assets and data have been removed.
h. If you expect problems from tax and customs officers, consider arranging an escort to exiting the country by trusted senior officials from ministries, the UN, or diplomatic missions.

Box 9.7   Exit Strategy Development

Step 1: establish closure approach (e.g., formal project management).

Step 2: determine roles and responsibilities for people managing the process.

Step 3: identify the factors that will determine when an office/project should close.

Step 4: develop exit strategy based on the kind of departure (rapid/forced, phased/planned).

Step 5: prepare closure plan including: implementation plan, timeline, risk identification (see devil's advocacy).

Step 6: finalize legal position (i.e., ensure that actions regarding termination of staff comply with local legislative requirements).

Step 7: determine organization and corresponding staff changes.

Step 8: determine financial impacts and prepare budget.

Step 9: develop communication plan (including engagement strategy and updates).

Step 10: identify impact on individuals and calculate the detailed termination data for each employee.

Step 11: determine the general range of assistance to be provided to staff leaving.

Step 12: formally consult with staff regarding closure and closure procedure distribution (need to know).

The step-by-step guide in Box 9.7 is based on the "Planning Checklist for Office Closure" by the EISF, provided in full in Appendix 9.2 of this book, as it pertains to the planning process only.[23]

It would go too far to explore the details and practicalities of office closure in this book. However, as mentioned in section 9.2, one of the most in-depth guidelines available to date, titled "Office Closure," is the toolkit developed by the EISF, which is highly recommended. Appendix 9.2 provides as an example the "Planning Checklist for Office Closure."

REVIEW QUESTIONS

- What is the purpose of operational planning tools?
- What does the analyst need to know before commencing with operational planning?
- Explain the utility of force field analysis.
- On which levels do entry point questions play out?

- Which brainstorming methods lead to quicker and better decisions in worst case anticipation, and why?
- What are critical failures?
- What can prevent the escalation of commitment?
- Which ethical concerns are relevant regarding points of no return?
- What is the purpose of scenario planning, and why is it particularly relevant for humanitarian organizations?
- Why are wildcards a problem for forecasting?
- What is the role of indicators in scenario planning?
- How does a *futures wheel* assist in developing scenarios?
- How does a planned office closure differ from forced office closures, and which approaches are applicable?

NOTES

1. Ben Ramalingam, *Tools for Knowledge and Learning: A Guide for Development and Humanitarian Organisations*, Rapid-Research and Policy in Development (London: Overseas Development Institute (ODI), 2006), 32, http://www.odi.org/publications/153-tools-knowledge-learning-guide-development-humanitarian-organisations.

2. Based on Sarah Miller Beebe and Randolph H. Pherson, *Cases in Intelligence Analysis: Structured Analytic Techniques in Action* (Thousand Oaks, CA: CQ Press College, 2011), 236.

3. Source 8, "Office Opening: A Guide for Non-Governmental Organisations," EISF publication (European Interagency Security Forum, 12 March, 2015), https://www.eisf.eu/library/officeopening/.

4. Ibid., 8.

5. Ibid., 10.

6. Dustin J. Sleesman, Donald E. Conlon, Gerry McNamara, and Jonathan E. Miles, "Cleaning Up the Big Muddy: A Meta-Analytic Review of the Determinants of Escalation of Commitment," *Academy of Management Journal* 55, no. 3 (June 2012): 541–62.

7. Sarah Miller Beebe and Randolph H. Pherson, *Cases in Intelligence Analysis: Instructor Materials* (Thousand Oaks, CA: CQ Press College, Sage, 2012), 24.

8. Ryan Hartwig, "7 Steps to Analyze a Problem—The Devil's Advocacy Technique," *Teams That Thrive*, accessed 7 January, 2016, http://www.ryanhartwig.com/7-steps-to-analyze-a-problem-the-devils-advocacy-technique/.

9. Alexander L. George and Eric K. Stern, "Harnessing Conflict in Foreign Policy Making: From Devil's to Multiple Advocacy," *Presidential Studies Quarterly* 32, no. 3 (2002): 484–508.

10. Oliver Markley, "More about a New Typology of Wildcards," *AFP Compass—Methods Anthology Special Edition*, April 2015, 2.

11. Jay Ogilvy and Peter Schwartz, "Plotting Your Scenarios" (Emeryville, CA: Global Business Network, 2004), 5, http://www.meadowlark.co/plotting_your_scenarios.pdf [highlighted by the author].

12. Ibid., 6.

13. Richards J. Heuer and Randolph H. Pherson, *Structured Analytic Techniques for Intelligence Analysis* (SAGE, 2010), Chapter 6.2.

14. Peter Schwartz, *The Art of the Long View* (Doubleday/Currency, 1991).

15. While developed for long-term predictions of 20–30 years, the tool is just as applicable to predictions of a project or program horizon for 1–5 years.

16. Andrew Curry and Wendy Schultz, "Roads Less Travelled: Different Methods, Different Futures," *Journal of Futures Studies* 13, no. 4 (2009): 40; Wendy Schultz, "Manoa: The Future Is Not Binary," *AFP Compass—Methods Anthology Special Edition*, April 2015, 22.

17. Safer Edge, "Office Closure," EISF publication (European Interagency Security Forum, 24 April, 2013), 15, https://www.eisf.eu/library/office-closure-eisf-guide/.

18. "Exit Strategy for Humanitarian Actors in the Context of Complex Emergencies" (Inter-Agency Standing Committee (IASC), 24 March, 2003), para. 8, https://interagencystandingcommittee.org/focal-points/documents-public/exit-strategy-humanitarian-actors-context-complex-emergencies.

19. Safer Edge, "Office Closure," 9.

20. Alison Gardner, Kara Greenblott, and Erika Joubert, "What We Know about Exit Strategies—Practical Guidance For Developing Exit Strategies in the Field" (Zambia and Zimbabwe: C-SAFE Regional Learning Spaces Initiative, September 2005), 8–9, http://reliefweb.int/sites/reliefweb.int/files/resources/A02C7B78FB2B-408B852570AB006EC7BA-What%20We%20Know%20About%20Exit%20Strategies%20-%20Sept%202005.pdf.

21. Sarah Lewis and Rachel Hayman, "NGO Exit Strategies: Are Principles for Closing Projects or Ending Partnerships Necessary?" *INTRAC Blog—Opinion and Debate*, July 18, 2014, http://www.intrac.org/blog.php/63/ngo-exit-strategies-are-principles-for-closing-projects-or-ending-partnerships-necessary.

22. Safer Edge, "Office Closure," 16–17.

23. Ibid., 56–57.

Conclusion

Recapitulating the Humanitarian Intelligence Cycle

This book introduced the concept of humanitarian intelligence and applicable tools to assess humanitarian disasters. By that we have built the bridge from traditional intelligence to humanitarian intelligence and from the intelligence cycle and project management cycle to the humanitarian intelligence cycle (see Figure C.1).

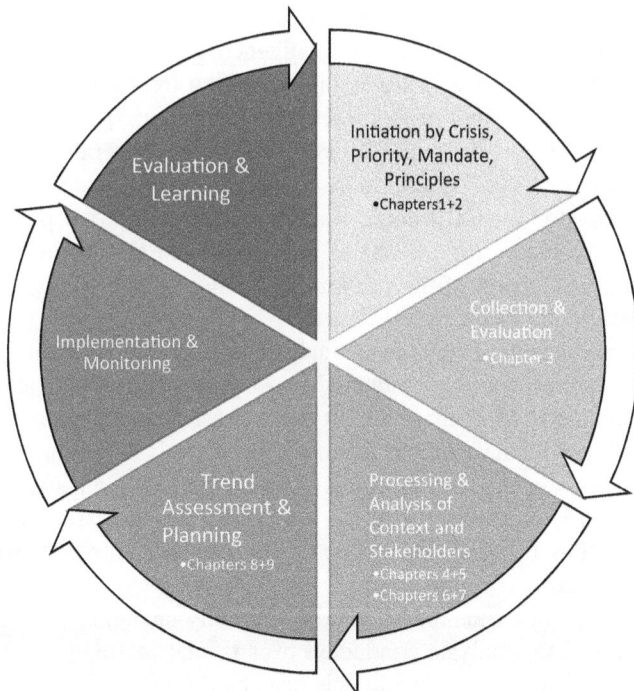

Figure C.1   Humanitarian Intelligence Cycle

185

The humanitarian intelligence cycle starts with the initiation of a response by crisis. The initiation is guided by humanitarian principles, the priorities on the ground, and the mandates of the respective humanitarian organization. The guiding principles surrounding the initiation of the humanitarian intelligence cycle, the logical framework (LogFrame), and the connection between intelligence and project management have been explained in depth in chapters 1 and 2. Before any planned response can take place, it is up to humanitarian analysts to collect the data necessary for such a response. Chapter 3 introduced the different modes of data collection and its evaluation for reliability and validity. The importance of the matter of reliability and validity cannot be overstated; all further analysis and intelligence production—coming from data to information and further to actionable intelligence—depend on the initial accuracy of the data. The data then has to be processed, that is, sorted for different categories such as the context dimensions or the levels of analysis, before it can be used for analysis.

Most donors require both context and stakeholder analysis (chapters 4–7). However, by now it should be clear that both context and stakeholder analysis are indispensable elements of any good analysis. Without knowing the context and the stakeholder field, a humanitarian operation is unlikely to succeed, and in any case it will be negligent by risking the safety and security of its staff and the well-being of its beneficiaries.

The next step in the humanitarian intelligence cycle, namely, the step from information to intelligence, consists of identifying trends and making information actionable by applying tools of decision-making (chapters 8 and 9). Throughout the book, the topic of indicators has been raised concerning the measurement of the context but also with regard to the monitoring of the situation. Indicators again become important during the two phases of the intelligence cycle that, for reasons of space but also given enough secondary literature, make part of the present book: monitoring during the project implementation and evaluation thereafter.

It was recommended that such an analysis if proposed in the humanitarian intelligence cycle would be conducted in analytic teams. It is clear that for reasons of financial constraints not all humanitarian organizations would be able to finance a whole analytic team. However, it is still recommended to enhance efforts of analysts and project planners by additional staff whenever possible in order to cross-fertilize the brainstorming processes by including a diverse background of disciplines and expertise, and in order to triangulate the analytic process to compensate for biases.

The landscape of humanitarian action is quickly changing with the ascent of drones, big data, analysis conducted by artificial intelligence, etc. However, when it comes to informed decision-making and taking responsibility despite all of these developments the human component in the humanitarian analyst and the decision-maker will not disappear, if only for ethical reasons. This does not mean that the data collection and processing will not change over time. It is all the more important that humanitarian analysts are well trained in second-guessing automated processes since no situation and the interaction of variables are ever the same in complex contexts. Furthermore, there is no one-size-fits-all panacea for humanitarian crises. So in the end the planning and decision-making will remain a value judgment—one that can responsibly and ethically only be done on the basis of sound evidence. This means that the humanitarian analyst is needed more than ever before.

Appendix 2.1

Sample LogFrame for a Rice Production Project

Narrative Summary	Objectively Verifiable Indicators	Means of Verification	Important Assumptions
Program goal: (broader objective to which this project contributes) Small farmer income increased in Northeastern Region	Measure of goal achievement: 1. Average farmer income raised from 100 baht/year in 1976 to 130 baht/year in 1978 2. Small farmer income raised from 70 to 110 baht in same period	• Sales and market price figures • Tax figures • Ag. extension agent reports • As for 1 above	Concerning long-term value of program/project: 1. Inflation doesn't exceed 12%/year 2. Sufficient "luxury" goods available for farmers to spend "disposable" income 3. Farmers protected from unscrupulous merchants
Project purpose: Small farmer rice production increased in Northeastern Region	Conditions that will indicate purpose has been achieved: End of project status 1. 30,000 farmers (owning 7 rai or less) increase rice yields by 50% between October 1976 and October 1978 2. Rice harvested by small farmers in 1978 is of better or equal quality (X% cracked) to rice harvested by same farmers in 1976 3. 95% of farmers buy HYV seed for 1979 planting season	1. • Harvest records: Dept. of Ag. (DOA), extension agents surveys • 1976 DOA records 2. Review and analysis by DOA experts 3. • Credit system records • Survey of farmers for program satisfaction	Affecting purpose to goal link: 1. Price of rice does not fall below X baht/ton in 1977, and Y baht/ton in 1978 2. Market absorbs total increased production each harvest 3. No spoilage or waste occurs in marketing/storage system

Narrative Summary	Objectively Verifiable Indicators	Means of Verification	Important Assumptions
Outputs: 1. Functioning fertilizer and high yield variety rice seed distribution system in place 2. Farmers trained 3. Functioning credit system in place	Magnitude of outputs necessary and sufficient to achieve purpose 1. • 10 distribution centers constructed by 12/78 • X tons fertilizer and Y tons seed distributed to target group by 12/78 • 96% of all purchases paid for within two months of purchase 2. • 35,000 farmers trained by 12/78 • 98% of those trained use new planting and cultivating techniques appropriately 3. • 8m baht issued in credits to 25,000 small farmers by 1978, by 30 credit area offices • Default rate does not exceed 21 of total loans • Credit terms acceptable to local farm leaders	1. • Project records • Project records, extension agent survey • Project A/C records 2. • Project records • Extension agent reports 3. • Spot check survey by project manager • Credit systems records • Ag. extension agent report	Affecting output to purpose link: • Extension agents correctly supervise farmer application of fertilizer • 10 inches of rainfall between May and October each year • Price of soya seed stays at 1976 levels so farmers will stay with rice project and not convert to soya
Inputs (activities and types of resources): 1. • Design distribution system • Construct storage facilities • Train staff 2. • Recruit farmers • Develop training facilities and materials • Conduct training 3. • Hire credit specialist • Develop system procedures • Train staff	Level of effort/expenditure for each activity: • 6 man-months/ US$15,000 • 12 man-months/ US$1,800,000 • 36 man-months/ US$150,000 • 24 man-months/ US$100,000 • 24 man-months/ US$200,000 • 36 man-months/ US$150,000	1. Project manager records 2. Subcontractor records and reports 3. Project manager reports	Affecting input to output link: • Farmers willing to accept new cultivation methods • Fertilizer prices do not exceed $__ per ton • Can recruit 150 agricultural extension agents locally

Appendix 5.1

Context Dimensions

Measurements and Indicators

The key questions are not restricted to one context dimension and its respective security alone but also include cross-cutting issues that allow a first assessment of interconnections between different context dimensions.[1]

For more indicators specific to different sectors or areas of specialization in humanitarian operations, the Sphere Handbook[2] and the Indicators Registry of HumanitarianResponse.info[3] are highly recommended (see also section 3.3).

ECONOMIC SECURITY

Main Issues of Inquiry

Income; employment/unemployment; macro-economic indicators; poverty; measures of inequalities; social public spending; prospects and restrictions of current productive structure; informal sector (gray and black economies); socio-economic and financial status; household spending; wages; social security or other forms of publicly financed safety nets; and identifying vulnerable groups.

Key Questions

1. What is the main source of income of the people?
2. What specifically generates economic security and insecurity in people?
3. Who is employed and unemployed?
4. What are the dynamics of economic performance (potential engines of growth or obstacles/barriers)?
5. What is the nature and scope of underemployment?
6. What type of support is available for people who feel economic insecurity?

7. What are the major economic problems or challenges facing the countries?
8. Is there possibility of self-employment, and if yes, in what form or areas?
9. How robust is the economy?
10. Is policy framework conducive to macro-economic stability?
11. Is policy framework conducive to micro-economic stability?
12. How sustainable is the state's environmental policy?

Indicators

- Unemployment/employment: long-term unemployment
- Productive employment for at least one household member; "productive = wage or other earned income sufficient to maintain the household"
- In case nobody is employed or self-employed in a household, receipt of an income in the form of social benefits
- Inflation, GDP per capita, budget deficit (corrects for currency fluctuation)
- Public/social expenditures per capita: military expenditures (effectiveness of government/diplomatic skills)
- Percentage of households with per capita consumption expenditure below a specified poverty line
- Percent of total consumption expenditure spent on food
- Resource flows and use (including investment and aid)
- Nature and type of subsidies
- Private/public ratio of economic performance
- Poverty and inequality indicators (Gini coefficient)
- Percent feeling economically insecure (in their employment, income, etc.)
- Energy input/GDP ratio (measure of energy efficiency, recycling)

FOOD SECURITY

Main Issues of Inquiry

Availability and access to, utilization and quality of food and nutrition; use and variety of coping strategies; identifying vulnerable groups.

Key Questions

1. What is the exact food security problem: availability, access, utilization, or quality? Also, what kind of nutrition (fat, protein and carbohydrates, vitamins, water) is not covered?
2. How does the political situation, the economy, and the environment impact on the identified food security problems?

3. What are the major specific health problems related to the lack of certain aspects of nutrition?
4. What is the cultural context of food production and consumption?
5. What are the actions taken by governmental and other actors to address food insecurity?
6. What are the local and individual coping mechanisms (e.g., food sharing patterns)?
7. To what extent is food a strategic asset used for purposes other than eating (i.e., in conflicts: a weapon in war)?

Indicators

- Food production index and calorie supply intake
- Food prices (and subsidies)
- Agricultural production
- Weight for height and height for age of children under five (as compared with a healthy and well-fed standard population)
- Body mass index
- Percentage pregnant women with iron deficiency anemia
- Percentage women breast-feeding their children up to six months of age (exclusive of other food or drink)
- Perception of availability, access, etc.
- Number of meals per day
- Percentage of income spent on food
- Cost of basic diet (appropriately defined by each country) as a percentage of family income

HEALTH SECURITY

Main Issues of Inquiry

Access to, and quality of, health services; diseases and infections posing major health threats; health spending; and identifying vulnerable groups.

Key Questions

1. What are the major causes of death in these countries?
2. What is the quality of nutrition and the environment (water, dwelling)?
3. What is the quality of health services and access to it?
4. How does the health security of men compare to that of women?
5. What is the level of health security among children?

6. What are the major demographic trends and their relation to health indicators?
7. What are the major diseases the group suffers from and are they communicable or noncommunicable diseases?
8. What percentage of people of this group is affected by the major diseases identified?
9. What are the influences of environment on communicable and noncommunicable diseases?
10. What are the influences of food security on communicable and noncommunicable diseases?
11. What are the actions taken by governmental actors to address health insecurity?
12. Are economic constraints of the group's aspiration for health security compensated by a national safety net?
13. What are the local and individual coping mechanisms?

Indicators

- Life expectancy and mortality rates by gender
- Maternal mortality
- Under five mortality rate
- Percentage births above 2.5 kg
- Number of cases of vaccine preventable diseases (especially diphtheria, measles, pertussis, tuberculosis, tetanus, polio)
- Number of reported cases of other major epidemic diseases (mainly malaria in the case of the TCR)
- Number of cases of HIV/AIDS
- Real cost of a childbirth as percentage of total household consumption expenditure
- Real cost of a routine medical consultation as percentage of total household consumption expenditure
- Percentage of children at risk (one-year-olds, except for BCG where WHO uses the number of newborn children as denominator) who have been immunized (BCG, DTP3, MCV, POL3, TT2)
- Percentage of couples with access to family planning advice
- Percentage households (or individuals) satisfied with arrangements for prevention/cure
- Number of cases of diseases and infections identified as threats
- Public/private health expenditures
- Doctor-patient ratio
- Hospital/Clinic-patient ratio

ENVIRONMENTAL SECURITY

Main Issues of Inquiry

Types of threats to the environment; water and sanitation quality, accessibility, and supply; land and soil degradation; desertification and productive land; forms and quality of irrigation use in agricultural production; source and effects of pollution; character of environmental damage and its effects; chronic and long-lasting environmental threats (deforestation, population growth, poverty, and land shortages) and sudden and violent changes (nuclear and oil spills, earthquakes, floods, landslides); identifying vulnerable regions and sectors.

Key Questions

1. Is economic growth in these countries heavily reliant on natural resources and the extent that this is affecting overall environmental security?
2. What is the role of population growth in increasing or decreasing levels of environmental security?
3. What is the nature and scope of the degradation of local ecosystems in these countries?
4. To what extent are resource (water) scarcity or poor distribution trends factors for ethnic strife, political tensions, and external conflicts?
5. Is there evidence of desertification, and what can it be attributed to?
6. Do these countries have plans for environmental protection and management?
7. Do these countries have plans to cope with natural emergencies and disasters?
8. What is the capacity of response to natural emergencies and disasters of the state and nongovernmental and community/social organizations and relief and aid agencies?
9. What are the main threats to the group by the environment?
10. What are the main threats to the environment by different actors?
11. How strongly do environmental threats impact on the social and (socio-) economic aspects of the actor?
12. How is food security influenced by environmental constraints?
13. How is health security influenced by environmental constraints?
14. How is economic security influenced by environmental constraints?
15. What are the actions taken by governmental actors to address environmental constraints? (Identify gaps and weaknesses.)
16. What are the local and individual coping mechanisms?

Indicators

- Nature and scope of productive structures (authentic competitiveness vs. spurious—dependent solely on natural resources)
- Indicators of pollution in air, water, and soil
- Water supply indicators, in terms of quality and access
- Indicators of forest land losses
- Salinization of land
- Urban/rural comparisons
- Awareness of environmental problems in different sectors of society
- Nature and scope of natural disasters
- Any health indicator, attributed to environmental hazards (e.g., polluted water contributed to cases of diarrhea)
- Number of earthquakes (over a 25-year period or whatever period is appropriate) by degree of severity
- Number of victims (deaths, injuries) from earthquakes
- Number of victims (deaths, injuries) from landslides
- Number of victims (deaths, injuries) from avalanches
- Levels of carbon monoxide (CO), sulfur dioxide (SO2), nitrogen dioxide (NO2), and lead standardized as appropriate in terms of GDP
- Proportion of the population that considers that arrangements to protect them from natural disaster are adequate
- Proportion of the population that considers that arrangements to protect them from environmental pollution are adequate

SOCIAL SECURITY[4]

Main Issues of Inquiry

Source of community security (family, community or social organization, local government, church, relief/aid agency); identifying emerging trends of social capital (if any); ethnic tensions; participation of communities and individuals in decision-making processes; cultural identity and set of values; identifying vulnerable groups; education (both from an individual and aggregate point of view).

Key Questions

1. What used to be the forms of social support?
2. What kinds of relationships were involved and what kind of support?
3. Have these forms been affected by the disaster, and how?
4. How are these forms of support affected by the intervention?

5. Can and should the intervention take into account these forms of social support?

Associated Questions

1. What is the status of family cohesion?
2. What is the level of education?
3. Are societies in greater or lesser risk today, and why?
4. Who are threatened most in these societies, and why?
5. What are the levels, shapes, and forms of social/community organization, and what are their role in societies?
6. To what extent are communities empowered to participate in decisions that affect their lives or security?
7. In what ways do individuals participate in decision-making at different social levels?
8. What is the cultural identity dimension to these societies, as well as the set of associated values, and to what extent do these two affect levels of human security?
9. What is the greatest source of community anxiety in these countries?
10. From which source (e.g., individual, group, the state) do people derive most security?
11. Is there any particular form of crime that is perpetrated against people that is common in these areas or that deserves special attention (e.g., violence against women, children, men, and/or ethnic groups)?

Indicators

- Rate of child abandonment
- Time spent at home by wage-earning mothers
- Literacy levels and school dropout and repetition rates
- Age of entry to preschool education
- Index of school efficiency (number of school years required for certificate/years attended)
- Any indicator of internal conflict and strife
- Indicators of social cohesion (e.g., number, density, and role of NGOs, social capital indicators)
- Levels of tolerance/intolerance for various community groups or sectors
- Indicators of discrimination or exclusion (if any)
- Structure of land distribution and tenure
- Number and nature of internal/external conflicts attributed to ethnic or religious tensions

POLITICAL SECURITY

Main Issues of Inquiry

Pacta sunt servanda, rule of law, perceived and real role of the state as a guarantor of basic standards of living; representativeness and accessibility of state institutions; level of respect for human rights; quality and transparency of the policy process; the capacity of the state to protect people against any form of repression; role of military/police forces; quality and scope of justice system; identifying relative level to which specific groups in society are affected by the above and how this is expressed in perceived levels of security.

Key Questions

1. Do people consider state institutions to be representative of the interests of society?
2. What are the policy development priorities of the government, and how are these expressed and reflected?
3. Is the state seen as providing adequate levels of basic social services?
4. Is the state seen as accessible to all citizens?
5. Do people in these countries live in societies that honor their basic human rights?
6. If not, what is the nature and scope of human rights violations?
7. Are people aware of their human rights?
8. Is there an ongoing democratization process, and if not, how can the political regimes be described?
9. Who are the major political actors?
10. How and to what degree do people participate in the electoral process?
11. Is there any form of state, political, and/or system repression?
12. How is the system of justice set up, and how are laws interpreted, administered, and enforced?
13. What are the major political problems or challenges facing the countries?
14. Are systems of grassroots democracy being established and developed, and to what degree do citizens participate in these?

Legitimacy of the State

1. Are there proper checks and balances in the political system?
2. How inclusive is the political/administrative power?
3. What is the overall level of respect for national authorities?
4. Is corruption widespread?

Rule of Law

1. How strong is the state judicial system?
2. Does unlawful state violence exist?
3. Does civilian power control security forces?
4. Does organized crime undermine the country's stability?

Respect for Fundamental Rights

1. Are civil and political freedoms respected?
2. Are religious and cultural rights respected?
3. Are other basic human rights respected?

Civil Society and Media

1. Can civil society operate freely and efficiently?
2. How independent and professional are the media?

Indicators

- Level of confidence in key state institutions as expressed in opinion polls
- Citizen's perception of the state and state institutions as measured through focus group-based scenario drawing
- Assessment of the state and state institutions through contents analysis of key media and professional journals
- Perceived level of corruption (opinion polls)
- Data on number of cases of corruption uncovered and classification according to the type of corruption
- Number of electoral processes, and the level of voter participation
- Number of political parties with members in parliament
- Number of major daily newspaper, radio, TV stations independent of government
- Representation of the minorities or disadvantaged groups in legislatures, the judiciary, and the executive arms of the government
- Legal provisions in respect of human rights specifically to safeguard minorities or disadvantaged groups
- Degree of ratification of international human rights treaties, covenants, and conventions
- Modification of the constitution and the law in conformity with the ratified conventions
- Revising administrative procedures (e.g., Ombudsman)

- Administration of justice indicators (e.g., court cases heard, trials, sentences, prisons, type of crimes, arrests and detentions, number of cases brought against state institutions)
- Attracting public support through civil society, the media, schools, etc.
- Number and type of cases submitted to the Ombudsman institution (if in place)
- Political refugees and Internally Displaced Persons (IDPs)
- Press freedom index
- Human rights and freedoms index

PHYSICAL SECURITY

This context dimension is an addition to the six previous dimensions. It is up to the analyst to determine whether the dimension is useful and necessary for the context analysis. It is certainly a dimension relevant for staff safety and security. In the years of teaching context analytical tools, however, it has shown to be overlapping so strongly with political and social security as to yield little additional analytical and predictive value.

Main Issues of Inquiry

Types of threats to human life (from the state, from other states, from groups or people, from ethnic tensions, from self).

Key Questions

1. What are the specific forms of threats to human life in these countries?
2. Are human lives in greater or lesser risk today, and why?
3. What are the nature and the scope of crimes in these countries?
4. Is there evidence of drug-related and organized-crime-related threats?
5. Is there any particular form of crime that is perpetrated against people that is common in these countries or that deserves special attention (e.g., violence against women, children, men, and/or ethnic groups)?
6. How high is the rate of violent nonpolitical crimes?
7. How high is the rate of hate crimes?
8. How high is the rate of economic crimes?
9. What are the actions taken by the government to address personal insecurity?
10. What are the local and individual coping mechanisms?

Indicators

- Crime rates, trends, and types
- Percentage reported crimes that are cleared up
- Ratio of reported/unreported crimes
- Percentage respondents who feel that insecurity from crime is a major problem for them
- Percentage respondents expressing confidence in the police
- Any indicator of internal conflict and strife
- Drug trafficking indicators (if any)
- Street security indicators (children, prostitution, gangs, organized crime)

Individual Risks

- Number of traffic accidents
- Number of persons killed in traffic accidents
- Material damage caused by fires
- The proportion of private cars insured
- Road reconstruction, however defined (km)
- Percentage feeling secure in respect of traffic accidents (and similarly in respect of other individual risks)

Housing and Associated Services

- Percentage households living in self-contained, permanent dwellings
- Percentage living respectively in owner/occupied and rented accommodation
- Percentage households with at least one room per adult equivalent
- Average number per day/hours of supply of domestic electricity
- Percentage households with piped water supplied from mains at least part of every day
- Percentage of households in accommodation with flush WC
- Monthly cost of electricity as percentage of total consumption expenditure

NOTES

1. This list of measurements and indicators is based on: European Commission, "Check-List for Root Causes of Conflict," 2007, http://www.eplo.org/assets/files/3.%20Resources/EU%20Documents/European_Commission_European_Commission_Checklist_Root_Causes_of_Conflict.pdf; Bratislava Regional Centre, "Human Security Measurements," 2003, http://www.undp.sk/uploads/ACF1EF1.doc; Marie V. Gibert, "Monitoring a Region in Crisis: The European Union in West Africa," Chaillot Paper (Institute for Security Studies (EUISS), January 2007), http://aei.pitt.edu/7413/01/chai96.pdf; Hazel Henderson, "Beyond Economics: New

Indicators for Culturally Specific," *Sustainable Development. Development* 3, no. 4 (1990): 60–68; Redefining Wealth, "Progress: New Ways to Measure Economic, Social and Environmental Change," *The Caracas Report on Alternative Development Indicators, The Bootstrap Press, New York*, 1990.

2. Sphere Project, *The Sphere Handbook—Humanitarian Charter and Minimum Standards in Humanitarian Response*, third edition (Rugby, UK: Practical Action Publishing, 2011), http://www.spherehandbook.org.

3. https://www.humanitarianresponse.info/en/applications/ir.

4. The following set of key questions and indicators illustrates the problematic nature of indicators, especially for the notion of social security. For example, the set of questions do not (yet) provide detailed definitions and operationalizations of the concepts concerned. That is, what is the definition of a family or a society? How to measure cohesion? What is meant by community anxiety? And: what to measure: does one focus on perceptions of people or on "objective" indicators? This list should therefore be viewed only as an illustration of what a checklist could look like and the types of questions it could consist of.

Appendix 5.2

Context Dimensions and Human Rights Correspondence

As can be seen from the table, the context dimensions relevant for humanitarian action, and which also reflect survival needs including safety needs ensured through social networks, can easily be translated into human rights. In this regard, the principle of nondiscrimination applies to all context dimensions. It also becomes clear that very urgent human needs such as food, health, and work are predominantly enshrined in the so-called second generation of human rights. This framework shows that the notion of generations of human rights cannot be extended to their priority of implementation and urgency in interventions. Also, this section includes the personal security context dimension.

Context Dimension	Relevant Human Rights Norms
Economic security	The right of people to work (Art. 6 ICESCR)
	Conditions of employment (Art. 7, 8 ICESCR)
Health and food security	Art. 11 para. 1 ICESCR: "right of everyone to an adequate standard of living [. . .] including adequate food, clothing and housing"
	Art. 12 para 1: "highest attainable standard of physical and mental health"
Environmental security	Indirectly enshrined in several legal provisions such as Art. 25 of the Universal Declaration of Human Rights or in Art. 11 and 12 of the ICESCR
Personal security	Right to life (Art. 6 ICCPR)
	Freedom from torture or cruel, inhuman, or degrading treatment or punishment (Art. 7 ICCPR)
	Freedom from slavery and servitude (Art. 8 ICCPR)
	Right to liberty and security of person (incl. prohibition of arbitrary arrest and detention) (Art. 9 ICCPR)
	Persons deprived of liberty shall be treated with humanity (Art. 10 ICCPR)
Community security	Freedom of thought, conscience, and religion (Art. 18 ICCPR)
	Right to hold opinions and freedom of expression (Art. 19 ICCPR)
	Right of peaceful assembly (Art. 21 ICCPR)
	Freedom of association (Art. 22 ICCPR)
Political security	The Rule of Law (Preamble para. 3 Universal Declaration of Human Rights)
	Equality before the law (Art. 26 ICCPR)
	Political participation (Art. 25 ICCPR)

Source: The table has been adopted from Andrej Zwitter, "Neutrality and Impartiality in Implementing Human Rights: A Framework for Measuring Human Security," in *Mainstreaming Human Security in Peace Operations and Crisis Management: Policies, Problems, Potential*, edited by Wolfgang Benedek, Matthias C. Kettemann, and Markus Möstl (Taylor & Francis US, 2010).

H-AID Trend Calculation

GENERAL VARIABLES

α = Security Aspect; [a, b ... f] = 6 Aspects of Security

$\alpha_{t=0}$ = Security Level [0, 6]

$\alpha_{t=0}$ = Lack of Security

$1 - \alpha_{t=0}$ Effect on security level; as security can never exceed 100 percent or go below 0 percent, the effect on security has to be calculated in relation to the current security level. The salience and capability of actors, respectively the force of a hazard and the vulnerability, have a positive or negative effect on the lack of security.

$\alpha_{t=0}$ Impact of actor on Security

$\alpha_{t=0}$ Trend of Security

ACTOR VARIABLES

S = Salience toward research object [−1,1]

S^+ = Positive salience of an actor toward the research object concerning [0,1]

S^- = Negative salience of an actor/hazard toward the research object concerning [−1,0]

$$S_\epsilon (S^+ + S^-).$$

C = Capability of an actor

P = Effective power is the actors' effect on a security aspect

$$P = \alpha_{t=0} + (1 - \alpha_{t=0}) \times SC.$$

HAZARDS VARIABLES

F = Force of a hazard [0,−1]
V = Vulnerability of the research object to the hazard [−1,0]
E = Effect of the Hazard

$$E = \alpha_{t=0} + (1 - \alpha_{t=0}) \times FV.$$

TREND CALCULATION

We can calculate and plot P and E. The trend is then the average of all impact on one security aspect in relation to its current security level.

$$\beta_{t=1} = \frac{\sum_{i=0}^{n}[Ei] + \sum_{i=0}^{n}[Pi]}{n}.$$

P and R as well as β can be expressed as a vector in a graph when they are put in relation to the current security Level ($\alpha_{t=0}$).

$$\begin{array}{c} v_{xt=0} \\ v_{yt=0} \end{array} = \begin{bmatrix} \alpha_{t=0} \\ 0 \end{bmatrix} \rightarrow \begin{array}{c} v_{xt=1} \\ v_{yt=1} \end{array} = \begin{bmatrix} \alpha_{t=1} \\ 1 \end{bmatrix}; \begin{array}{c} v_{xt=1} \\ v_{yt=1} \end{array} = \begin{bmatrix} E \\ 1 \end{bmatrix}; \begin{array}{c} v_{xt=1} \\ v_{yt=1} \end{array} = \begin{bmatrix} P \\ 1 \end{bmatrix}$$

Appendix 9.1

Agency Needs Form
for Office Opening*

Title	
Project name	
Country/region/city or village	
Tenure (freehold or leasehold) (rent/buy)	
Location	
Describe any preferred location	
Would you consider any other area? Which ones, and what are their advantages and downsides?	
Functionality, headcount, and quality requirements	
Main use of space	
What is the functionality of the new space and how will that affect the layout and infrastructure (e.g., open plan layout, storage space, etc.)?	
How many employees will the space house?	
Are there other elements that will impact on space needs and utilization to be taken into account (e.g., size of warehousing)?	
How long do you anticipate being in this space?	

*Adapted for humanitarian operations from: Source 8, "Office Opening," 40–42.

What is the estimated headcount growth in short to medium to long term (two weeks, two months to one to three years)?	
Will you be open to consider converted residential space?	
Space requirements	
What is the space requirement?	
How flexible can you be in the terms of space requirements?	
For instance, would you consider a large space and partition a section off for future growth?	
Do you have any particular requirement/ standard in terms of the depth of the floor plate/ceiling height, etc.?	
Is the preference to be on one floor or several floors?	
Parking/public transport	
What is the number of parking spaces required?	
Can it be secured if necessary?	
Is covered parking desired?	
How much visitor parking is required?	
Is access to public transport important?	
Neighbors	
Are there any other NGOs or industries that you wish to be located with or near?	
Are there any NGOs, companies, or entities that you do not want to be located with or near?	
Security	
Other than organizational guidelines, are there any other special security requirements required in the specific location?	
Health and safety	
Other than market legislation and your organizational standards, are there any specific health and safety standards that should be considered?	

Other than market legislation and your organizational standards (please provide), are there any specific fire safety infrastructure standards required?	
Timing	
When does the new space need to be operational?	
Is there a key lease event that needs to be respected (break option or lease end), and what is the notice date?	
Is your timeline flexible?	
Are there any internal or external factors impacting on the definition of the budget?	
Telecoms	
Describe any unique telecoms need.	
Other	
Is there any further requirement to take into account? For example, if sharing, would it be preferable to share with another organization being funded by the same donor?	

Appendix 9.2

Planning Checklist for Office Closure*

	Steps/Activities	Person Responsible	Timeline	Comments
1	Establish closure approach (e.g., formal project management)			
2	Determine roles and responsibilities for people managing the process			
3	Identify the factors that will determine when an office/ program should close			Ensure closure strategy aligns with organizational strategy.

4	Develop exit strategy			Exit strategies should consider:
				• different types of closure:
				  o full or partial
				  o phased or rapid
				• the ongoing needs of the organization and beneficiaries
				• what will be the replacement structure

5	Prepare closure plan Identify all elements to be considered Implementation plan Timetable for implementation Risk identification and mitigation actions			This document can be provided to unions/staff representatives as a basis for consultation as required. Check with HQ HR/Country HR as appropriate to confirm proposed closure details.

*Safer Edge, "Office Closure," 56–57, based on tools developed by Oxam GB Organisational Closure Guide.

6	Finalize legal position			Ensure all actions regarding termination of staff comply with local legislative requirements prior to finalizing closure plan.
7	Determine organization and corresponding staff changes			Detailed analysis of employment issues will be required, e.g.: financial costs of termination, timings and impact of contract end dates, criteria and methodology for selecting remaining posts, identify staff who have priority status, by being "at risk of termination." There should be some consistency in the methods of assessment for same/ similar roles, but it is not necessary to have identical approaches, as the actual selection criteria will influence which methods should be used for assessment.
8	Determine financial impacts and prepare budget			
9	Develop communication plan, including: "engagement" strategy for remaining staff, regular update points, selection process for remaining posts			Although the decision to close is not negotiable, staff should be encouraged to comment on the process and their suggestions incorporated into the overall plan. This is particularly important for risk mitigation.
10	Identify impact on individuals and calculate the detailed termination data for each employee			
11	Determine the general range of assistance to be provided to staff leaving			This will cover financial support (both legal and organization entitlements) and nonfinancial support.

12	Formally consult with staff, including: distribution of closure proposal, consultative meetings with staff representatives (collectively and/or in each office), staff meetings, incorporation of appropriate comments, finalization of proposal			It is important to stress that the proposed changes are to positions and not people If the formal process is followed, but agreement can't be reached, may need to refer it to Industrial Court for arbitration (depending on local legal requirements).
13	Conduct selection process as appropriate			Keep documentation of procedures for future reference and to defend any complaints made.
14	Finalize arrangements and terminate positions Provide written confirmation to staff regarding their particular situation Ensure final termination payments are made appropriately Ensure that staff return any outstanding monies and equipment owed/belonging to the organization			
15	Track and monitor the change process Keep appropriate records Inform relevant authorities Prepare regular closure reports and updates Before ending the closure process, prepare a "lessons learned" paper for future reference Ensure all personnel records and files are properly destroyed or transferred to appropriate location			

Bibliography

Adinolfi, Costanza, David S. Bassiouni, Halvor Fossum Lauritzsen, and Howard Roy Williams. "Humanitarian Response Review." Independent Report Commissioned by the Under-Secretary-General for Humanitarian Affairs. New York and Geneva: Office for the Coordination of Humanitarian Affairs (OCHA), August 2005.

"Aid Worker Security Report 2013—The New Normal: Coping with the Kidnapping Threat." Aid Worker Security Database (AWSD). Humanitarian Outcomes, 2013. https://aidworkersecurity.org/sites/default/files/AidWorkerSecurityReport_2013_web.pdf.

Anderson, Mary B. *Do No Harm: How Aid Can Support Peace or War.* London: Lynne Rienner Publishers, 1999.

Ban Ki-Moon. "Safety and Security of Humanitarian Personnel and Protection of United Nations Personnel." Report of the Secretary-General to the General Assembly, August 18, 2008.

Barnes, Alan. "Making Intelligence Analysis More Intelligent: Using Numeric Probabilities." *Intelligence and National Security*, 31 no. 3 (2016): 327–44. doi: 10.10 80/02684527.2014.994955.

Beebe, Sarah Miller, and Randolph H. Pherson. *Cases in Intelligence Analysis—Instructor Materials.* Thousand Oaks, CA: CQ Press College, Sage, 2012.

Bishop, Peter, Andy Hines, and Terry Collins. "The Current State of Scenario Development: An Overview of Techniques." *Foresight* 9, no. 1 (2007): 5–25.

Blaikie, Piers, Terry Cannon, Ian Davis, and Ben Wisner. *At Risk: Natural Hazards, People's Vulnerability and Disasters.* New York: Routledge, 2004.

Bratislava Regional Centre. "Human Security Measurements," 2003. http://www.undp.sk/uploads/ACF1EF1.doc.

Bryson, John M. "What to Do When Stakeholders Matter." *Public Management Review* 6, no. 1 (2004): 21–53.

"Burkina Faso—Food Security Outlook: Tue, 2012-07-31 to Mon, 2012-12-31." *Famine Early Warning Systems Network.* Accessed April 24, 2015. http://www.fews.net/west-africa/burkina-faso/food-security-outlook/july-2012.

Burt, Ronald S. "Structural Holes versus Network Closure and Social Capital." In *Social Capital: Theory and Research*, edited by Nan Lin, Karen S. Cook, and Ronald S. Burt, 31–56. New Brunswick, London: Transaction Publishers, 2001.

Clark, Robert M. *Intelligence Analysis: A Target-Centric Approach*. Washington, DC; London: CQ Press College; SAGE [distributor], 2013.

Clarke, Walter, and Jeffrey Herbst. "Somalia and the Future of Humanitarian Intervention." *Foreign Affairs* 75, no. 2 (April 1996): 70.

Collinson, Sarah, Michael Bhatia, Martin Evans, Richard Fanthorpe, Jonathan Goodhand, and Stephen Jackson. "Politically Informed Humanitarian Programming Using a Political Economy Approach." Network Papers, HPN Resources. London: Humanitarian Practice Network, Overseas Development Institute, December 2002. http://www.odihpn.org/hpn-resources/network-papers/politically-informed-humanitarian-programming-using-a-political-economy-approach.

Collinson, Sarah, and Samir Elhawary. "Humanitarian Space: A Review of Trends and Issues." London: Overseas Development Institute—Humanitarian Policy Group, April 2012. http://www.odi.org/sites/odi.org.uk/files/odi-assets/publications-opinion-files/7643.pdf.

Curry, Andrew, and Wendy Schultz. "Roads Less Travelled: Different Methods, Different Futures." *Journal of Futures Studies* 13, no. 4 (2009): 35–60.

Daniell, J. E., B. Khazai, and F. Wenzel. "Uncovering the 2010 Haiti Earthquake Death Toll." *Natural Hazards and Earth System Sciences Discussions* 1, no. 3 (2013): 1913–42.

Dearden, Philip, CIDT, Steve Jones, and Rolf Sartorius. "Tools for Development—A Handbook for Those Engaged in Development Activity." London: Department for International Development (DFID), March 2003. http://webarchive.nationalarchives.gov.uk/20090119062531/http://www.dfid.gov.uk/pubs/files/toolsfordevelopment.pdf. http://webarchive.nationalarchives.gov.uk/20090119062531/http://www.dfid.gov.uk/pubs/files/toolsfordevelopment.pdf.

"Drones and Crisis Mapping—Digital Aid in Vanuatu." *ReliefWeb*, April 14, 2015. http://reliefweb.int/report/world/drones-and-crisis-mapping-digital-aid-vanuatu.

ECHO. "ECHO Manual: Project Cycle Management." Brussels: European Commission Directorate-General for Humanitarian Aid—ECHO, June 2005. http://ec.europa.eu/echo/files/partners/humanitarian_aid/fpa/2003/guidelines/project_cycle_mngmt_en.pdf.

Edward Freeman, R., and William M. Evan. "Corporate Governance: A Stakeholder Interpretation." *Journal of Behavioral Economics* 19, no. 4 (1990): 337–59. doi:10.1016/0090-5720(90)90022-Y.

European Commission. "Check-List for Root Causes of Conflict," 2007. http://www.eplo.org/assets/files/3.%20Resources/EU%20Documents/European_Commission_European_Commission_Checklist_Root_Causes_of_Conflict.pdf.

"Exit Strategy for Humanitarian Actors in the Context of Complex Emergencies." Inter-Agency Standing Committee (IASC), March 24, 2003. https://interagencystandingcommittee.org/focal-points/documents-public/exit-strategy-humanitarian-actors-context-complex-emergencies.

"Exiting Emergencies: Programme Options for Transition from Emergency Response." Executive Board Decision. World Food Programme, December 30,

2004. https://www.wfp.org/sites/default/files/Exiting%20Emergencies%20-%20 (2005).pdf.

"Fact Sheet: Timeline and Figures/Syria Displacement Crisis." UNHCR, September 2013. http://www.unhcr.org/5245a72e6.pdf.

Flanagan, J. C. "The Critical Incident Technique." *Psychological Bulletin* 51, no. 4 (July 1954).

Freeman, R. Edward. "The Stakeholder Approach Revisited." *Zeitschrift Für Wirtschafts-Und Unternehmensethik* 5, no. 3 (2004): 228–41.

———. *Strategic Management: A Stakeholder Approach.* Cambridge University Press, 2010.

Friedman, Jeffrey A., and Richard Zeckhauser. "Handling and Mishandling Estimative Probability: Likelihood, Confidence, and the Search for Bin Laden." *Intelligence and National Security* 30, no. 1 (January 2, 2015): 77–99. doi:10.1080/02 684527.2014.885202.

Gardner, Alison, Kara Greenblott, and Erika Joubert. "What We Know about Exit Strategies—Practical Guidance for Developing Exit Strategies in the Field." Zambia and Zimbabwe: C-SAFE Regional Learning Spaces Initiative, September 2005. http://reliefweb.int/sites/reliefweb.int/files/resources/A02C7B78FB2B-408B852570AB006EC7BA-What%20We%20Know%20About%20Exit%20 Strategies%20-%20Sept%202005.pdf.

George, Alexander L., and Eric K. Stern. "Harnessing Conflict in Foreign Policy Making: From Devil's to Multiple Advocacy." *Presidential Studies Quarterly* 32, no. 3 (2002): 484–508.

Gibert, Marie V. "Monitoring a Region in Crisis: The European Union in West Africa." Chaillot Paper. Institute for Security Studies (EUISS), January 2007. http://aei.pitt.edu/7413/01/chai96.pdf.

Gould, Roger V., and M. Roberto Fernandez. "Structures of Mediation: A Formal Approach to Brokerage in Transaction Networks." *Sociological Methodology* 19 (1989): 89–126.

Granovetter, Mark. "Economic Action and Social Structure: The Problem of Embeddedness." *American Journal of Sociology* (1985): 481–510.

Groupe URD. "Quality COMPAS Companion Book." Version 9.06-EN. Plaisians (France): Group Urgence Réhabilitation Développment, 2009. http://www.compasqualite.org/Setup/en/V9.06-EN_Quality_COMPAS_companion_book.pdf.

"Guidance Note on Using the Cluster Approach to Strengthen Humanitarian Response." New York, Geneva: Interagency Standing Committee (IASC), November 24, 2006. http://www.humanitarianresponse.info/system/files/documents/files/IASC%20Guidance%20Note%20on%20using%20the%20Cluster%20 Approach%20to%20Strengthen%20Humanitarian%20Response%20(November%202006).pdf.

Hall, Wayne Michael, and Gary Citrenbaum. *Intelligence Analysis: How to Think in Complex Environments.* ABC-CLIO, 2009.

Hanneman, Robert A., and Mark Riddle. *Introduction to Social Network Methods.* Riverside, CA: University of California, 2005. http://faculty.ucr.edu/~hanneman/nettext/C10_Centrality.html.

Harris, Josh. "Haiti Earthquake Response: Key Findings from ALNAP's Mapping and Analysis of Evaluations." *Trust.org—Thomson Reuters Foundation*, April

13, 2011. http://ww.trust.org/item/?map=haiti-earthquake-response-key-findings-from-alnaps-mapping-and-analysis-of-evaluations/.

Hartwig, Ryan. "7 Steps to Analyze a Problem—The Devil's Advocacy Technique." *Teams That Thrive*. Accessed January 7, 2016. http://www.ryanhartwig.com/7-steps-to-analyze-a-problem-the-devils-advocacy-technique/.

Hassard, John. "Aspects of Time in Organization." *Human Relations* 44, no. 2 (February 1, 1991): 105–25. doi:10.1177/001872679104400201.

Henderson, Hazel. "Beyond Economics: New Indicators for Culturally Specific." *Sustainable Development* 3, no. 4 (1990): 60–68.

Heuer, Richards J. *Psychology of Intelligence Analysis*. Center for the Study of Intelligence—Central Intelligence Agency, 1999. https://www.cia.gov/library/center-for-the-study-of-intelligence/csi-publications/books-and-monographs/psychology-of-intelligence-analysis/index.html.

Heuer, Richards J., and Randolph H. Pherson. *Structured Analytic Techniques for Intelligence Analysis*. Washington DC: SAGE, 2010.

Heyse, Liesbet, Andrej Zwitter, Rapahel Wittek, and Joost Herman. *Humanitarian Crises, Intervention and Security: A Framework for Evidence-Based Programming*. London: Routledge, 2014.

Holland, Jeremy. *Tools for Institutional, Political, and Social Analysis of Policy Reform: A Sourcebook for Development Practitioners*. World Bank. Washington, DC: World Bank, 2007. https://openknowledge.worldbank.org/handle/10986/6652.

Hovland, Ingie. *Successful Communication: A Toolkit for Researchers and Civil Society Organisations*. Rapid-Research and Policy in Development. London: Overseas Development Institute (ODI), 2005. http://www.odi.org/publications/155-successful-communication-toolkit-researchers-civil-society-organisations.

Humphries, Vanessa. "Improving Humanitarian Coordination: Common Challenges and Lessons Learned from the Cluster Approach." *Journal of Humanitarian Assistance* (April 30, 2013). http://sites.tufts.edu/jha/archives/1976.

Joint Chiefs of Staff. *Joint Intelligence*. Joint Publication 2-0. Defense Technical Information Center (DTIC), 2013. http://www.dtic.mil/doctrine/new_pubs/jp2_0.pdf.

Lancaster, Warren. "The Code of Conduct: Whose Code, Whose Conduct?" *Journal of Humanitarian Assistance* (April 18, 1998). http://jha.ac/1998/04/18/the-code-of-conduct-whose-code-whose-conduct/.

Lewis, Sarah, and Rachel Hayman. "NGO Exit Strategies: Are Principles for Closing Projects or Ending Partnerships Necessary?" *INTRAC Blog—Opinion and Debate*, July 18, 2014. http://www.intrac.org/blog.php/63/ngo-exit-strategies-are-principles-for-closing-projects-or-ending-partnerships-necessary.

Macrae, Joanna, Mark Bradbury, Susanne Jaspars, Douglas Johnson, and Mark Duffield. "Conflict, the Continuum and Chronic Emergencies: A Critical Analysis of the Scope for Linking Relief, Rehabilitation and Development Planning in Sudan." *Disasters* 21, no. 3 (1997): 223–43. doi:10.1111/1467-7717.00058.

Macrae, Joanna, and Adele Harmer. "Humanitarian Action and the 'Global War on Terror': A Review of Trends and Issues." HPG Report. Overseas Development Institute—Humanitarian Policy Group, July 2003.

Mardiasmo, Diaswati, and Paul H. Barnes. "Community Response to Disasters in Indonesia: Gotong Royong; a Double Edged-Sword." In *Proceedings of the 9th Annual International Conference of the International Institute for Infrastructure Renewal and Reconstruction*, edited by Paul H. Barnes and Ashantha Goonetilleke, 301–307. Brisbane, Australia: Queensland University of Technology, 2015. http://digitalcollections.qut.edu.au/2213/.

Markley, Oliver. "More about a New Typology of Wildcards." *AFP Compass—Methods Anthology Special Edition*, April 2015.

"Measuring Malnutrition (Module 7)." *Unite For Sight*. Accessed April 23, 2015. http://www.uniteforsight.org/nutrition/module7.

Miller Beebe, Sarah, and Randolph H. Pherson. *Cases in Intelligence Analysis: Structured Analytic Techniques in Action*. Thousand Oaks, CA: CQ Press College, 2011.

Mitchell, James Clyde. *Social Networks in Urban Situations: Analyses of Personal Relationships in Central African Towns*. Manchester University Press, 1969.

Mitchell, Ronald K., Bradley R. Agle, and Donna J. Wood. "Toward a Theory of Stakeholder Identification and Salience: Defining the Principle of Who and What Really Counts." *The Academy of Management Review* 22, no. 4 (October 1, 1997): 853–86. doi:10.2307/259247.

Needs Assessment Task Force (NATF). "Multi-Cluster/Sector Initial Rapid Assessment (MIRA)." Geneva: Inter-Agency Standing Committee (IASC), March 2012. https://docs.unocha.org/sites/dms/Documents/mira_final_version2012.pdf.

Newman, Edward. "Exploring the 'Root Causes' of Terrorism." *Studies in Conflict & Terrorism* 29, no. 8 (2006): 749. doi:10.1080/10576100600704069.

Norwegian Agency for Development Cooperation. *The Logical Framework Approach—Handbook for Objectives-Oriented Planning*. 4th edition. Norwegian Agency for Development Cooperation, 1999. http://www.norad.no/en/tools-and-publications/publications/publication?key=109408.

OCHA. "Ebola Crisis Page—Humanitarian Data Exchange." Accessed March 30, 2015. https://data.hdx.rwlabs.org/ebola.

———. "Indicators Registry." *Humanitarian Response*. Accessed March 25, 2015. http://www.humanitarianresponse.info/applications/ir.

Office of Knowledge Exchange, Research and Extension. "Guide to the Project Cycle—Quality for Results." Rome: Food and Agricultural Organization, 2012. http://www.fao.org/docrep/016/ap105e/ap105e.pdf.

Ogilvy, Jay, and Peter Schwartz. "Plotting Your Scenarios." Emeryville, CA: Global Business Network, 2004. http://www.meadowlark.co/plotting_your_scenarios.pdf.

Pictet, Jean. "The Fundamental Principles of the Red Cross: Commentary." *ICRC*, January 1, 1979. https://www.icrc.org/eng/resources/documents/misc/fundamental-principles-commentary-010179.htm.

Practical Concepts Incorporated. "The Logical Framework: A Manager's Guide to a Scientific Approach to Design & Evaluation." Practical Concepts Incorporated (PCI); 1730 Rhode Island Avenue, NW #200 Washington, DC 20036, November 1979. http://pdf.usaid.gov/pdf_docs/PNABN963.pdf.

Prunckun, Hank. *Handbook of Scientific Methods of Inquiry for Intelligence Analysis.* Plymouth, UK: Scarecrow Press, 2010.

Ramalingam, Ben. *Tools for Knowledge and Learning: A Guide for Development and Humanitarian Organisations.* Rapid-Research and Policy in Development. London: Overseas Development Institute (ODI), 2006. http://www.odi.org/publications/153-tools-knowledge-learning-guide-development-humanitarian-organisations.

Raymond, Nathaniel, Caitlin Howarth, and Jonathan Hutson. "Crisis Mapping Needs an Ethical Compass." *Global Brief*, February 6, 2012. http://globalbrief.ca/blog/2012/02/06/crisis-mapping-needs-an-ethical-compass/.

Renault, Val. "Chapter 3. Assessing Community Needs and Resources—Section 14. SWOT Analysis: Strengths, Weaknesses, Opportunities, and Threats." In *Community Tool Box.* Work Group for Community Health and Development. University of Kansas, 2015. http://ctb.ku.edu/en/table-of-contents/assessment/assessing-community-needs-and-resources/swot-analysis/main.

Rowley, Timothy J. "Moving beyond Dyadic Ties: A Network Theory of Stakeholder Influences." *Academy of Management Review* 22, no. 4 (1997): 887–910.

Safer Edge. "Office Closure." EISF publication. European Interagency Security Forum, April 24, 2013. https://www.eisf.eu/library/office-closure-eisf-guide/.

Savage, Grant T., Timothy W. Nix, Carlton J. Whitehead, and John D. Blair. "Strategies for Assessing and Managing Organizational Stakeholders." *The Executive* 5, no. 2 (February 1, 1991): 61–75.

Schultz, Wendy. "Manoa: The Future Is Not Binary." *AFP Compass—Methods Anthology Special Edition*, April 2015.

Schwartz, Peter. *The Art of the Long View.* Doubleday/Currency, 1991.

Selten, Reinhard, and Rolf Stoecker. "End Behavior in Sequences of Finite Prisoner's Dilemma Supergames—A Learning Theory Approach." *Journal of Economic Behavior & Organization* 7, no. 1 (March 1986): 47–70. doi:10.1016/0167-2681(86)90021-1.

Sleesman, Dustin J., Donald E. Conlon, Gerry McNamara, and Jonathan E. Miles. "Cleaning Up the Big Muddy: A Meta-Analytic Review of the Determinants of Escalation of Commitment." *Academy of Management Journal* 55, no. 3 (June 2012): 541–62.

Slim, Hugo. "Doing the Right Thing: Relief Agencies, Moral Dilemmas and Moral Responsibility in Political Emergencies and War." *Disasters* 21, no. 3 (1997): 244–57.

Source 8. "Office Opening: A Guide for Non-governmental Organisations." EISF publication. European Interagency Security Forum, March 12, 2015. https://www.eisf.eu/library/officeopening/.

Sparrow, Malcolm K. "The Application of Network Analysis to Criminal Intelligence: An Assessment of the Prospects." *Social Networks* 13, no. 3 (September 1, 1991): 251–74. doi:10.1016/0378-8733(91)90008-H.

Sphere Project. *The Sphere Handbook—Humanitarian Charter and Minimum Standards in Humanitarian Response.* Third edition. Rugby, UK: Practical Action Publishing, 2011. http://www.spherehandbook.org.

Stoddard, Abby. "Humanitarian Firms: Commercial Business Engagement in Emergency Response." In *Humanitarian Assistance: Improving U.S.-European Cooperation*, edited by Julia Steets and Daniel S. Hamilton, 246–66. Washington, DC:

Center for Transatlantic Relations, The Johns Hopkins University/Global Public Policy Institute, 2009.

Thürer, Daniel. "Dunant's Pyramid: Thoughts on the 'Humanitarian Space.'" *International Review of the Red Cross* 89, no. 865 (2007): 47–63.

Tilly, C., and R. E. Goodin. "Chapter 1. It Depends." In *The Oxford Handbook of Contextual Political Analysis*, 3–32. Oxford: Oxford University Press, 2006.

UN OCHA. "What Is the Cluster Approach? Humanitarian Response." Accessed February 3, 2015. http://www.humanitarianresponse.info/coordination/clusters/what-cluster-approach.

USAID. "Ethiopia Food Security Update June 2007: Humanitarian Crisis Possible in Somali Region." Text. *Famine Early Warning Systems Network*, June 21, 2007. http://reliefweb.int/report/ethiopia/fews-ethiopia-food-security-update-jun-2007-humanitarian-crisis-possible-somali.

Value for Money Department, FCPD. "Guidance on Using the Revised Logical Framework." How to note—DFID Practice Paper. Department for International Development, February 2009. http://mande.co.uk/blog/wp-content/uploads/2009/06/logical-framework.pdf.

van der Heijden, Tamara. "Countering Piracy in Somalia—A Social Network Approach to Stakeholder Analysis." Master's thesis, University of Groningen, 2013.

Wasserman, Stanley, and Katherine Faust. *Social Network Analysis: Methods and Applications*. Cambridge University Press, 1994.

Wealth, Redefining. "Progress: New Ways to Measure Economic, Social and Environmental Change." *The Caracas Report on Alternative Development Indicators, The Bootstrap Press, New York*, 1990.

Weihrich, Heinz. "Analyzing the Competitive Advantages and Disadvantages of Germany with the TOWS Matrix—An Alternative to Porter's Model." *European Business Review* 99, no. 1 (1999): 9–22.

———. "The TOWS Matrix—A Tool for Situational Analysis." *LRP Long Range Planning* 15, no. 2 (1982): 54–66.

Wellman, Barry. "Structural Analysis: From Method and Metaphor to Theory and Substance." In *Social Structures: A Network Approach*, edited by Barry Wellman and Stephen D. Berkowitz, 19–61. Cambridge University Press, 1988.

"WHO Factors That Contributed to Undetected Spread of the Ebola Virus and Impeded Rapid Containment." *WHO*. Accessed January 17, 2016. http://www.who.int/entity/csr/disease/ebola/one-year-report/factors/en/index.html.

Yakura, Elaine K. "Charting Time: Timelines as Temporal Boundary Objects." *Academy of Management Journal* 45, no. 5 (October 1, 2002): 956–70. doi:10.2307/3069324.

Zwitter, Andrej. *Human Security, Law, and the Prevention of Terrorism*. Vol. 88. Taylor & Francis, 2010.

———. "Humanitarian Action, Development and Terrorism." In *Research Handbook on International Law and Terrorism*, edited by Ben Saul, 315–32. Cheltenham: Edward Elgar, 2014.

———. "Humanitarian Action on the Battlefields of the Global War on Terror." *The Journal of Humanitarian Assistance (online Journal)*, October 25, 2008. http://sites.tufts.edu/jha/archives/223.

————. "Neutrality and Impartiality in Implementing Human Rights: A Framework for Measuring Human Security." In *Mainstreaming Human Security in Peace Operations and Crisis Management: Policies, Problems, Potential*, edited by Wolfgang Benedek, Matthias C. Kettemann, and Markus Möstl. New York: Taylor & Francis US, 2010.

————. "The United Nations Legal Framework of Humanitarian Assistance." In *International Law and Humanitarian Assistance: A Crosscut through Legal Issues Pertaining to Humanitarianism*, edited by Hans-Joachim Heintze and Andrej Zwitter, 51–69. Berlin, Heidelberg: Springer Verlag, 2011.

Index

About the Author

Andrej Zwitter is dean of the University College Fryslân, as well as director of the Data Research Centre, Campus Fryslân, University of Groningen. Zwitter was the previous NGIZ Chair of International Relations and Ethics at the Faculty of Law, the University of Groningen. In this function he headed the Political Sciences Department and the research group Research in Ethics and Globalisation (GSG-REG). Prof. Zwitter is also a senior research fellow at Liverpool Hope University.

Zwitter consults and trains practitioners in the field of Humanitarian Intelligence and Big Data Ethics, such as EUROSTAT, German Central Bank, and the Dutch Ministry of Foreign Affairs.

Andrej Zwitter studied general law (master's) and received his PhD with summa cum laude in International Law and Legal Philosophy. During his PhD research he received a Marie Curie Fellowship of the European Commission and conducted his research at the Institute for International Law of Peace and Armed Conflict (IFHV) at the University of Bochum, Germany. Right after the completion of his doctoral studies in 2008, Zwitter was appointed assistant professor for International Relations at the University of Groningen, the Netherlands. Subsequently, in 2012, he became chair of International Relations and Ethics endowed by the Dutch Society of International Affairs (NGIZ).

His current research foci include law and politics of humanitarian action, humanitarian analysis, emergency legislation and practice, as well as Big Data, humanitarian innovation, and ethics.

His recent publications include among others:

- Bunnik, Cawley, Mulqueen, Zwitter (eds.), *Big Data Challenges: Society, Security, Innovation, and Ethics*, 2016.

- Zwitter, Lamont, Heintze, Herman (eds.), *Humanitarian Action: Global, Regional and Domestic Legal Responses*, 2014.
- Heyse, Zwitter, Herman, Wittek (eds.), *Humanitarian Crises, Intervention and Security—A Framework for Evidence-Based Programming*, 2014.
- Zwitter, *Human Security, Law and the Prevention of Terrorism*, 2012.

www.ingramcontent.com/pod-product-compliance
Lightning Source LLC
Chambersburg PA
CBHW021813270326
41932CB00007B/172